DODDIE'S
DIARY

DODDIE'S DIARY

The Highs, the Lows and the Laughter from My Fight With MND

DODDIE WEIR

with Stewart Weir

BLACK & WHITE PUBLISHING

First published in the UK in 2021
This edition first published in 2022 by
Black & White Publishing Ltd
Nautical House, 104 Commercial Street, Edinburgh EH6 6NF

A division of Bonnier Books UK
4th Floor, Victoria House, Bloomsbury Square, London, WC1B 4DA
Owned by Bonnier Books
Sveavägen 56, Stockholm, Sweden

This book is a work of non-fiction, based on the life, experiences
and recollections of the authors. The authors have stated to the publishers
that the contents of this book are true to the best of their knowledge.

Front cover and author photo on p.314 © Sean Cahill
Back cover photo © Ian Rutherford / Alamy Stock Photo
Jacket design by Richard Budd

All plate section images, except those otherwise credited, © The Weir Family.
The publisher has made every reasonable effort to contact copyright holders
of images in the picture section. Any errors are inadvertent and anyone who
for any reason has not been contacted is invited to write to the publisher so
that a full acknowledgement can be made in subsequent editions of this work.

A CIP catalogue record for this book is available from the British Library.

ISBN: 978 1 78530 386 9

1 3 5 7 9 10 8 6 4 2

Typeset by Iolaire Typesetting, Newtonmore
Printed and bound in Great Britain by Clays Ltd, Elcograf S.p.A.

www.blackandwhitepublishing.com

To the tens of thousands who have contributed, and to my countless friends, rugby colleagues and the Trustees who have made the Foundation so successful, a massive thank you.

My love and gratitude to all of my family and relations but in particular to Hamish, Angus and Ben and especially to Kathy for everything they have done and continue to do for me.

All my love.

FOREWORD

GREGOR TOWNSEND

I've always looked up to Doddie, and not just in the literal sense. When I was in my last year of school back in 1990, I had dreams of playing for Scotland and I took a lot of inspiration from Doddie, who had broken into the Scotland team that year. His selection and performances gave other young players in the Borders the belief that it was achievable.

Two years later I found myself involved with the national team for the first time as I got called up to tour Australia. Doddie, despite only being twenty-one at the time, was now established in the team and when I joined the group it seemed like he'd been in the side for years. Again, I looked to him to find out how he had become so experienced and accepted in such a short time. I soon discovered that it all came down to respect. Doddie had earned respect on and off the field, through his courage and his personality – and above all by being a team man.

Playing through the pain barrier against England in 1991 after a burst eardrum showed his toughness – and stealing some lineouts in the game exemplified how much of a valuable asset he had become for our national team. Before and after games, he was the key person driving the positive energy, having fun, and making

1

everyone laugh. Big, daft Doddie had taken to international rugby very quickly.

Doddie, like me, grew up in the Scottish Borders. It's a place we still call home today. It's a sparsely populated region, with small towns, villages and farms scattered across the rolling hills and countryside. However, the rugby landscape is much more close-knit. Doddie played for Melrose and was coached by the great Jim Telfer. Melrose is famous throughout the world as the birthplace of the seven-a-side game and for its annual Sevens tournament. Back in the early 1990s, Melrose were the dominant force in Scotland – winning multiple premierships and producing a number of Scotland Test players.

Four miles up the road were their arch rivals, Gala; a team that Doddie's father and two brothers played for, and also my home-town club. Gala came close to winning a title on a couple of occasions in those glory years for Melrose, but we couldn't quite manage to stop the Melrose machine. Would we have got over the line if Doddie had chosen the beautiful maroon jersey just as the rest of the male contingent of his family had done? I firmly believe he would have made that winning difference . . .

There will be a generation of people who won't be aware of Doddie Weir the rugby player. They will know Doddie for what he has done since his rugby career, whether that is the after-dinner speaking, his tartan suits on TV or since he has been on his quest to raise awareness and funding for MND research.

Doddie was an outstanding rugby player both at club and Test level. He won a premiership for Newcastle Falcons and many more for Melrose before he crossed the border. He was a Lion in 1997 and played for Scotland on sixty-one occasions over a ten-year Test career. Playing in three World Cups was also a tremendous achievement, and remarkably his final games in each of those tournaments were all against New Zealand. That comprised two quarter-final defeats in 1995 and 1999, as well as a third versus fourth place play-off loss against the men in black in 1991. That was Scotland's best-ever result at a World Cup, and Doddie was at the heart of this performance. Even more impressive was Doddie becoming a try-scoring machine in 1995 against the All Blacks, going over the whitewash on two occasions. One more on the day than the unstoppable Jonah Lomu.

Mention of Jonah does strike a chord, as I see a lot of similarities between the two men. Jonah had a presence about him that lit up a room – physically imposing but also such a kind man that people gravitated towards him. They are game-changers too – Jonah transformed rugby union through the impact he made in that World Cup in 1995, Doddie has undoubtedly transformed how MND is viewed by the public and highlighted how important it is to put more funding into finding a cure to this terrible disease. Both are legends of our game that have transcended rugby.

18 November 2017

The referee calls 'Two minutes, Scotland', and I know it's time to head up to the coaching box. This is the players' time and I can sense that they are in the zone – aware that this will be one of the biggest games of their careers. In a few minutes they will be playing the mighty All Blacks, a team Scotland has yet to defeat in over a hundred years of playing the men from New Zealand.

As I leave the changing room and enter the Murrayfield tunnel, I see Doddie and his three sons – Hamish, Angus and Ben. Doddie is resplendent in a wonderful blue tartan suit, but I can sense that he is nervous with what awaits him. The All Blacks have kindly agreed to do their Haka earlier to enable Doddie to walk out onto the field with his three boys prior to the kick-off. He was all set to be welcomed by 67,500 supporters, with the crowd eager to show their appreciation.

What unfolded was an incredibly poignant and soon to become iconic moment for Doddie and his family, for Scottish rugby, and for those who were watching in the stadium and throughout the world. It was almost as if time stopped, as the captains of both teams – John Barclay and Kieran Read – waited for the crowd's applause to end.

Doddie had been with us that week, watching us train, joining us for lunch then speaking from the heart to our players about what he was going through and what it meant to him to be supported by the current Scotland team. His speech was moving, self-deprecating and honest, and I knew our players had extra motivation to perform well against New Zealand. His walk onto the field added even more fuel to this burning desire our players had to succeed and it undoubtedly helped us put together one of our all-time best performances, with the final play of the game coming very close to us pulling off a historic win. It was a special night, an emotional night – where we were privileged to share a special moment together.

Doddie's walk out onto the Murrayfield pitch not only had a lasting impact on those in attendance that night, but it also launched the My Name'5 Doddie Foundation. What followed was a frenzy of fundraising events all over Scotland and the rest of the world. There were some memorable dinners held in Doddie's honour from London to Hong Kong, and so many individuals or groups of people did things to show their appreciation and love for Doddie, as well as doing something to help find a cure for MND.

To date, the Foundation has raised millions of pounds, an incredible achievement. Doddie has been the driving force behind this, being present at so many events and encouraging those who have taken the initiative to make a difference. These efforts have shown rugby and humanity in its best light, with our game supporting one of their own, but this compassion also extends beyond sport.

A dinner in aid of the Foundation in Kelso was one of the best nights I've ever experienced – it felt like a celebration, reunion and party combined in an event to honour Doddie and raise money for his Foundation. You could feel the love for Doddie in every interaction and it was such a special atmosphere, a community coming together.

This feeling is enhanced further when the man you are honouring is so humble and has no ounce of self-pity, despite the challenges he is facing.

8 September 2019

It's 5.30 a.m. and I look out my window to see a car pulling up in the driveway. As I grab my golf clubs, Doddie climbs out of the car to greet me, excitement in his eyes and a can of gin and tonic in his hand. What had started as a way to raise some funds for MND through his brilliant Foundation became something we were both looking forward to and didn't know how it would unfold. A golf challenge – playing one hole at each of the twenty-one courses in the Scottish Borders, from Langholm in the south to Peebles in the west and over to Eyemouth on the North Sea coast in the east. We began the day with an hour's drive just as the sun was rising to Newcastleton, a town and golf course I'd never been to before.

As we came into the town, Doddie and I discussed what we might expect from each golf club we visited. Both of us hoped that someone would be at Newcastleton to tell us what hole we were allowed to play, but feared that we'd be on our own, seeing that it was still just 06.20 on a Sunday morning. We needn't have worried, as we were greeted by a lot of smiling faces, and a make-shift barbeque had already been fired up to provide us with some food ahead of a long day in the sun. This became the pattern as we travelled from course to course over the next fifteen hours, with members having raised money to hand over to Doddie and me. Each club had done things their own way, many decking out their clubhouse with Doddie's tartan, and some drawing in many people from the villages to come and support us. They were so appreciative and thrilled to see Doddie, which gave us a boost as we went through the day.

Scottish rugby legends joined us for a hole of golf, from Greig Laidlaw and Stuart Hogg in Minto, Jim Renwick in Hawick, and John Rutherford in Selkirk. It was great to raise more money for the Foundation, and it was also brilliant to spend the day with Doddie. We had a great laugh. Doddie had brought two dozen cans of gin and tonic and announced that whenever I got a double-bogey I had to see one off. He promised to join me each time.

Luckily, my golf held up okay in the morning and I only had to down one can, but in the afternoon and evening things went downhill – as there were a few 5s and 6s on the scorecard. This meant that by the time we got to St Boswells around 8.30 p.m., for our final course of the day, we had almost finished the drinks between us.

The following day I joined up with the Scotland squad as we were off to Japan for the Rugby World Cup. I was a little dry in the mouth, but still buzzing from the events of the day before.

Being in Doddie's company has always been a pleasure, as he tries to make you laugh – and have a few drinks. These last few years have also been a privilege, because you know that you are in the presence of a great man – someone who has put others before himself as he also battles against such a debilitating disease. He's the most courageous person you could ever meet.

Go well, big guy, we all love you.

INTRODUCTION

Thanks for joining me to share the inside story of everything that has happened over the last three years in this new book, which takes us from the launch of my first (award-nominated!!) publication, up to the present day. It has been an amazing time where, individually, I have done so much, been to so many places, met so many people, and been blown away by their generosity. And it has been the reaction of folk who I have mostly never got to know that has been so incredible, both in terms of your financial and moral support. I say 'your' because, if you're reading this, the chances are you've helped in some way over these years and for that I'd like to take this opportunity to thank you.

It's been three years where the My Name'5 Doddie Foundation and I have worked so hard to bring people together – the experts, the professors, the doctors who study and know about Motor Neuron Disease – in the fight against this horrible condition. And, with their help, we have done our best to invest wisely the many millions raised in our name to try to beat, stop, halt or at least delay the onset of this dreadful disease. In these three years we have moved our understanding of MND on a bit further, along with the science and the use of medicines that might combat it. It's been three years, for me, on the frontline of this battle. And three years in which words like coronavirus, Covid and pandemic have become the norm, as they impact on everyone's day-to-day living, existence and survival.

Ultimately, however, it is three years where I still have to ponder if and when we'll find a cure for MND, three years further down the line in my journey. And those three years really have flown by.

Hopefully, my diary will give you an insight into the incredible things that have happened, the special moments, the love and support, the laughter along the way, the astonishing fundraising efforts which have gone well beyond anything I could ever have imagined – and will also bring you closer to what life has been like and to the reality of what I and so many others face in our daily lives. One of my favourite expressions is 'we are where we are' and, after reading this, you'll have an idea of how we got here and where we might go next . . .

2018

When you see that, you do allow yourself a wee smile and one of my imaginary air punches. Who'd have thunk it? Me, a bestselling author!

OCTOBER 2018

Friday 12 October

Who would have thought there was so much work involved in producing a book? Certainly not me, but even after *My Name's Doddie* has gone to press, after all the various additions and edits and checks and changes, what comes after it appears on the shelves is something I'd never bargained for: photos, the launch party, media interviews, reviews, festivals, TV and radio appearances.

We were always coming away on holiday to Majorca for a week, at the lovely villa owned by Graham Wylie, a big supporter of Newcastle Falcons. Firstly, it gives us time to get away as a family while the schools are on holiday, secondly, it's a lovely place to visit for Kathy's birthday, and thirdly, I can get some sun and a bit of a solar recharge before – if my schedule is anything to go by – what will be a full-on blast all the way to Christmas.

We arrive in advance of the weekend before the kids join us, so it's just me and my adoring wife in the villa. Idyllic, peaceful and picturesque. And the house wasn't bad either.

Having arrived late in the evening, we were just in the door and hadn't even unpacked the bags, but I needed something to eat, being a wee bit peckish, so I decided to have an egg and some toast.

I didn't get a chance to enjoy it. I choked on a piece. I tried to cough it up. Nothing. I tried to swallow. I only made it worse. I tried to shout, but wheezed. Kathy was aware of the commotion and came to the rescue.

I wasn't in a panic, well not immediately. However, I was aware that the toast wasn't going anywhere, but also that I wasn't breathing the way you're supposed to. In fact, I wasn't breathing at all. After everything, was this it?

I knew only too well what Motor Neuron Disease could do, particularly what it did to your breathing and when swallowing. Was this me witnessing those horrors, first-hand, so unexpectedly? Not that I had time to dwell too much on that. This was, as the last few years had been, survival time.

My life wasn't quite flashing before my eyes – well, it wasn't until Kathy started laying into me. Kathy wasn't really an exponent of the Heimlich manoeuvre (look it up in all good first aid journals), but she gave it a go. Nothing. Maybe it was me being too tall for her to get enough purchase. She did, though, have a good idea how to make something – a horse, a sheep, a retired rugby international – cough something up in a hurry, by thumping me on the back.

It was a while since I'd been pummelled like that. I was half expecting to see someone in a Harlequins or All Blacks jersey. But she was a life-saver. Out the toast popped, in went a gulp of air. I appeared to be sweating, and so was Kathy, although in her case it seemed to be brought on by desperation, and I may add, a soupçon of anger. She scolded me like a child for being so bloody stupid. She did have a point.

Five, then ten, then fifteen minutes passed and I was noticing my breathing was a bit on the painful side, in particular my back, and specifically where Kathy had been unleashing her hammer-like blows. What was causing more discomfort was my throat.

It felt totally raw, so painful that I couldn't make out whether or not I still had a lump of bread wedged down there. After some to-ing and fro-ing, the good lady and I decided there was only one thing to do – phone Annabel Howell from the Borders General Hospital. Dr Howell, when she's doing her day job, is associate medical director at NHS Borders and lead for Palliative and Realistic Medicine. Annabel, through being local and because of MND, was now playing a more significant part in our daily lives. Now we really needed her advice.

I know you might be thinking, why not call a local GP, or the hospital, or an ambulance? However, whether we could have made ourselves understood during such a fraught and frightening episode was just something that could have added to our predicament, rather than bringing a solution.

Annabel was great, and so calm hundreds of miles away, down the phone, coming up with lots of suggestions as to what I might try that would be of benefit, without creating even more of a drama. She had me eating butter, sipping water and drinking fizzy Coke, all of which cleared my airway and eased the rawness in my throat, though the pain was still very uncomfortable.

A trip to the doctor was in order first thing on the Monday and he was terrific, understanding and very comforting. Nothing was broken, but he gave me some painkillers. It could, without being too dramatic, have been a trip to the mortuary rather than to see the local GP.

Mary Doll, that's Kathy to you, by the way did say – and she was kidding – that had this dice with death happened at the end of the holiday, rather than on the first night, she might have been less attentive and could have had another few weeks in the sun out of it. At least, I think she was kidding.

Kathy may have saved my life, no question, but had she buttered right up to the corners this would never have happened. Well, that, and me trying to stuff too much in my gob. One of us was to blame ...

Wednesday 17 October

Kathy's birthday. Thirty-nine, or thereabouts. We enjoyed it, in much the same way as I enjoyed every special or festive occasion. Without being too dark, you can never be sure how many you will be able to enjoy – so enjoy it we did. No toast on the menu though ...

Tuesday 23 October

The Big Launch – 'I Name This Book ...'

Actually, the name of the book was something that had been decided upon even before me and my esteemed co-author Stewart had signed the contract. *My Name'5 Doddie* would get my foundation and charity a mention every time the book was talked about on radio, TV, asked for in a book shop, or just mentioned in the passing. A bit, according to Stewart, like Paddy Power of Paddy Power doing Paddy Power's advertising promotions, or Cliff Richard getting two or three mentions in his early interviews because folk called him 'Cliff Richards'.

Way above my head, but Stewart can be like that on some things, a lot of things. The *My Name's Doddie* thing came about from Lee Alexander, who worked with me at the time, and pointed out that's what I say to people on the phone when I explain who I am and what I'm about. He'll claim that anyway.

Months earlier, I'd attended a photo shoot in Edinburgh, in a weird and wonderful studio down in downtown Leith. It was one of these places, like rabbit holes, with doors here, corridors there, where you felt like leaving some chalk marks on the wall so you could find your way back out. The photographer, Sean Cahill, was from Dublin and worked regularly with the publishers. Sean had also produced the cover for Sean Cavanagh, the legendary Gaelic footballer, and his autobiography, *The Obsession*.

It reminded me of some top secret mission, when the publishers explained the photographer 'was being flown especially just to do you'.

Sean, the snapper (although there are worse terms that can be used for camera operators), was a lovely guy and very easy to work with. I say easy, but I'd taken along a couple of suits. Ever the professional, that's me. But hindsight is always 20/20. Had I known how many photographs he'd take, I'd have never doubled my workload by taking along two suits!

Still (one for the more artistic among you and no pun intended), his portrait of me, eventually used on the front cover of the book, I think really captured me and what I was maybe thinking and feeling at that time – like how long am I going to be in the studio, and will we ever see the outside world again.

At times, putting the book together seemed to take an age as well, but credit to my co-author Stewart, he kept the process (and me) going, although I think once or twice I might have tested his patience just a wee bit.

Some people were quite impressed at how quickly I wrote the book – that should be 'we wrote the book' – because we didn't really start discussing the content seriously until the end of May, and by September, the entire manuscript (hark at me and my literary terms) had been delivered.

Maintaining the top secretness of the operation, the first printed edition arrived through my door a couple of weeks before the launch, but other than flashing the cover around the house, I couldn't let anyone else see it. I must admit, I felt rather chuffed that I, sorry 'we' (and not in the royal way either) had produced a real, live book. Were there times when I thought it might not happen? Yes, several. But there was a real sense of achievement in having and feeling the real thing in my hand.

But writing the book and seeing it in print was only the first bit of the deal. As a first-time author, I wasn't really aware that there was more work to be done once you had the solid copy. By work I mean radio, TV and media interviews.

The big date for the launch would be 25 October, but we had a bit of promotional work to do down in London the day before, as a build-up to the main event, put together by the publishers and Stewart, who appears to know nearly as many people in different places as I do. Quite handy on occasions, and this was one of them.

Stewart meets me off the train and the two of us headed through the Underground and out towards our hotel. The Tube is always an adventure, a chance to marvel at its complexities and wonder even more when people constantly moan about it. Try commuting anywhere when every road is covered in a foot of snow.

It's also a great source of people watching, sitting there in the carriage wondering what he does, where she is going, what's in her bag, whose text he's laughing at. And they're sitting across from me, wondering who is this giant galoot that's staring at me? Some recognise me, some elbow their friend and say, 'that's him', some know me by name, and maybe make reference to having seen me play or speak at a dinner, and others ask the question, 'You are the Scottish rugby player, aren't you?'

I have been known to reply, 'Yes, Gavin Hastings,' or whatever name has come into my head first. Never Stuart Grimes or Carl Hogg though . . .

Now, some people may be upset if that happened to them and think, 'Oh, they don't know my name.' But not me. They might not have any interest in sport, or rugby, but just have an idea who you might be. Or, of course, they could be saying it in a way that means you are '*the* Scottish rugby player', in which case they are both observant and correct. Fortunately you can hear that inflection in their voice. The hurtful part is when they add, unprompted, 'It is Gavin, isn't it?'

We arrive at the hotel and check in – always amusing when there is more than one Weir involved. In the case of me and Stewart, it's usually about whether we are related or not, and, stranger still, are we brothers? If you haven't seen us together, Stewart is a sort of normalish height, maybe a foot or so shorter than me. So my favourite replies are: 'No, we're twins,' which usually means the person on reception lifting their head up from their computer terminal and taking a closer look at the two of us, and wondering if we could be the Scottish equivalent of Arnold Schwarzenegger and Danny DeVito. Another stock answer is, 'No, grandson and grandfather,' which gets an even more studious look from those on the other side of the desk.

A box of books has been couriered to London, gifts for those nice people who we'll be meeting the next day. Some of them received the manuscript of the book in advance, so they could give it a quick read and have an idea what it was all about. That would put them one up on me.

Stewart and I, after charging phones, making calls and having a shower (although not together), agree to meet in reception where he, as has become the norm, does the top button on my shirt. This is now a necessity, nearly two years after my diagnosis with MND.

We have no idea where we are going. Not strictly true. We do, we are just not sure where we are and how to get from here to there. We wouldn't be straying too far from base, though. After cutting about for a bit, we hit on a very busy Italian restaurant, but not before we stop someone and ask them if they know where the nearest Italian restaurant might be, a wee tad embarrassing as we are standing right outside of one. We don't get out in big towns much.

The wee girl at the door stalls us, saying they are fully booked, but her boss weaves between the tables, slalom-style and says hello – with that look of 'I know you' – and guides us to a table. How very kind. I've already made up my mind, though, that if he says, 'It's Gavin, isn't it,' I'm walking out. Maybe he recognises me as someone who played against Italia, the Azzurri, all those years ago, in that very first Six Nations match in 2000.

Turns out he and all the staff are Polish. How does that actually work? That minor detail becomes funnier as the evening progresses through the pasta and into the Chianti and Peroni.

We decide to have one for the road and end up in a gay bar, not noticing the rainbow banners on the exterior. The regulars probably just see us as a slightly odd couple, but the Peroni in frozen glasses was perfect. Our one for the road becomes four or five roads.

Unfortunately, we couldn't have too many (although it had never stopped us before), because tomorrow – which was now today – would be long and busy.

Wednesday 24 October

The day starts with a 6.45 a.m. taxi to New Broadcasting House and doing the rounds with the BBC; Nicky Campbell on Radio 5 Live *Breakfast* then on to the *Today* programme on Radio 4, interviewed by Rob Bonnet, and then a piece for *Sportsday* for the BBC News channel, and then a planning meeting with the *One Show* for the following week. In between times we meet Carol Kirkwood (her with the nice weather fronts), and Beverley and her fantastic bearded Collie called Oscar, who is a blind dog. He is actually blind, but beautiful with it. It turns out Oscar was on more drugs than me to keep him going. Maybe he should try Peroni?

I've never been one to get nervous before doing radio or TV work, or broadcasting. I admire those who ask the questions, do the links, and manage the interviews, and impressed with how cool and calm they are while they are doing it. It appears easy, but I know how hard it is to try and talk while someone is chirping in your ear. It is easier said than done, but each to their own.

Before we depart Broadcasting House, we also meet the lovely Jade, one of the producers at the Beeb, who has helped set a lot of these things up on the day. Stewart knows a lot of influential people. I suppose I do as well. I'm great with faces but I am hopeless with names and where I've met someone. Fortunately 'wee man' is a phrase that seldom, if ever (unless I come up against another lock or a basketball player), fails to get me out of a pickle.

'Wee man' doesn't work for everyone. I'm thinking about the ladies here. But I have an array of greetings for them. And a wee kiss usually works as well.

Job and kisses done, it was a quick (if there is such a thing in London) taxi ride across the river to the talkSPORT studios.

Everyone there was nice and very kind, maybe down to everyone knowing Stewart – or at least his voice. He later admitted that he'd only met a couple of the producers and presenters in the flesh, despite being a regular on air. At talkSPORT, the likes of Mike Graham (who Stewart did know well, as he is his former boss), Daisy McAndrew, Paul Hawksbee and Andy Jacobs – the famous H&J – looked genuinely vexed as a I gave them a stark reminder of what this condition would eventually do to me. Already my hand and arm movement and strength is limited, but eventually I will stop walking, talking, swallowing AND breathing as my body closes down.

The questions they asked were entirely reasonable, and answerable. There was nothing untoward and they listened intently. While

I'm moving from studio to studio, Stewart is away doing his bit with his pal, Ray Stubbs.

Between shows, Jim White, something of a Scottish broadcasting legend as an instantly recognisable anchorman, firstly with STV but for much longer with Sky Sports, came to see us after he had finished his shift. A small gesture perhaps, but nice that someone would seek you out because they'd heard 'Doddie is in the building'.

With the last of the interviews done, we stepped outside the talkRADIO studios and heaved a sigh of relief, me because all my talking was done, Stewart because the big box of books he'd been lumping around had now shrunk to just a handful in his rucksack.

Time for lunch – a massive combo for starters, then fish and chips (we are still growing boys, although I had an excuse) – accompanied by a few beers (rude not to) before we said our farewells; Stewart heading back to get ready for Thursday, me heading back to get changed into another suit – tartan of course – then to head to a dinner in the company of the Princess Royal, who I first met years ago in her official capacity as the Scottish Rugby Union patron.

Over lunch, Stewart lets me into a secret of how he remembers things, like people's names, places and who won the FA Cup in 1937. It is so simple. It is, however, easier just to think there is something seriously wrong inside his head.

Thursday 25 October

Before I know it, it's another early taxi ride, this time with Jill (with a 'J') Douglas for company, headed for the station and the train back to Edinburgh for the big unveiling of my autobiography. Naturally, we were late in to Waverley, but Cameron Buttle from the BBC had a car waiting, which meant he also got some footage for the documentary the Beeb were working on, and we got to Murrayfield in double-quick time. Safe to say our excuses for being late had already been made in advance. We just blamed the trains.

It was interesting on the day of the launch, at Murrayfield, that while many had seen the cover either in adverts or websites, nearly all of the press photographers flicked open the book to see if any of their own photographs had made the final cut. Of even more interest was who had taken the cover shot.

'Who is he?' one demanded to know.

'He's a guy from Dublin who the publishers had used before,' Stewart explained.

'What, are us Scottish photographers not good enough or something?' one exclaimed.

Thankfully, Stewart was on hand to quell any international incident, with his unique, diplomatic style.

'Correct . . .'

However, whether the photographers are from Dublin or closer to hand, they do like to get their money's worth out of any photographic opportunity, their cameras clicking away, accompanied with calls and instructions to look up, look down, right, left, of 'over here' and 'just one more', which in reality means another twenty minutes. But I wasn't complaining. It was lovely to see so many of them there, and again, as I was hearing all the time in my ear, 'Think how this will help with the sales.'

Inside though, I was complaining, or at least my hands were. I may only have had to smile and hold up a book or two, but I was getting tired. Holding on to the books was difficult, and after not too long, holding them up was impossible. People see a relatively healthy individual, walking, talking, laughing and joking, and think I'm fine. But that couldn't be further from the truth. Doing the most basic things brings on fatigue. How can just holding a book be tiring? Trust me, it feels like an anvil after a bit.

All through my playing days, I'd had a really good relationship with photographers. They seemed a good bunch, a bit more demanding than the journalists in terms of what they want from you, but always appear less stressed, and a bit more jovial in their work. I've never had any issues or problems with them. They have a job to do, and in this case all they were asking was for me to stand still for thirty seconds. What was difficult about that? Quite a lot for some, but let's not go there.

Of course, they were open to a bit of bribery, which way back worked both ways. If you saw a particular photograph in a paper, a good action shot from a big game, you might find out who the photographer was, maybe Jim Galloway, or Ian Rutherford, or Eric McCowat, and ask him for a copy or a print. I think in my playing days, they were a bit more relaxed about ownership and copyright and dishing out photographs. Indeed, prints became almost like a currency; you'd get a picture from them, then they would offer you other shots they had taken, knowing that at some point they might need a favour from you. Bartering at its best.

I only realised how many such 'transactions' had taken place when I began sourcing pictures and photos for *My Name'5 Doddie*. There were thousands of them, no kidding. I had bundles, but so too did Mum. In fact, she had more than me, being the official curator of my unofficial museum. She had them from Melrose, Scotland, Newcastle, Borders, the Lions, the Barbarians, from Famous Grouse, from other sponsors and advertisers, from local papers, national papers, from club games, Sevens, internationals. I laugh, because I think every time she got a good one she promised, 'I'll get that one framed.' She never had. She'd have run out of walls by now, or had to hang them in the byres or other farm buildings around Cortleferry. It might brighten the place up, come to think of it.

Once the snappers had all the photographs they could ever have needed, then there was the written press to be dealt with, with various media scrums, for daily and Sunday titles. Some wanted exclusive interviews, but to be honest, there would have been just too many to do. One chap turned up late, and asked if he could just have five minutes on his own, a request which was denied.

I didn't have a problem with that, but Stewart reckoned it was just a ruse, so one newspaper could claim an exclusive, have their own headline, or splash, and present some details differently to everyone else. And that wasn't happening. Oh well, he knew best.

Radio and TV had to be done, which included another sit down in the stand with Rona Dougall of *Scotland Tonight* (remember the wee blether we had in the stand at Melrose to launch the Trust and Foundation?), but the media call wasn't over. Anything but.

A film crew was on hand from World Rugby, who were going to be doing some very public 'secret' filming for a package they were editing together for their awards night in Monaco. Down in the bowels of the stadium, they had me walking into the dressing rooms, out of the dressing rooms, around the dressing rooms, sitting down in the dressing rooms, pointing to my number, my name, my name and number hung on the wall in the tunnel, saying hello to people on the Murrayfield tour, saying cheerio to the people on the Murrayfield tour. And then they'd change the lighting and I'd need to do it all again. Is it like this in Hollywood?

Eventually, I was left with one more scene to shoot. I was to march up the tunnel and out onto the pitch, a walk I'd made a few times over the years, from my first cap (though Murrayfield is unrecognisable from that day in 1990) to my famous walk onto the pitch for the All Blacks game with my three boys.

For this, they were going to use a drone, which would go from ground level all the way into the sky above Murrayfield. After a few test runs, it was time to go for a 'take'. Then another, then another, and another. I was too quick in my walk out the tunnel, too slow, the drone's rate of climb was too steep, not steep enough, too fast, not fast enough. I asked the 'pilot' if he'd done this sort of thing before. If looks could kill! I'd have liked a wee shot myself, but the old thumbs don't work like they once did, and I could see 'insurance claim' written across the cameraman's face.

In the end, they called it a wrap. I'm into my technical terms. I don't know if they got what they wanted or not, or had just run out of time and patience. It had squeezed my day, but there was one more photograph to be had, with a new friend – the Doddie Weir Cup. With big lugs and tartan trim, we could have been twins.

All of which meant I was up against it, time wise, on that Thursday. Where had the day gone? And I still had to go and beautify myself and prepare for the evening reception in the Up & Under Bar.

The SRU had kindly booked a room and use of the spa at a nearby hotel, so I could have a kip, freshen up and have my nails done. In the end there was too much going on for me to shut my eyes, but my nails looked braw. And then we were into the final leg, the main event, the big book launch, meeting and greeting the guests, friends and family, and signing some books, lots of books.

The invites were a bit last minute, my fault mostly. Make that my fault entirely. There were just so many people I wanted to invite. Mary Doll and I pored over the list endlessly. Names were added, some taken out, then resubmitted, with a few more that we'd just remembered thrown in. I think we managed to reach eight or nine 'definitive' lists before we got the emails, social media and WhatsApp messages fired out; there was simply no time to post them. In the end, the publishers booked for three hundred to attend, but they did add that, in their experience, usually only half the invites were taken up for various reasons. For our launch, nearly three hundred turned up on the night.

It was an evening where I could have happily settled down quite easily with a few pints and a bit of chat, there were just so many people I was happy to see and would have been happy to be in their company for the night. But I had duties to attend to. What I didn't know was that Gregor Townsend was going to break off (or maybe that should have been break out) from the Scotland team hotel to join us, and kindly add a few words.

Jill Douglas, Gary Armstrong, Stewart Weir and myself took part in a Q&A, and that was when it hit me. As I sat on the stage and looked out, there was my entire life before me – my family, people I'd gone to school and college with, guys from my playing career with Melrose, Newcastle Falcons, Scotland, people from the SRU, those from the farming community, and people I'd got to know through business after my career had ended. All there to see and hear me, no doubt wondering if I'd mentioned them in the book. If I didn't, blame Stewart.

But seeing all those faces. Remember what I said about being blindsided? I might see them all again – albeit from on high – in rather more sombre circumstances in the future. But right now, given my mindset, that's way in the future. Nevertheless, being handed the microphone and being left on my own to put some words together, hell that was hard. Easier, though, than signing three hundred books!

Saturday 27 October

Stewart, although it pains me to say so, is quite good at this PR-thingy. He knows nearly everyone and has a lovely way of diplomatically saying 'no' to some of them, but usually finds a way to accommodate most requests.

Saturday, and it feels like I'm getting prepped and psyched up for a game. In actual fact, I am about to make my debut on BBC Scotland's *Off the Ball* with Tam Cowan and Stuart Cosgrove. I ask them to be gentle with me but I needn't have worried; they give me a great platform to chat about the book, the Foundation and me.

Team GB hammer thrower Chris Bennett is also with us in the studio, and for what is often seen as a football show, having a rugby player and an athlete on as guests shows that the whole world of sports doesn't only revolve round eleven-a-side, two set of goals and a round ball . . . perhaps just ninety-five per cent of it.

Speaking to Chris, there is so much about his professionalism that takes me back to my amateur – or 'shamateur' – days when, although you were expected to perform at the very highest level, ultimately, so much of the hard graft was left up to you, on your own, usually in the pissing rain. He and many like him have my admiration. There is one difference in that he gets paid to do it – but even that is performance related. The side of sport few see. That, and throwing in a park most days, not a purpose-built stadium.

'Are there dog walkers where you train?' I enquire.

'There used to be.'

I change the subject, hastily.

NOVEMBER 2018

Thursday 1 November

So much of rugby is based on momentum, moving forward, then keeping going in that direction. After the launch of the book and the Foundation, I genuinely feel a surge of interest in me, MND and what I am trying to do. It's the kind of support that confirms that what we're trying to do is right, and it's a great lift when doubts creep in, or when you feel a little low.

Today I'm London bound, the first leg of a long – a very long – weekend, kicking off with an appearance on *The One Show*, BBC 1's early evening offering of chat, human interest and the occasional funny. Which makes me the ideal guest.

I'm not alone on the couch. Actress Samantha Womack was with me, as were the Hairy Bikers, top chefs and topper blokes Dave Myers and Si King, who I'd met before. (Oh, I know all the celebrities, me.) Sam mentioned before the show that she'd appeared in a film about rugby called *Up 'N' Under* during the 1990s, but that it was about rugby league. Maybe why I'd missed it.

I've been invited to talk about me, my book and life with MND. Alex Jones and Amol Rajan were the presenters and, ahead of the show, they briefed me on what we'd be seeing and what they'd be asking. All straightforward, except it never really is. Even when you are relaxed you are slightly on edge, almost expecting the unexpected.

While you might answer a few questions easily enough, occasionally even the most tame request can throw you off your train of thought and catch you completely off-guard. You might feel your lip tremble, or feel the tears well up, or shiver a little, because a nerve – even though some of them aren't working the way they should – has been struck.

However, it all passes off without incident. I'm asked about being diagnosed, about cures and drugs, and about life expectancy. Between one and three years I reply, a stock answer. 'That's so quick,' says Sam, disbelievingly. What I'm aware of is an audible – well to me – 'sssst' from Si, as he sucks the air through his teeth, accentuating the shock of what he'd just heard. The stark reality often has that effect on folk.

And, as quickly as they've told us we are live and on-air, it's all over and done with, although there was time to plug the book and the charity, and glance occasionally at the monitors around the studio, just to make sure the suit looks good. Fair dapper.

Backstage, I switched my phone on again as I'm chatting away with my fellow guests, lovely people. I hope they didn't think I was being rude, as my phone began to make all sorts of noises, with various messages beginning to drop, some wishing me well, the latter ones saying how well I'd done, all mixed in beside texts and screen grabs from the publishers and my co-author, each accompanied by a celebratory emoji.

If you wanted to see the power of television in all its glory, then my appearance on the Beeb that evening was a real eye opener. How many had been watching the show? Quite a few if the social media updates were anything to go by.

The book, which had been doing reasonably well sales-wise and had been in the top 50 sports books before the show, was suddenly in the top 10, then it was the number one rugby title, then the top sports book overall, and then it was up there with the bestselling books across all categories on Amazon, all evidenced by the snapshots being forwarded on to me.

When you see that, you do allow yourself a wee smile and one of my imaginary air punches. Who'd have thunk it? Me, a bestselling author!

Friday 2 November

I rise early, have breakfast, and soon I'm on my way down to the West Country on the train. It has become my favourite way to travel. Sit back, relax, and let someone else find the way there. At the other end I'll meet up with Kathy, who has travelled down and spent the night with Jill with a 'J' and Hoggy.

Feeling a bit fidgety, probably because we are not going quickly enough, I occupy myself by reading all those tweets and messages again, then read up a bit on those I'd shared centre stage with the previous evening. I decide to look up that film Sam Womack had been telling me about. One of the first things to pop up on Google was a publicity photograph of Samantha in her rugby gear, smiling, posing with some rugby league sorts. I flick through them, then flick back the way. Did I really see that? I did!

Here was one of the photographs where she is being held off the ground by three rugby players, none other than Neil Jenkins, Mike Catt and, wait for it, Duncan Hodge. Jenks, the Lions full-back during the successful tour to South Africa in 1997; Catty, a World Cup winner with England in 2003; and then Hodgy, whose claim to fame was that he spent less time than me on the pitch when Scotland won the final Five Nations in 1999.

But Jeez, Samantha had taken a massive chance appearing in that promotional photograph, trusting that trio not to drop her!

The messages and texts just keep on coming, either saying how well I'd done on the Beeb the previous night or singing the praises of the book. I'm sure in this electronic blizzard, I'll miss something of importance. There is no official book signing appearance (what is wrong with you, Cardiff?), but I have some radio interviews to do ahead of the big gala dinner in my honour at the Principality Stadium, which is all part of the build-up to the inaugural game for the Doddie Weir Cup, contested between Scotland and Wales.

We all arrive in good time in Cardiff. We want to look our best and it takes some (mentioning no names, Hoggy) a bit longer than most to achieve it. But I just want to chill a bit, recharge the batteries and have a good kick at the ball later on.

Around lunchtime, we start getting phone calls from those who had departed Scotland early on Friday morning. For want of a better description, Wales was shut to visitors, or at least those who were coming via the M4.

An accident just to the east of Cardiff meant the tailbacks stretched right over the Second Severn Crossing, and back on to the southbound M5 for twenty miles. While his wife Anne was flying back from a business trip to China, my brother Tom was stuck in the middle of it with his three kids, Douglas, Amy and Lucy, and basically just had to bide his time and wait for the issues to clear. He estimated he was travelling at a snail's pace for at least four hours.

Stewart was also headed south, but on hearing of the impending block, said he just took a right turn somewhere and ended up in deepest, darkest Wales. Progress was similarly torturous. In one town, Stewart's better half Nicola jumped out of the car, dashed into a shop for some sandwiches and drinks, then thought it wise to stock up on Sharpie pens for the usual autograph frenzy later. She says she walked to the shop, stood in the queue, was served, then went into WH Smith's, bought the pens, waited again while the assistant checked the price as they were reduced but the true price wasn't showing up at the till, paid for the goods and then walked down the street fifty yards and got back in the car – and Stewart hadn't even needed to pull in and park up.

All parties reckoned that they would make the start of the evening on time. Incredibly, they were on the money, although Stewart and Nics made it with a minute to spare. Despite Stewpot not quite adhering to the speed limit on some demanding A-roads, Nicola had still managed to do her hair and make-up before they arrived.

On arrival at the hotel, however, they found their room had been taken by a Mr Stewart Weir – except it was one of my dad's friends, who just happened to be called Stewart! There were no rooms left at the inn, but the staff promised to rectify the misunderstanding by bedtime. About 4 a.m., then.

Stewart reckoned they'd got changed in a broom cupboard, but later in the evening broke the great news that they'd been upgraded to a laundry closet.

The evening couldn't have gone any better, with several Welsh and Scottish players from yesteryear – Scott Quinnell, Robert Norster and Rupert Moon – who was wearing a Welsh kilt the last time I saw him – with Gazza, Scott, Kenny and JJ upholding Scottish honours. And Hoggy was there as well.

After the dinner, auctions and all the formal welcomes and speeches, we were joined for a quick Q&A session with two surprise guests, none other than Wales and Lions coach Warren Gatland and his counterpart, my old pal and often teammate, Gregor Townsend.

The reception they received was a measure of just how much people appreciated them taking time out from their hectic schedules to add their weight and support to the cause. A great gesture from two great individuals.

It was then time for the informal interlude, where everyone could let their hair down and participate in some traditional rugby games. That involved drinking. Gats and Toony hung around for that as well, although maybe they were wise after the event.

Now, while we are all rugby supporters at heart, there is a mantra we live by which is that what goes on tour stays on tour. That also applies to dinners and functions. So, when Gary lined up the pints of Guinness to see who could sink theirs the quickest, the last thing we wanted to see were dozens of mobile phones suddenly videoing events.

Very politely, they were asked to put them away, and anyone who failed to do so would be fined twenty quid. All for a good cause you understand. There were a few who just weren't listening and had to forfeit their hard-earned cash – twenty pounds a pop – but, eventually, we could bring everyone under starters orders.

Stewart appeared to have been sipping at his pint while the terms and conditions were being applied, but still finished last. He can drink a lot of them, just not very quickly. Gats won. Once a hooker . . .

As Warren took his acclaim and headed back to the team hotel, Hoggy presented me with £100. 'What's that for?' I asked.

'I had to fine three people,' he replied. Three times twenty equals a hundred? Maybe he should have been fined himself for extortion.

Eventually the night concluded. Us old timers headed for food, then a nightcap, then bed. The younger generation – my sons, their cousins, and anyone else they could rope into getting up to mischief – headed into the Cardiff night, looking for a good time. I've heard that one before.

Saturday 3 November

Game day, a leisurely paced morning, breakfast and a blether, time to listen to the tales of woe from the previous evening after the young team had hit the high spots of Cardiff, and then time to amble along to the stadium again, this time for lunch.

The Beeb decided they were going to join us, doing a bit of an atmospheric scene-setter for their live network coverage. I know all the jargon, I do. Because it was all a bit stop-start, while they got different shots and moved the cameras, the walk took longer than we'd expected as people took advantage of seeing me in the street to say hello and pass on their best wishes. Very kind. Not one of them, however, said they were hoping for a Scotland win. Very disappointing.

All of my sizeable entourage were given superb tickets for the game, and Kathy and I were treated like royalty. Just how big an occasion this was began to hit me.

There had been some criticism in the media that the SRU and the WRU weren't doing enough in terms of supporting me or the Foundation. Everyone is entitled to their opinion, but honestly, some had written articles with no knowledge whatsoever of what goes into putting on a game of rugby at the highest level. The Foundation had looked at putting on a benefit match featuring players of past and present, but once you'd hired a stadium and staffed it, invited players and paid for their accommodation, travel and insurance, and being in the lap of the gods as to how many would turn up and support such a game, the costs and risks involved made it quite prohibitive.

Pairing up with the WRU, and especially the SRU, around an Autumn Test match, made much more sense. Even then, this game – with both sides playing for the Doddie Weir Cup – was always more than about how much the Foundation would benefit financially. We always earmarked this occasion as a way of driving awareness and publicity around MND and the Foundation.

The sceptics will, even now, still be saying, 'Well, you would say that.' But this gave us such a massive platform and vehicle to drive the Foundation forward that it was always going to be too much of an opportunity to pass up on. And if there are any doubters, ask nicely and we might show you the spreadsheet of what came in online off the back of this game.

For me as well, there was also the honour of being able to present a trophy carrying my name. Cups named after people is nothing new but, as I've said a number of times, not too many get to see that while they are still around.

It would have been great if Scotland had been able to take the cup back to Edinburgh, having posted a win in Cardiff. It had been so long ago since we'd last achieved that feat that Bill McLaren was still commentating, although it was the last game he commentated on for the BBC.

Wales probably deserved to edge it. Scotland got to within four points of the hosts early in the second half, only for Jonathan Davies to show his world-class credentials, as I'd witnessed in New Zealand in 2017 with the Lions, to run in a match-winning and Doddie Weir Cup-winning try.

What I remember most about the match really had nothing to do with what was going on down on the pitch. The TV cameras focused in on me and Kathy, minding our own business, watching the game. This was 'Kiss Cam' at work, the idea being that if the cameras zoomed in on you, you kissed whoever it was sitting next to you. Thankfully JJ was a few rows away. However, as soon as our mugs flashed up on the big screen, people started cheering and chanting, 'Kiss, kiss, kiss!'

We looked at each other. This was pressurised stuff, and Kathy went all shy and embarrassed. It had been a while. I'm joking. However, by the time we'd smiled at each other a few times, and giggled like young things caught by their pals, the cameras had left us and gone back to matters rugby. Phew, that was a close thing. But at the next breakdown and pause in proceedings, the director had got his camera trained on us again. Well, here goes – but again, we took so long in summoning up the passion, Kathy and I went to plant a big smacker on each other's lips – and the footage again went back to the game. We did though get a cheer, as the more observant noticed this time we made contact, but totally missed the target. I think I kissed Kathy on the nose!

However, that wasn't a good enough effort for the full house watching on. And when the cameras panned in for a third time, we went for it – direct hit, and arguably the biggest cheer of the day. Oh, how we laughed. Actually, we blushed more, but still. A magic moment.

Alun Wyn Jones is a latter-day legend of Welsh and Lions rugby, and a top bloke on top of that. I dearly wished it had been a countryman of mine who was getting the silverware in this inaugural encounter, but alas it wasn't to be. AWJ was a deserving recipient, and there will be another game between these Celtic friends along in the near future.

One young man who would never forget this game was Edinburgh's Darcy Graham. Having come through the ranks of the Sevens game and earned a contract with Edinburgh, this match marked his international debut. Again, a win would have been lovely, but it gets his name up on the wall at Murrayfield. Better there than not. As it was his first cap, at the after-match gathering he had to stand up and sing to the invited company, and he gave a belting rendition of the Hawick Song. It was well received by the other folk who were there from Hawick.

We had a private function room booked back at the hotel. Not sure how private it was supposed to be, but it appeared several hundred had got the invite. There were loads of faces I knew, many of them I'd not seen in ages. The noise level in the room was steadily going up, generally a sign that alcohol was being accompanied by some decent chat.

I glanced around, getting my bearings and finding where everyone was, just in case I required any assistance. Always better to be safe than sorry. I spot my mum and dad in very close proximity to Stewart and, it appeared, through choice. On closer inspection, auld Jock appears to have a decent glow about him, while Mother is armed with a knife, a cucumber and a tube of plastic cups. I have my suspicions as to what is going on, but my attentions are channelled elsewhere when some London Scottish boys arrive.

A merry old time was had by all then last orders were called, but the night was still young. We headed to the hotel bar, managed to secure a few seats together and then gently spread out into other folk's territory. A well-practised ploy. And there were more of us than them – and who would say no to a man with MND. It does have its advantages, occasionally.

Stewart arrives in the bar, towing what appears to be a pull-along shopping trolley full of bottles of drink. He looks like an airline steward. Mum is right behind him, with her tube of plastic cups not as tall and with only half a cucumber. Then comes my sister-in-law Anne, Sean McGrath (the Foundation's Medical Strategy Lead, and the conduit between what we wish to do and who can do it from the world of medicine, science and research), a couple of my parents' friends and a long line of others. Talk about the Pied Piper of Hamilton!

Stewart's portable minibar was very popular, but not with the hotel management. Two security staff confront Stewart: 'You are not allowed to bring drinks into the bar, sir.'

Quick as a flash, Stewart replied, 'These are the raffle prizes for Doddie's charity.' And they bought it, hook, line and another triple Balvenie for Jock, despite Anne spraying everyone with her gin and tonic as she tried, unsuccessfully, not to laugh out loud at Stewart's quick-wittedness.

Drinks were taken, and everyone got one – or at least a

measure – of the 'raffle' prizes, even in the lift back up to our bedrooms, although I was in the particular lift I took for a very long time. It was one of those nights.

Sunday 4 November

The morning after the night before had more casualties than twenty-four hours earlier. I was up early with the rest of the trustees as there was some business to take care of and books to sign. Lots of them, which was all good news.

I knew Scott Hastings was the Foundation chairman for a reason. In the part of the bar we were using, Scott casually enquired if we could order drinks. When the reply came in the affirmative, Scotty ordered Bloody Marys for everyone, and then gave the barman direction on what should be in it. The good news was that there was so much vegetation and tomato juice, it qualified as one of our five-a-day! The bad news was it also counted as our alcohol intake for that week. Bloody Mary? It was bloody good. So good that we all had another. It made signing a couple of hundred books a bit easier, but once they were done, the party was over. Jill and Stewart packed up the books in boxes, to go here, there and even Kelso, and then it was time to head home.

A good weekend had been had by all. Anyone who didn't, it's your own fault. Here's to the next one when, hopefully, Scotland will fill that space left in the Murrayfield display case with the Doddie Cup.

Tuesday 6 November

My homecoming as an author. The good people of the Borders Book Festival have put on an 'evening with' at the Volunteer Hall in Galashiels. Poor Campbell (Brown) from our publishers, Black & White, is looking quite harassed. There aren't as many books for sale or signing as he would like and he can see that demand on the night could be about to outstrip supply, which is a good and bad thing – or that should be a bad and good thing – in many ways, but either way is close to a publisher's worst nightmare.

The one thing you need to be aware of when appearing in front of those who know you best is that you can't come across as a Flash Harry. There are just too many there who will know you so well.

MC and host for the evening is Alistair Moffat, a weel-kent face in these parts and someone who has done this gig on numerous occasions, and joining me on stage is my sidekick in crime (especially if we are sued for anything that has appeared in writing), Stewart Weir. But of course, they've come to hear me.

The BBC Scotland cameras and John Beattie are floating around, getting various shots for a documentary they are filming. I hope they catch my good side.

The crew had turned up at Kirsty's house late afternoon to do some atmospheric and background shots, namely of the entire Weir clan eating. Kirsty had produced a couple of industrial-sized shepherd's pies – her own making, not M&S – and told everyone to help themselves. The Weir weans – Stewart's youngest, Callum and Zara – showed their West of Scotland upbringing by being first in with the serving spoons, much to the embarrassment of Nicola, their mum. You could tell that they definitely had the Weir genes when it came to food.

There was plenty for everyone and, noticing the rather famished expressions on the faces of those from the Beeb, Kirsty offered them a plate as well. I don't think she had quite bargained on being asked for a receipt at the end, but you know what these BBC lot are like around expenses.

From there, it was a quick dash into Gala, get some books signed in advance, a bit of blusher, and then on stage. The front row was entirely Weir women, arms folded with 'right, entertain us' expressions on their faces. The bright stage lights made it hard to see folk too far back in the hall, which was packed, although I can make out the profile of a certain Jim Telfer. No doubt he'll have his views on how to do a Q&A session. He has views on most things.

Alistair leads off by asking a few questions about me, and how I was, before turning to Stewart.

'And how long did it take you to write the book?'

Stewart explained that after nearly twenty years in the planning, he started at the end of May and handed over the complete manuscript in mid-August.

'So May 2017 to August 2018?' Alistair quizzed him.

'No, May to August this year.'

'So, 75,000 words in three and a bit months?'

'Ahuh . . .'

I think that was the last question he was asked. I don't think Mr Moffat could quite believe the turnaround time, but it was true. Ask the cleaners and bar staff at the hotel he went to for his summer holidays in Gran Canaria!

I'm able to contribute a few yarns before turning my attention to some of the locals. Always good for a laugh. Everyone sounds as if they are having a good time – as I say, I couldn't see everyone – and we close the evening with an open mic session with questions from the floor.

Mr Telfer, in his capacity as local resident and rugby guru, gets two questions, but the belter of the night brings the curtain and the house down on a fantastic evening.

The microphone is passed to someone right at the front, and I manoeuvre myself into a position where I can make out local farmer, Jimmy Morton.

'Aye Doddie,' he begins. I'm now wondering what literary insight he is looking for, or what particular memory from my career he might recall. 'Is there any reason why you didn't buy as many sheep from me this year?'

Only in Gala. Time for bed.

Saturday 17 November

There is, seemingly, a very fine dividing line between genius and madness. I have always known Rob Wainwright to be a clever guy; a doctor, an army officer, a Lion, an outstanding player and captain with Scotland, and the man who introduced me to the finer points about whisky, something I will be forever grateful for.

He is a great man to visit on his island of Coll, where he fishes and catches his tea, and is a more than exemplary host whenever you pay him a visit up there. More than once, though, I have thought that the whole island way of life has been a wee bit too quiet for our Rob, allowing his thoughts to run away with him. And this is where that rather blurred line I mentioned earlier, between brilliance and bonkers, comes into play.

You'll know what I mean when I mention the Doddie Gump, a fundraising event for the Foundation, the first of which took place when Scotland visited Italy in the Six Nations in early 2018. Rob, through a wonderful social media campaign, set out to drum up the support of a thousand fans to march on Rome and ended up with just about every Scot in the Italian capital turning up.

So, when he hatched plans to do the same again, this time closer to home, needless to say he set the bar a good bit higher when it came to his ambitions – namely getting ten thousand to parade from the city centre to Murrayfield ahead of Scotland's Autumn Test against South Africa.

Rob has a persuasive streak in his armoury and no sooner had he posted his intentions than the big sign-up began, and with a special edition headband being rolled out to swell the coffers of the Foundation further. To make sure no one missed out, me, the

Wainwright, Ian Smith (three members of the Row 19 club – if you want to know more, buy the first book), Gary Armstrong (any excuse to get out/drink), and two of the fastest men ever in a Scotland jersey, Roger Baird and Iwan Tukalo, hit the bars in Edinburgh on the Friday night, mixing sales with research and a beer-tasting session. Not often you go out, get fu' and come back with nine grand in your pocket!

So, if anyone was going to join me on the Mercat Cross to get the march started on match day, it was going to be the Gumpmeister himself.

I'll admit, I cut the timing a bit fine. It is always difficult to work your way through the hordes when everyone knows you. But Bailie Norman Work did a sterling job of stalling, before passing me the microphone. Me, a PA system and a crowd? I needed no second invitation.

Still, there were a couple of words that just didn't come out as I'd wanted – because they didn't come out. Looking across the throng, I could see family, friends, folk from all over the Borders, folk from a host of different rugby clubs. Emotion got the better of me as I tried to tell people what a wonderful guy Rob is. No, not here, not now. Deep breaths, Dodgy. A hug and a laugh from Wainwright, and we were back on song. The scrum before me, nervously looking at their watches, told me it was time to get going, but I wouldn't be marching as it might have been a wee bit too far for me.

Instead, I had been provided with a chauffeur-driven car, or that was the script. The reality came as something of a shock – a lowered, modified, minimalised Land Rover dragster, complete with the noisiest tuned V8 engine I'd ever heard. The driver says something to me, I nod, because I haven't a clue what he has said. And from his reaction, I think the police providing our escort were wondering if it was entirely street legal.

By the time I was dropped off at Murrayfield, in addition to my loss of hearing – I think I would have had a decent claim for industrial deafness – the vibration of the power unit had me tingling in places I'd forgotten I had!

I had a few duties to do on the field that afternoon, nothing too taxing, mainly giving a bit of chat about myself, the Foundation and the game, alongside Al Kellock, and Jo Wilson from Sky – actually I think it's Perth – but you see what I did there.

The one good thing working with this Jo is that you always get a kiss at the end. I see it as one of the perks of the job, or perhaps, my condition. I then seamlessly move on to do an interview with the equally lovely Sonja McLaughlan of the BBC, again nothing too taxing, mainly about me!

And guess what? Another wee kiss at the end of the interview. I won't say it too loud, but there are going to be some seriously angry ladies around when they find out there is nothing wrong with me!

There is still time at the end of the day to meet up with some of those who have put so much time, effort and willingness into their own and our fundraising. The people from STRIVE in Stonehaven, Willie Tulloch, wife Jane and quite a few others have gone from complete novices in the world of event management to experts after staging a cycle ride and a veterans rugby tournament which saw Tom Smith, Marcus di Rollo, Stuart Grimes, Nikki Walker, Barry Stewart, 'coach' Kevin McKenzie and a few others – well over two hundred Scotland caps between them – represent the King Penguins touring team. They even installed our good pal and comedian Scotty Glynn as their King Penguin, and a Gala Ball to help swell the Foundation's funds by another £85,000.

Quite a figure, as was that cut by no. 1 son Hamish, who represented me and the Foundation at the dinner, chaperoned by Edinburgh's Grant Gilchrist and the Foundation's money man, Jim Robertson.

There was even a guest appearance from Rob Wainwright who just happened to be cycling past, as you do! I won't expand too much, but their collective childminding skills could be improved slightly as Hamish and, going by the photographic evidence afterwards, some of the local youngsters enjoyed a very, very big night. I'll leave it there, but 'Hamish on Tour' T-shirts could be appearing soon.

The only thing wrong with the day was the end result, with South Africa winning 26–20. Ho hum . . .

Friday 23 November

To paraphrase a saying from the world of rock and roll, if it's Paris, it must be Tuesday. Or was it Berlin, it must be Thursday? Or even London, it has to be Saturday? You'll soon catch my drift. Sometimes you are just so busy that you only identify what day of the week it is by where you find yourself. This week, I fancy, might be a bit like that.

Today is Friday and therefore it has to be Edinburgh, the day divided into two equally important halves. During the daylight hours, me, wife Kathy and the boys have been at Murrayfield at lunchtime to witness the 'Captain's Run', in the company of Scottish Rugby Union patron, Her Royal Highness, The Princess Royal, who has been such a fantastic supporter of the game in Scotland, and a source of encouragement for me and the Foundation.

The players, too, are in good spirits. Their performance a week ago may have deserved a better outcome, but I'm sure they'll win this one.

That done and dusted, it was on to the City Chambers for my evening appointment with the Edinburgh Lord Provost Frank Ross who would present me with the Edinburgh Award for 2018.

The criteria set out for being considered for this award is very specific: I hadn't been previously awarded the Freedom of the City; I wasn't a previous winner of the Edinburgh Award; I'm not a serving politician. All ticks, but the biggest one was had I been born in Edinburgh or lived in the city for the past twelve months? Easily forgotten, given my links to the Borders, that I made my debut in Edinburgh.

All these honours I have been collecting – each of them well deserved I should add – have been a fantastic accolade for me, but they've also identified the work and effort put in by all Foundation members and the wider public as well. These credits and awards I've gathered, I genuinely consider to be real achievements, comparable with anything I did as a player.

At first, it might have been a bit of a laugh, a bit of fun, something to add to my after-dinner routine. Nevertheless, thinking it through, these awards recognise the work and assignments I have taken on over the last few years, specifically in the fight against MND and seeking a better deal for fellow sufferers. That makes them truly special.

It is a splendid evening. When I see names like Ian Rankin, J.K. Rowling, and Richard Demarco as previous recipients, you find yourself giving a wee nod of the head in acknowledgement at what they've achieved, and now someone has deemed I'm on a par with. It was a lovely touch as well that some previous winners were there on the night for the ceremony, like Sir Tom Farmer, Ken Buchanan and Sir Chris Hoy.

The thing that always surprises me is just how small some of these boxers are. I know, most people in my world are tiny, but Ken isn't big in stature at all. That said, he must make up for it on the inside, with the size of heart he must have to do what he did for a living. An undisputed world champion – imagine having that title. You won't, though, find me being condescending to any boxer, lacking in stature or not. I once did that with Paul Weir on a photoshoot years ago, who gave me a couple of 'playful' digs in the ribs as his payback. A lesson never forgotten.

It was a great night. I've noticed at such occasions and events that people can't help themselves from having a wee nosy behind closed doors. Have you seen that? It's not just members of my family either.

Neither will I ever forget Carl Hogg's words on the night. I think his good lady Jill may have helped along the way, but it was touching and moving. It would have made a nice eulogy, but we're a bit away from that stage just yet.

All in all, it was just a great night and a great privilege. I ask Frank if there are any other perks with this award, like my own lane to drive in when in and around Edinburgh. He replies that he doesn't even get that. If only he knew a politician in high office . . .

Saturday 24 November

Scotland play Argentina. Almost exactly twenty-eight years before, a skinny, lanky laddie, five foot eighteen inches – maybe more – and thirteen and a half stone (it does look better in kilograms) was nervously waiting to take his place in a Grand Slam winning team for what would be his international debut. More than quarter of a century ago. It seems like yesterday in so many ways, but I can still remember what the old Murrayfield looked like back then.

That day, we hammered the Pumas 49–3, me giving the scoring pass to Chick (Craig Chalmers) for the final score. To be honest, I was going to make a charge for the line myself, but I had nothing in the legs and it was easier to let my Melrose teammate romp home.

This time around, Scotland still won, albeit by the slightly less impressive tally of 14–9. A win is a win, but we wouldn't be hanging around in the capital to celebrate. We'd bigger fish to fry.

Compared to twenty-eight years ago, my activities on game day are less frenetic, with a bit of chat in the hospitality suites, alongside a certain Gary Armstrong who I followed out of the tunnel all those years ago. Amazing how things pan out.

Sunday 25 November

Kathy and me are up first thing and on the move. We have a big date tonight. In Monaco. I know, what a pair of jet setters.

Monte Carlo, home to the mega rich and mega famous. And the dynamic duo from Blainslie, guests of World Rugby for their annual awards celebrations, will be rubbing shoulders with them (although not too closely in case it costs us money).

The 'what should I wear?' question, needless to say, was not one I needed to ask. While it was officially black tie, I couldn't see anyone taking issue with me turning up in a tartan suit, especially when it was the My Name'5 Doddie tartan. But just to abide by convention, I did wear a black tie with it. A tartan tie would have been better, but in the end no one seemed too worked up over my fashion faux pas.

Kathy looked beautiful, using up the few hours I was away filming for World Rugby to give herself a make-over. We scrubbed up well. While I'm well used to these sort of functions, it is fair to say Kathy isn't entirely enamoured with them, and certainly wouldn't want to be the centre of attention in any shape or form, oh no.

On our way from the hotel to the venue we just happened to bump into Keith Wood and his lovely wife Nicola. What she sees in him, I'll never know. Don't they have free eye tests in Ireland? It was great to see and catch up with one of my favourite people in rugby. And Keith is pretty popular as well.

I think it was around then that the anticipation started to hit me. I'm not the nervous sort, but whether it was the location, or the importance of the occasion, I did feel a few flutters, although I couldn't let Kathy see that I was in any way apprehensive. Still, the good thing was, in her mind, that we wouldn't be anywhere near the front, table 10 was as good as it got for us, so we might as well get ourselves settled.

It was at this point, the maître d' approached and asked to see our guest invite. Kathy presented him with the card, which he turned upside down. '01? You are on the top table, sir . . .'

The colour just drained from Mary Doll's face, as we found ourselves in the company of His Serene Highness, Prince Albert II of Monaco. I don't think my boyish giggling was appreciated by my good lady, but the evening turned into a great one, as I collected the World Rugby 'Award for Character' – which Ireland's Jamie Heaslip presented to me – for our crusade against MND.

The interview stuff I'd done in the afternoon had all been edited into a package, and finally I got to see what that fella at Murrayfield had been doing with that drone a few weeks previous. I might not be ready to challenge Gerard Butler just yet, but it only goes to show what a good video editor can do.

I did have to do a live interview on stage with Alex Payne, and yet again the ovation I received from the body of this rugby church just about set me off. Be brave, Dodgy.

Apart from Woody, or should that be including Woody, it was great to catch up again with Sean Fitzpatrick, who I played against in my very first World Cup, and Bill Beaumont, always someone to share a glass – or two – with. JJ was there too, in whatever capacity he had that week with World Rugby, with another couple of my former sparring partners, Will Greenwood and Lawrence Dallaglio also in attendance. Johnny Sexton took the top prize as player of the year. There was also a Welsh boy, Geraint Thomas there, but I couldn't remember who he played for . . .

As they might say, it was a good night for us Scots as Jamie Armstrong, founder of Trust Rugby International, collected the 'Spirit of Rugby' prize for his concept of 'unified rugby', where players with a disability play in the same team as non-disabled players. That's the kind of person who deserves an award. Someone who turns up in full Highland Dress, not with a tartan suit and a black tie!

However, I couldn't get too carried away, even in such great company. We were back home tomorrow and then it was on to Glasgow – and another award.

Tuesday 27 November

While my muscles may not be quite what they once were, our postie is beginning to develop thighs like Chris Hoy given what is delivered to the house of a week. One letter that arrived during the summer came from the Glasgow Caledonian University. Addressed to me? Surely some mistake?

If you are like me – and not a lot are – then opening mail always follows the same chain of thought; look at the envelope front and back, open it. Scan the address to make certain it's for you, glance down the page to see if there is a '£' sign anywhere, if there is, are you receiving or paying out, and finally, who signed it off.

This morning, in world-record time, I'm reading 'Annie Lennox, Chancellor'. Now, I've heard of her, Annie 'Sweet Dreams' Lennox, and on behalf of the GCU, she informs me I am being awarded an Honorary Degree of Doctor of Science. I will be Dr Weir! Specialist in line-outs, sheep, the Scottish Borders, spotting dafties from Langholm and beer, but primarily for my 'outstanding contribution to the sporting community and commitment to fundraising for the Common Good'. The business cards are going to cost a bit more to get all of that on them!

Primarily, I'll accept because it is a lovely honour and so fantastic that people are thinking about me now for what I am trying to do around MND. But, and by no means secondly, I cannae wait to tell Armstrong, JJ, Scotty, Finn, Grimes, Taity, Hoggy, Chick, Tukalo, anyone by the name of Dods, or Redpath or Milne, Baird and Benzo – especially Benzo – and my three sons, that I am now a doctor. Sorry, I may have got carried away for a second.

Now the big day has arrived. Timetable worked out, hair

nicely spiked, what to wear? Oh, I know. Something off the peg.

Once there I am introduced to my fellow recipients. David Duke is the CEO and founder of Street Soccer, formed to help people who had fallen on hard times to make a change to their lives and come together with others through football. A fascinating story.

Then there was Gary Lewis. I recognise him off the telly.

'You were in Billy, er, the wee boy, the dancer?'

'Elliott.'

'And the *Gangs* thingy with Di what's his name . . .'

'*Gangs of New York*, with DiCaprio.'

I get the feeling Gary knew I had exhausted my knowledge of his works, but he kindly further explained where else I might have seen him. I just agreed, but the more I looked at him, the more I was seeing him in character in other roles and films he would have played, except I didn't know the names of any of them. But a nice guy. My biggest fear was he'd mention *River City* when I'm a devotee of *Emmerdale*.

And then there was Janet Harvey, receiving her Honorary Degree of Doctor of Engineering. She's ninety-six, and being recognised for the work she had done, during the war, as an electrician in the shipyards. This wee woman, a shipbuilder? Amazing.

Speaking to these lovely people, very unassuming but evidently very talented, I couldn't avoid that while here we were, all in the same place at the same time, and all being acknowledged by the university, we had all taken very different routes to arrive at where we were in life. It reaffirmed my thinking that there isn't a right way or a wrong way, or a good or a bad way, of going about your life, but ultimately it's your way – or 'My Way' as Frank Sinatra sang, although he wasn't graduating that day. But here we all were, being celebrated for what we'd achieved.

That said, it was nothing compared to the hard work, and I'd imagine, sweat and tears, that some of the younger graduates had put in to get their degrees and qualifications. I'm not saying I was there under false pretences, but what I had done couldn't possibly have equated to some of the sacrifices those who had studied had undergone. They all deserved the acclaim and applause they received during their moment in the spotlight.

My laureation is delivered by Professor Cam Donaldson. It really is lovely hearing people say nice things about you, but this association is a two-way street.

A few weeks back, I was able to meet with the Early Career Research Group at GCU to talk to them about living with MND, giving them a bit of insight into how it feels to actually live with one of the diseases they are researching, and to explain the human cost of the disease on an individual basis. Hopefully it was a good learning process for them and it's always great to be able to deliver my message to a new audience.

Now, remember I mentioned what to wear?

People expect me to wear tartan. It is my trademark, my signature, so I was not going to disappoint on yet another big stage. I was resplendent in my Doddie tartan suit, which everyone had taken an interest in and the tale behind it. If you don't know the story, why didn't you buy the first book?

But, and it is a colossal but, probably only understood by those who have themselves suffered a wardrobe catastrophe, what I hadn't realised was that I'd be donned in ceremonial robes, and I'd need to wear these for the inauguration.

They were blue and red with a yellow trim, thrown over the blue, black, white and yellow of my tartan suit, creating a bit of a colour clash that was likened to an explosion in a paint factory. Looking back at the photographs, they weren't wrong. However, there was one saving grace.

We also had to wear a hat – I'm informed it's called a Tudor bonnet – which was a smidge too big for my dainty cranium and would slide down occasionally. Thankfully my lugs prevented it from falling over my eyes, but it did prove to be a minor distraction to what was going on downstairs with the fashion show. Which was no bad thing.

But a lovely day all in. Me, a doctor. When will they deliver the TARDIS?

Thursday 29 November

'Would you like to sit on the couch with Lorraine Kelly?'

Would I? I don't think it was a question that needed to be answered. Lorraine *is* morning television, so having the chance to talk about me, the Foundation and my book wasn't something I was going to kick into the long grass.

The only thing I had to consider was managing my travel and rest. It wasn't too taxing, but I'm conscious of how easy it is to be caught up in the moment, doing too much too easily, and then paying the consequences for a couple of days. What with my graduation, it had been a full-on week already for the good doctor.

All the work had been done behind the scenes between those at Black & White Publishing and Stewart, so all I had to do was jump on the train, get picked up, go to the hotel, eat, sleep, get picked up in the morning and be taxied to the studios to start talking.

The young woman who met me said Lorraine knew I was there and that she would come in and see me in a few minutes. Next thing, there she was, TV royalty, gorgeous, lovely and supportive. We didn't have long for idle chat off-air, but she wanted her photo taken. Secretly, so did I, and just for effect she'd come in with her flat shoes on, to accentuate the height difference, although in truth, she could have been on stilts and I'd still have been a foot taller.

I've been getting quite an exclusive photo album assembled. Not that I have an actual album, with all the wee spaces for the individual snaps. I've got dozens of them from years ago, but do they actually still exist today, or are we all mobile phone dependent?

Lorraine hurriedly went through the brief, but said I'd be fine. Microphones on, waistcoat buttoned up, and we were good to go. I did have the usual dab of makeup, but, as you will have noticed, it isn't really something I need, unlike others who appear on TV.

If I was asked once, I was asked ten times, if I wanted something to drink. I did, but only took a sip. Put it this way; what goes in, has to come out again, and I'm not really currently cut out for a quick dash to the wee boys' room, to get unzipped, have a pee, then zip back up, ready for action, all in sixty seconds before going on air. Best not to take that risk.

Lorraine, true to her word, kept to what she was going to speak about, which was fine, but you could really feel her empathy, maybe it was sympathy, as to where I had now found myself. She had a wee press at those emotion buttons, but I'd switched them off. Nevertheless, the interview itself went well, not too harrowing, and afterwards Lorraine thought it had been brilliant, which I'm pleased about because she was just so nice and is a very special lady.

Then it was off-set, time to say our farewells, until next time, and I was off back to my billet by taxi. All the way back I was thinking what lovely people I'd met, particularly Lorraine, and how it had been a good, if a wee bit early, start to the day. For someone who'd always played down being on telly, even being dismissive on occasions, I was liking sitting in front of the cameras, and more importantly, in front of millions of viewers.

I daydream in the cab, glancing at the skyline, at the hustle and the bustle around me. Just losing myself in the moment. The trip seems to take just a matter of minutes. Back in my hotel room, I realise all those niceties had utterly blindsided me, distracted me into making what would best be described as a schoolboy error, although not too many schoolboys wear a waistcoat on a daily basis. But, disastrously, I was still wearing mine.

If I have difficulty in buttoning things up – shirts, jackets, coats, trousers and waistcoats – then undoing them is just as difficult, make that impossible. And here I was, in a room, on my own, trussed up like a corseted turkey.

I had been so busy enjoying the moment with Lorraine and her crew, I'd completely forgotten to ask someone to unbutton me, a request you kind of only make within earshot of those you know or trust. Hence why a telephone call to reception might have landed me in bother. Best not to take that risk. I'm in enough trouble without bringing myself to the notice of the hotel management, or worse.

Extracting myself from the waistcoat wasn't easy; basically I lay on the bed and just wriggled up and down, anchoring my arms in various positions, digging my heels in, and shoving myself around until I got it off.

There were a few hairy moments, including nearly going off the bed, upside down and backwards, the consequences of that doesn't need thinking about, plus when it felt as if my arm and head were trying to go through the same hole. But we got there eventually, a hell of a lot more sweaty, and a hell of a lot wiser in as much as I wouldn't make that mistake again, and a bit happier to be free. It was, despite being a complete pain at the time – and goodness knows how long I'd spent being Harry Houdini – quite funny in a stupid way.

It only brings home again just how organised you need to be when stepping out of your usual and trusted environment. I'm lucky, having so many people who I can call upon, or who are willing to help in almost all eventualities. Similarly, you ponder the difficulties of others in my situation, who maybe don't have siblings, or friends, or ex-teammates to help them. They have my sympathies, but they need more than that. They need assistance, help, or a cure. All in, I'm lucky among the unlucky.

One of my 'carers' is Jill Douglas and this afternoon we'll be on a very nice mission – to sign off on a gin that will carry my name. I'll be honest, I've never been a gin drinker (I leave those duties to Kathy), but Jill knows what she likes on that front, and will no doubt shove me along in the right direction. If it all goes too well, she might end up pushing me back to the hotel.

This tasting thing is a real eye opener. Producing gin is just a big chemistry process, although I never got to try anything like this when I was at school.

From what is the basic spirit, various potions, flavourings and ingredients are added – and some are taken back out again – until such times as you arrive at a taste and flavour that is pleasing on the tongue. I have a confession to make; I may have been somewhat intoxicated by the time it came to nod approval for the winning mix, and I have a real suspicion that this might have been more to suit Jill's palate than mine. I'm not saying I got drunk, but my recollections the next day were somewhat hazy.

Nevertheless, another great venture to be involved with and hopefully the bottles will fly off the shelf. All in a good cause you understand . . .

Friday 30 November

Jill leaves and Stewart arrives. I have never been this popular.

Stewart is here because we have another book signing to do, this time at Waterstones in Leadenhall Market. It should be busy, with a number of factors playing into that theory. The first is I've been longlisted for the *Telegraph* Sports Book of the Year award, in the category of best autobiography.

I say I've, but maybe that should be 'we've', given Stewart's input into this venture, just twenty years in the making. I'm quite chuffed about being recognised in such a way, but Stuey appears thoroughly delighted with the prospect, exemplified by him grabbing my head in his hands and planting a kiss on my forehead. He's just taking advantage of me, but explaining the significance of this nomination, I might just join in his celebration, minus the kisses.

As part of the build-up to the awards, Sky Sports have come along to film an interview with me, and have sent the gorgeous Jacquie Beltrao along for the chat.

After the introductions, we grab a corner and a coffee, and get the interview out of the way before the official book signing begins upstairs.

Jacquie has had her own health issues over the years and although we don't quite compare notes, there is certainly a connection between the two of us, the kind perhaps you only really understand when your health and wellbeing – and indeed your life – is threatened.

Having met and spoken to various people in a similar predicament to myself, I think a great many folk – once the initial shock and fear has subsided – take quite a philosophical view about where they are; namely, while I'm still here, we may as well make the most of it; and enjoy the moment.

While you don't know quite what is ahead of you, Jacquie confirms that these challenges make you stronger, steelier and less frightened. It helps if you have enough in your life, or you can get on with things that occupy you, rather than dwelling on what might happen – although it might never happen for some. Not a category I currently belong to.

Jacquie wants a selfie or two, and says she'll be sending one to her Sky News colleague, fellow Scot Niall Paterson, who she says is quite envious of her getting to do this shoot.

Jacquie says I'm the nicest man she has ever interviewed. I bet she says that to all the boys, but there is a real warmth in her every word, maybe because she's been through the mill herself. Hugs and kisses approvingly received, Stewart and I continue with the signing. And there is a queue.

We have become quite a good double act; he knows the page to open the books at, I sign them, he does his squiggle, and then fills in any messages as it would simply take me too long to do it, and anyway, you'd like to be able to read the message inside your bestseller. He now reveals why that *Telegraph* commendation is key; a great many wait for books to be recommended, and in the world of sports books, the *Telegraph*'s tick of approval is as good as it gets.

He also mentions that we are a little more than a month away from Christmas – the key time of year for book sales. Add those two factors together and hence why you have a line stretching out the door and around the corner.

Stewart writes 'a Merry Christmas' as often as he does his scrawl, where every sale and signing means another photograph of me. I don't mind. All part of being a bestselling author I suppose.

Eventually we are done. In my case, I'm exactly that. It is very tiring doing the book signings, because not having any dexterity in my fingers or hand, the only way I get anything like an autograph on the page is to shift my entire arm, which weighs a ton after five minutes. Those beads of sweat are for real.

We take a taxi to the station. I'm going to Edinburgh, Glasgow for Stewart. We get into the Virgin VIP lounge and grab a seat. Do you recall what I said about all those kisses being a bonus? They're not the only things that come with recognition.

'Can I buy you lads a pint?' comes the very kind offer from a complete stranger. It would have been rude not to.

DECEMBER 2018

Saturday 1 December

Saturday, and I'm working for Premier Sports, covering Glasgow Warriors versus Scarlets at Scotstoun with Rory Lawson and Richie Rees. I seldom get out these days.

Wednesday 5 December

Another batch of books has arrived from Black & White, last minute signings to be sent out for the Christmas market – and the North Pole. I have no idea how many we've signed now, thousands I reckon. But the sales appear to have been very good, everything I hoped for. While it's nice people are supporting me this way, I also hope they read the book and the messages contained. If it inspires one individual to make a difference, or to seek a change, or to live for a bit longer, then it would be job done.

Monday 10 December

Like every other household, the Weirs are gearing up for Christmas, although perhaps with a little less of the madness of a year ago. Who wants what – and more important who is getting what they want – is all a matter of debate and compromise. So how come compromise, which is supposed to be about all parties getting an equal part of what they want, costs me so much?

Tuesday 11 December

This year has been an absolute blur at times. There has been so much to cram in, what with appearances, book launches, meetings and gatherings, and that's just me and the Foundation. There is also the small matter of being a husband and a dad, and the support I receive from Kathy, Hamish, Angus and Ben, and the rest of my immediate family, has been quite incredible. Without them, I wouldn't be able to spend my time working on behalf of the Foundation and tackling the challenges of MND.

Today we are in Edinburgh, for the last meeting of the trustees and the board this year. Compared to where we were at the start of the year, we really have a focus and a route to what we want to achieve, in terms of setting up the business – because ultimately that is what your charity becomes – but also in putting some of the key component parts of what we do in place: namely, how do we spend the small fortune that people have collected for us, and how can that be best spent.

To that end, formulating our medical advisory panel has been essential; who do we get to run it, who should we involve, who should we take counsel from, who is to be listened to, and above all else, what is the best way we can utilise the resources we now have. A lot of thought has been given to this, and mental fatigue does set in occasionally.

We need to relieve that stress – so today we're having our Christmas party. Our first, and definitely not our last. A chance to let our hair down, and even raise a glass to what we've done and what we will do. Glad to report that everyone behaved.

Hmmm ...

Monday 24 December

Some days and dates are especially memorable; your anniversary, your kids being born. Others become etched in the memory for very different reasons, and this is one of those for me.

Two years to the day, I was given the news I had MND. There has not been a day when I haven't played that message back in my mind, of what it meant to me from that moment and to others going forward. The pessimism of that day – the worst of it being told that in a year I wouldn't be walking – hasn't materialised, though it will, eventually and inevitably.

Right now, I'm still able to put my best foot forward, capable of walking where I want to go. Ask me if I'm still able to do that tomorrow night after several glasses of falling-down juice . . .

Thursday 27 December

All of these honours and awards have been a major surprise. I do question what I've done to deserve them, or warrant consideration for them, because I don't think I've done much to deserve them, not like some people.

Some months ago, a very nice envelope popped through the letter box. It looked more official than the most official envelope I'd ever seen previously, which was probably from HMRC. Then it dawned on me what it was. Oh my God!

It's strange when something like that arrives; you kind of know what it might be, but I don't think you can ever believe it. Me and Mary Doll just looked at one another, then looked at the letter again. I think I had a quick look around the kitchen just to make sure there wasn't a secret camera set up, like for a Jeremy Beadle sketch.

Previously, I would hear people saying that it wasn't just for them but for everyone involved in whatever venture they were being recognised for. I wish I could have been different and say no, it's got my name on it, get your own, it's all down to me.

But that really would be denying the people who have worked endlessly for the Foundation, not just the trustees, and those close to them, but for all the people who entered into fundraising events, organising all the daft things you could ever imagine, just to help our cause against MND.

You get a lot of forms and things to return, just to say whether you accept, or not, although I can't imagine why you'd do that because there must have been people thinking you were worthy of such an honour. Whatever, and each to their own.

In saying that, I did wonder what I should do because part of my after-dinner routine is about slagging off all my old teammates who had OBEs, MBEs and the like off the back of me doing my job so supremely well. Gary Armstrong, OBE, for services to rugby, namely taking the ball off a plate I'd served it up on. But I'm not bitter.

In the end I decided I would accept because I could always change my routine. I'm clever that way.

Mary Doll was just as shocked. She'd need a dress! It looked like she had quickly got her head around the reality of the situation.

The main thing, obviously, was that we couldn't tell anyone – and I mean no one – and we had to be totally discreet.

I put the envelope to one side, out the way, for safe keeping – and then completely forgot all about it. Now, I know you will be thinking how can you forget that, or let it completely slip your memory. But trust me, it was quite easy.

You have to remember there was so much going on in my life, I was living for the day, and incredible as it sounds, things do fall into your mental spam folder. We hadn't replied.

Then an unsuspecting Jill received a call from the Home Office, a rather perplexed Home Office, saying that they hadn't received either an acceptance or a refusal from me, and 'Did George Wilson Weir want to accept his OBE?'

'I just forgot' sounded a bit lame. Not like me, at all, but thankfully they understood the circumstances and we were good to go. And we knew Jill wouldn't say a thing.

But sitting on the news was quite difficult. I became quite paranoid about the story breaking. There were some people who would say certain things, almost like they were poking, trying to tap you for information. I was really impressed with myself in those weeks up to the announcement, saying nothing.

Not long to go now. This is the final day of silence. Hogmanay would soon be here.

None of our immediate family knew. We were instructed to say nothing, and we stuck rigidly to the guidelines. Kathy and me just didn't see the reason why you'd want to let it out the bag, just for someone else to broadcast it. No, that wasn't the way it worked.

On 28 December, it was Hamish's eighteenth birthday party. That was a big day for him, and a big day for me – one of the reasons I was still here. We had a few people around to the house and had a few drinks.

Then out of the blue, a message, then another, and another. What was going on? Not now, with just a few days to go! Had the cat jumped out of the bag and run around the country telling everyone that it would now be Dodgy OBE? How did they know, and who told them? Obviously, I had to ignore them. Then a call and a message from Stewart. Right, to the bottom of this.

What I didn't know was – although it might have been on one of those sheets of paper in the envelope – was that the day prior to the announcement, and before the embargo can be broken, people in the media have access to the list.

New Year Honours it said. The 28th was not New Year. I wish I'd read the small print.

But what to do. Should we say now, or still play to the rules? Kathy and I had a five-second conversation. We'd leave it as is. Say nothing. Play dumb. Amazing how easy that was.

Then, about 10.30 that evening, the brother-in-law, Dougie Mundell, came up and asked, 'Is this news right, have you got a gong?'

Of all people in the western world, Mundell had the BBC news app on his phone. People will be aghast at this revelation. This is the man who tried to take his tractor through the McDonald's drive-thru in Gala.

But there it was, me and Nicola Benedetti being two people, out of the dozens of Scots who would have been honoured, to be featured on the BBC News page.

And when one person knew, so too did someone else, and the phones really began to light up. It was lovely being congratulated, but deep down, I hadn't expected it to happen this way and I wouldn't have wanted it like this.

This was Hamish's big day, the day the biggest boy becomes a big man and can now do so many things only an eighteen-year-old can do – or, at least, can now do them legally. I really didn't want to distract from his party, his time. If I had to do it all again, I would do exactly the same. And Hamish appreciated that. No, he didn't actually.

Although it was his party, and he was really happy for me, he gave me a right bollocking for not telling him in advance. The same applied to my sister, Kirsty, and in time, my other boys, my brothers, folk in Gala, Melrose, folk in Newcastle, Ireland, Wales, everywhere, upset for not celebrating that night. See, that's what playing to the rules gets you!

Tricky when you get on in later life, even the simplest of decisions, or at least what you consider simple, can have ramifications.

It was, and is, a fantastic honour and accolade, just like the others I've received.

But what perks come with being an OBE? Free parking? Driving in the bus lanes? Whatever, I won't be going out blinged up. That just isn't my style.

2019

*That union between us is almost like a living history
in today's rugby world. It meant a great deal then.
And those friendships mean even more now.*

JANUARY 2019

Tuesday 1 January

Happy New Year one and all. Compared to a year ago, the Hogmanay celebrations were slightly more reserved – although not by much. From my perspective, this life and living thing is everything it's cracked up to be. Challenging, of course. But better to be here doing what I can than not. Not sure what the New Year will bring. But after the often hectic schedule I had to end the year, I'm going into 2019 at a much more leisurely pace. I'm sure you can understand why.

Monday 21 January

Can you imagine not liking haggis?

I've had it countless times, but I've seldom enjoyed it in more salubrious surrounds than where I'm visiting this evening – a certain 10 Downing Street.

There are some places that just blow you away, because of size, importance, or notoriety. But tonight I got to step though arguably the most famous front door in the world.

The fantastic invite to join Prime Minister Theresa May to celebrate Burns Night comes from John Lamont MP, and I'm glad to have accepted. It is my City of Edinburgh tartan suit for this evening, and as always it attracts a fair bit of comment – from the PM and others.

'How many do you have?'

'Who makes them?'

'Do you ever not wear a tartan suit?'

For future reference, currently I have ten, they are not made they are built, and finally yes, but only so I can put on my tartan jammies.

The kids of the Ayrshire Fiddle Orchestra are providing the music and seem delighted to be doing so – if a little nervous. But what an experience to look back on. They will never forget it.

Sir Boyd Tunnock, 'The Caramel Wafer King', was there, a great supporter of the traditions of Burns especially with youngsters in our schools, according to those in the know, and so too was John Barrowman, as well as a couple of 'faces' I recognised and then spent the rest of the night trying to work out how I knew them.

They knew me, always slightly embarrassing that. But I concluded this was neither the time or place to greet people with: 'How are you doing, wee man?'

Friday 25 January

Once more I'm in the company of Frank Ross, the Lord Provost of Edinburgh as his guest of honour at his annual Burns Supper at Prestonfield House. I'm introduced to other guests and declare that it is such a long time since I've had haggis. Some nod in agreement.

Once again, Provost Ross will use the evening to raise funds for the OneCityFirst charity, as well as the Foundation, and this year will be making the involvement of children and young people as a real focal point in so much of what they support. I like children. I was one myself once.

When I heard that, and having been in discussion with the

Provost and his office, I thought it only right that I offer the services of my resident 'Addresser of the Haggis' – it's a technical term – Callum Weir, who a year ago had done such a grand job at the Newcastle Falcons Burns Supper. What a delivery in front of so many people – although he showed the kind of wicked sense of humour that appeals to me, and that had his parents in a pickle when he asked a minute before going on stage, 'And how does it start again?'

Having arrived by train, I accepted the kind offer of a lift home in a Bentley Bentayga, provided by one of the sponsors of the evening, but only after I'd given Callum a spin around the block. What a machine, and the effortless ride back to the farm in a beast weighing a couple of tons and capable of doing 180 m.p.h. had me wishing I'd arrived in such style as well.

I suppose we had better take Callum back to Edinburgh now …

Wednesday 30 January

Bluecairn, our wee farm tucked away in the Scottish Borders, is a busy place at the best of times but especially crowded today and will be for much of this week. We are sticking the 'pod' on to the side of the house, a self-contained unit – for want of a better description, a fully functional wet room – for me to use whenever my mobility becomes an issue.

While I am still able to roam around, indeed like a mad giraffe, there will come a time when that isn't so easy. It is better therefore to be prepared for all eventualities, because with MND you never really know what could happen and when.

Designed by James Cromarty at Yeoman's in Berwick Upon Tweed, Kevin Armstrong (you may recognise the surname) has been charged with producing this piece of domesticated wizardry. The pod is finished off site, then is hoisted into place, sitting atop stilts, and bolted on to the side of the house. The beauty of this is that the house can be restored to its usual workings once the pod has outlived its purpose.

And once secured, all the plumbing work and electrics can be completed. Simple. I can see the fancy toilet and even fancier showers becoming tourist attractions for anyone visiting.

Not only can Gary make a mean pass, he is also a master behind the wheel of a truck. Incredibly, in all the years I've known him, I've never sat beside him in a big rig (trucker jargon that is) before. We need to go and collect the pod, which only just fits on the lorry. There is a bit of an overhang on my side, which I have to say was coming quite close (or so it appeared) to collecting trees, traffic lights and road signs along the way, but thankfully it all arrived, dent-free.

Gazza wasn't concerned at all and told me to have another Yorkie – I'd taken some along just to get into character – although one did melt on my denim jacket. Well, I needed to look the part as well.

However, the road trip was nothing to seeing Gary reverse the lorry down the narrow driveway into the farm. I suppose it's difficult to go through life without being good at something.

Kevin and his team (which excludes Gary as he is only a driver and he drinks too much tea as well) are getting on with their work while I supervise. Actually, that should be make nuisance of myself. They really don't need me for anything and, such is their desperation to get me out of the way, they allow me to go digging holes around the farm buildings in the mini-excavator they are using.

Twenty-seven holes later (all of various lengths, depths and widths, though none are filled in), the guys are ready to use a crane, forklift and whatever other machinery is required – along with no small measure of brute strength and ignorance – to get the pod in place.

At this point I lose the keys to the digger – well, they were not lost, just taken from me – and my tunnelling is made good before the final hoist, with me nowhere to be seen, takes place. Job's a good 'un.

Credit where it is due, Kevin is a talented lad. Good that there's one brother in the family who is. Me, I'm costing up one of those wee dinky diggers for next Christmas . . .

FEBRUARY 2019

Sunday 10 February

The auld ferm can be a mucky place, especially during winter, with rain and snow turning the surrounding lands – when they are not frozen solid – into mud baths and any hole becoming more a water splash than a puddle. Important then that you keep on top of basic cleaning duties.

Sunday is a good day for a wee spruce up, before another week begins (although they never really end), and because there tends to be willing, helping hands (sons) around to join in. Still, I like to do my bit. Just give me a power washer and I'll stay amused for hours.

Lance in hand, I was as happy as a pig in the proverbial. That was up until I decided to unfankle myself from the hoses to go elsewhere. Wham.

I'm not sure if I knocked myself out. If I did it was for a split second. But I really banged my head, face down on the terra firma, with the emphasis and the impact on the firma. A bit dizzy – but what's new – I waited until my head cleared as assistance arrived. And ouch.

I was too busy wondering if I'd damaged my boyish good looks to realise I was hurting elsewhere. Hurting a lot.

Anyone who has ever done something like this will know that your thought process speeds up to ten times its normal rate. What was I doing, where was I going? Well, Pitlochry and Monaco in the next week for starters. Hopefully not the hospital. Simultaneously, I find myself answering questions like, 'Are you okay?' and 'Where does it hurt?' I can barely draw the strength or power to say 'yes' or 'no', never mind give a running commentary because by now I'm acutely aware that I have sore bits elsewhere than my napper, namely my chest, or rib cage. Time for some medical attention.

The doctor said I'd probably punctured a lung, which I was assured would rectify itself – 'usually' – but in the meantime take some painkillers and I'd be assessed again in a week.

Saturday 16 February

Had been due to have a date last night with Stewart at the Winter Words Book Festival in Pitlochry. I'm ruled out through injury, so send them a wee video explaining the situation, apologising and telling the people who'd bought tickets that I would see them in 2020. Stewart had to fly solo, an 'impact substitute', something he was quite good at according to Twitter. He always said I cramped his style. Don't think I'll invite him next year . . .

Sunday 17 February

A week gone and the pain is as excruciating as it has been most of the weekend. I have a pretty high pain threshold, but breathing was making me yelp. I had damaged ribs before but it was nothing like this. Second opinion time. The lung needed re-inflating. I visualised a trip to the garage for some compressed air. No, rather than the local service station, a trip to Borders General Hospital was the order of the day.

As excuses go, having a message sent through to Iain Clark of Laureus that I wouldn't be able to attend because of a punctured lung wasn't bad. Thankfully, Iain understood and came up with a solution – that Hamish would represent me and he could take a guest. Me? Nah. It was Monte Carlo or bust – and I was bust.

Hamish's cousin Graham Dun was added to the squad as a late replacement and the pair were packed off with their heads full of instructions.

Monday 18 February

Who'd have thought me and the NHS were so close? But, here I am in their care for something else other than my usual ailment. It sounded such a simple procedure. They always do. However, what it meant was a drain – slightly less intrusive than the ones I used to put in for Hutchison's when I installed sewage tanks for a living – 'Your number twos are my No. 1' – that had to be inserted in my chest to remove the fluid in my lung, which was causing the inflammation and adding to the pain. Harking back to my MND diagnosis, I needed a lumbar puncture during the many tests I had. That was gruesome and sore, ten out of ten on the Doddie ouch-o-meter. Sticking this drain between my ribs, we touched nine a few times.

Once inserted, you could see the gunge starting to drip out into the wee pot you have to carry around with you. My new fashion accessory would have proved troublesome getting on a flight to Monaco. The reality was I wasn't fit to fly on one lung anyway. Instead of a five-star hotel, I was given an extended bed in Ward 7 of the BGH and an extended stay of three nights, full board. Melrose rather than Monte Carlo for me.

In my hospital bed I'm adjacent to a fella, eighty years old, who not only had taken a nasty tumble well over a month ago, he'd landed up against a radiator which scalded him. Poor old bugger. What have I got to moan about?

Not much really. Creamy, Gary and Hoggy pay me a visit,

nice of them although I was enjoying the R&R. Out of the blue, Toony pops in. He's taken time out from preparing for the next international against France in Paris (a place he and I have happy memories of) to come and see me. No grapes or Lucozade, but it's the thought that counts. Being the Scotland rugby coach, he is box office material. You can see that through the reaction of the nurses. 'Another ginger nut, Mr Townsend?' Pfft.

I was having more than ginger nuts. One night I had a wee whisky tasting, and on the last night in a private room, some wine and cheese. All part of the recuperation process, you understand. This unanticipated spring break has given me a few days to put my feet up and ponder. The damage to my lung was never life threatening, but my capacity has probably deteriorated by around ten per cent in the past eight months.

The last thing I want to be doing is causing myself unnecessary damage, which ultimately takes time to repair – although, I know, probably never fully.

By the end of the week I've had enough of hospital life – mind you, the food wasn't bad – and maybe they've had their fill of me as well.

Back home, Hamish is full of stories from his meanderings around the Mediterranean. With Sir Chris Hoy and Sean Fitzpatrick keeping a worldly eye on them, Hamish and Graham did a bit of talent spotting on the big night: Novak Djokovic, Boris Becker, David Coulthard, Bryan Habana, Arsène Wenger, Cesc Fábregas, Eliud Kipchoge and Tony Hawk to name but a few.

But did I win? Remember, the only reason this harum-scarum duo were out there was because I was up for the Moment of the Year award after my now-famous walk onto the Murrayfield pitch ahead of Scotland's game against the All Blacks back in 2017.

No is the simple answer, beaten by double amputee Xia Boyu who climbed Mount Everest. Must just have pipped me . . .

Saturday 23 February

Scotland lose in Paris. Ach, well. Hope Gregor taking a timeout to come and see me in the hospital wasn't the root cause of that loss.

I'm home but still confined to barracks, although there are other events on my schedule this week that I was looking forward to. I can get up, slowly, and walk about, but I'm really very aware that I feel as if I am walking around at times with my hands in my pockets, something you're told as a kid not to do – and by Jim Telfer regularly. However, in my case, the feeling is there simply because they are not much use to me should I have to move speedily, as in, say, preventing a fall.

I've had a couple of slips and falls now. The one last week could have happened at any time, to anyone. Today, in contrast to fifteen years ago, or with an able-bodied person, is that now, for me, such an eventuality carries slightly more risk of a catastrophic conclusion. But what to do; sit and look out the window and stay safe, or lead a life that keeps me content?

I'll carry on as normal. But my fall was a big warning to say: you are not that well, behave yourself. But where is the fun in that? I'm just doing what I always do, and that's whatever I can do to make the most of every single day.

Training yourself to respond differently, to change how you've always previously reacted when you get your feet tied up or lose balance is easier said than done. Like when I came off second best to a cow coming out of the horse box on my sister's farm. 'I'll stop this,' my brain was saying, but my body and the cow were saying the total opposite. Smack, one busted eye. Easier said than done and I'm not sure how exactly you go about disciplining yourself to counter your natural instincts.

Maybe I need a jacket like an air bag. Now there's a thing worth inventing. Actually I think there is something like that on the market for eventing, on the horses. I may have to invest in one, or one of the rugby scrum caps – in the Doddie tartan, but of course.

Thursday 28 February

This is where I get frustrated. The legacy of my fall has resulted in grief and pain, me spending three days in hospital, missing a trip to Monaco, another appointment in Pitlochry, and now I am unable to fly to Guernsey to fulfil an engagement with Gazza. Basically, every time I fall, I one, hurt myself and two, I hurt my reputation. It is frustrating to say the very least. I have two options going forward: firstly, don't fall, and secondly, learn to bounce. That would take practice. So perfecting number one it is ...

MARCH 2019

Wednesday 6 March

My motto 'if you don't use it, you lose it' applies not just to muscle and sinew, it also applies to keeping my brain active and pushing myself to go that little bit more than I should, probably, even in a working environment.

Today is the middle of another very, very, VERY busy week, one when I'm constantly on the move. Makes me a more difficult target...

This morning I'm in Edinburgh for a photo shoot to launch the official partnership between the Foundation and Purple Bricks, the... well, if I need to tell you what they do then their advertising campaign hasn't been working!

They have very kindly come aboard and will make a donation based on every house transaction they are involved with. I don't see myself using their excellent service – I'm far too happy at Bluecairn – but I'll be really interested to look out for their 'SOLD' signs in the My Name'5 Doddie Foundation tartan. Another tremendous example of business supporting our campaign against MND.

I think I'm on hard standing when I say that writing a book and

MND has, maybe individually, perhaps inseparably, taken me into the thoughts of a different audience and a different generation to those who might recall me as a rugby player. Now I'm seen as an MND warrior, although some days I toil to fight sleep.

If every day is a school day, then I learned a great deal going back to school tonight, when I was invited to participate at an 'in conversation' evening at North Berwick High School. Unluckily for the packed audience, Stewart came along as well, though he does come in handy opening books for me to sign.

Having met various children and teachers in advance, we took to the stage to begin the cross-examination. The kids chosen to ask some of the questions were very polished and free of nerves, more than could be said for the MC, Mr Orr. As a punishment exercise, we let him lie on the floor – in his new jacket – so we could explain the difference between rucking in today's game and twenty-five years ago. He did take a bit of a shoeing and a couple of wee digs for his troubles. I'm not sure who enjoyed seeing a teacher being set about the most, the kids or the parents.

I think we can call it a dead heat... and Mr Orr a very good sport, even if his dress sense leaves something to be desired.

Thursday 7 March

My diary is chock-a-block. This morning I'm on the 11.12 out of Carlisle, bound for Cardiff where I'm due to appear on the BBC Wales *Sin Bin* rugby show that evening with Gabby Logan (I'm beginning to think there are three of her), Gareth Thomas (there's only one of him), Carol Vorderman and Jamie Roberts, who, like me, is a doctor, but one who studied to earn that title.

At the same time, Gary and big boy Hamish are filling in for me (it takes two of them to do what I do on my own) at the Sport Newcastle Annual Dinner where I have been awarded the Wilkinson's Sword for Lifetime Achievement, something I'm immensely proud to accept off the back of everything I've achieved career-wise with the Falcons. I told you the diary was rammed. And still more to tick off.

Friday 8 March

I'm becoming a bit of an anorak when it comes to train times and stations. And 10.05 a.m. is when I step back onto the big chuff-chuff (although I don't know the last time this train would have made that sound) going north back to Carlisle, but not before I've spent the early morning at BBC Wales again, doing breakfast TV and radio. They're getting their money's worth. A night in my own bed beckons ...

Saturday 9 March

... and back on another train, this time from Tweedbank to Waverley where I am hosting the 'big room' – otherwise known as the Thistle Suite – ahead of the Six Nations game against Wales. Not one to get teary eyed and all sentimental, but this will be my last one. After 61 international caps, someone has calculated that I've now made 39 starts for Scottish Rugby in hospitality – leaving me one hundred not out.

I'm laughing at thinking how it all started, when, to be totally honest, getting a second booking was a shock. But we've gone from there to me nearly understanding what a running order and timings were about, to live calls, dressing room interviews and, but of course, special guests. Some have been much better than others. Scott Quinnell, for instance, has his own radio show in Wales. Probably the only people who understand him. And he was funny, nearly as good as me. Others were a bit uncomfortable having the spotlight on them. No names, but Al Kellock knows who I mean.

Joking apart, all the guys I had the joy to work with were great fun, and we had some legends on stage. David Campese was always up for a bit of craic – and abuse – and the Irish fellas, like Shane Byrne and Alan Quinlan really got what it was all about, namely entertainment.

You had a laugh, dished it out, took it back – and in the case of some of the English boys, they gave it me tight, what with my track record against them. All, though, in the name of rugby and enjoying yourself.

But, above all, those I'd really like to say thank you to were the Scotland team members who at times really didn't want to have a microphone thrust under their nose, especially after a tough loss – or any loss – and in particular any of the Scotland captains I've interviewed. It can't have been easy sounding positive or upbeat, not so much on the tail of a loss, but with the daft questions I was asking you.

But all good things must come to an end, and after giving it a bit of thought and a bit of chat with those at the SRU, I decided the game against Wales in the Six Nations would be my swansong. Putting in a five or six hour shift prior to and after an international is hard work for healthy lads. But given my condition, and that things don't come as easy as they once did, it's nice to go when people are talking about me for the right reasons. And, after all, what better way would there be to bow out than celebrating Scotland beating Wales to win the Doddie Weir Cup – surely, this time?

Many will not have realised, however, how close I came to making the type of catastrophic blunder that would have had me sacked on the spot (even though I'd already quit). All the SRU senior management were standing up the back of the room, watching and listening to my last spiel, when I decided it might be a good idea to summon up a member of the audience, and preferably a small-looking guest.

Given that I can spout out verbal abuse quicker than an Uzi submachine gun and, of course, with the PA system on 11 so I'm the only person you can hear, for once I didn't enter into any banter, or abuse, didn't say anything about height or appearance, until I saw who the person I'd selected was as he had his back turned to me. I picked him, really, because he should have been watching and listening.

He turned and stood up – indeed, a diminutive gentleman, quite possibly because he seemed to me to be of Far Eastern descent. 'Ooh ya . . .' – that was a close one, particularly with what I'd normally have said as someone was getting to their feet!

I could see the headlines flashing up before my eyes. Thankfully, I regained my composure and changed the script: rapidly. However, I think there were a few of my employers – with their hands over their mouths – who realised, in aviation terms, that was a near miss.

Before everyone left, all the guests – probably more than five hundred of them – came outside and into the main stand to have one last photograph taken with me and members of the Scotland team that afternoon. A perfect picture – albeit one missing the Doddie Weir Cup. We lost 18–11.

So much for the best laid plans . . .

Monday 11 March

Having travelled on Sunday to arrive in time for dinner (and what a splendid dinner it was), Boughton House, courtesy of Richard Scott, Duke of Buccleuch, is the location again for the Foundation's scientific advisory board meeting.

I feel we are headed in the right direction with a real semblance of order in what we do, steered greatly by Jill, Sean and Scott. I'm not really into legacy and the likes. I am trying to do what is best for all MND sufferers and that includes me. Accelerating the processes alone would be of some comfort and hope to those most acutely shaken by this disease.

Thursday 14 March

On our way to London, again. Maybe we should invest in time travel?

The passenger rail service between the two capitals is certainly an easier way to travel to the south than the one adopted by Rob Wainwright and Mark Beaumont, that intrepid and incorrigible pair, who are cycling from Murrayfield to Twickenham with a match ball. What these guys do for the Foundation. What they do to get out of the house.

I keep an eye open for them, but maybe they've taken a different route, or they know a shortcut.

Kathy – we're seeing a lot of each other lately – is with me as the train makes its way south, not quite at the speed we were requiring to make the Rugby Players Association lunch at Gaucho's on time. As a result, me and the good lady miss the bubbles and reception. Fortunately, unlike the train, we can make up for lost time.

Lots of acquaintances, old associates and even older friends make it a lovely afternoon. You can, however, feel the hostility being cranked up for the weekend. England are very confident ahead of the Calcutta Cup clash. I would be as well if I hadn't lost this fixture at home since 1983 . . .

Friday 15 March

I don't, and never would, whinge about my schedule. I take it on, I say yes. No one twists my arm – although Jen (my PA), Jill, Scott, Stewart, Kenny and Gabby, Gary (have I mentioned Jill?) – have given me the equivalent of a Chinese burn occasionally, just to coax me into doing something I'm slightly against. They tend to be right.

However, today is one of those shifts you just know is going to be a long one – start one day, probably finish the next – although that would absolutely be through choice. A big double dunt.

Covent Garden is where we have to be during the day to conduct an interview with Ed Jackson for Channel 4's *Big Tackle*. Nice chap, nothing too strenuous. That is the starter, though, before the main course, the Auld Enemy Dinner at the Grosvenor House in London, an event the Foundation benefits from greatly and one I'm keen to support.

As always, there are enough old-timers, has-beens and never-beens to make it a thoroughly memorable occasion. I should say that Stuart Reid, the former Scotland No. 8, who is the brains and driving force behind the dinner, doesn't fall into any of those categories. But you can imagine, with some fifty former players from down through the ages in attendance, there was plenty of flak given and taken. Highlight for me was former England prop Phil Vickery wearing a shirt with a huge Saltire on the front. Maybe he's a late convert. I hope he wears it tomorrow.

Saturday 16 March

Scotland are playing England today at Twickenham in the Six Nations. Call me defeatist, but although Kathy and I had very kindly been invited to the match as guests, after two exhausting days in London on business, I thought it wise we headed home to my own bed, rather than stay down south and wake up on Sunday slightly hungover, caused not by drink but by an inevitable loss. With all of that considered, we are taking the 08.00 out of King's Cross bound for the Scottish capital.

I had seen this movie before. Indeed, I'd had a walk-on part a few times. World Cup semi-finals, Grand Slam deciders, twice. I had witnessed first-hand what it was like not to get your hands on the Calcutta Cup, several times over. Of course, I wasn't alone. Did I mention that not since 1983 had Scotland beaten England on their own patch?

All of these contributing factors meant grabbing an early train back to the Borders made perfect sense. The shoogle of the train, plus a bit of fatigue means I have no bother in nodding off, then do the same once we are home.

I wake up and check my phone. England are rampant, 31–0 up and only a try on the stroke of half-time from Stuart McInally gave the scoreline some respectability. My expert judgement had been vindicated. I also learned later that Gary Armstrong had taken that as a cue to walk the dog, while some at the game headed for the pubs of Richmond to beat the rush and drown the sorrows.

The buzzing in my pocket meant something was happening, but I thought it might be a couple of my English friends on to wind me up. Then curiosity got the better of me. Scotland not only had made a remarkable comeback, I was still reading the messages when they went ahead. Expert?

There was no glorious finish, though. England managed to grab a draw, which must have felt like another defeat for the Scots. I think Gregor felt like that. He didn't enjoy the last eighty seconds. It reminded me a bit of that World Cup quarter-final against Australia when we just couldn't close the game out.

Nevertheless, I knew I'd be proven right! However, that has to go down as one of the most amazing games in the long history against the Auld Enemy.

The best part was still getting to lift the Calcutta Cup, having retained the famous old pot. But still not a win at Twickenham, something else I'm expert in.

Saturday 23 March

A much quieter week all told with a trip to Glengoyne Distillery with Gary and a meeting the next day with Annabel. Sober on both occasions. I will share a beer or two today, however, back in the Toon as Newcastle Falcons play Sale Sharks in a match labelled 'The Big One'. And they don't come much bigger than St James's Park, which is packed for this game.

For the occasion, the Falcons kit providers ISC produce a special limited-edition jersey in keeping with the occasion featuring the black and white stripes of Newcastle United, with the MN5DF logo on the front and the My Name'5 Doddie tartan across the shoulders. And going by how many I signed, it proved very popular, as did the match.

In total, 27,284 people were there to see the Falcons win 22–17. But they are still fighting relegation. We'll need a few more results like that to avoid the drop. But the crowd who turn up to see a bottom of the table team – Newcastle is just sport mad.

Sunday 24 March

Thanks to the success of Stewart's solo talk at Pitlochry, we have been cordially invited to the Aye Write Festival in Glasgow, at the Royal Concert Hall. I do love that festival title and on a Sunday afternoon we have a great crowd in – not just in terms of size but also in their participation – which makes it all the better.

There are the usual rugby fans, a good selection of Warriors and Scotland tops in evidence, but also the real book and literature lovers as well. Having been astonished at the response initially, I can honestly say I think we've hit the mark with the book. It is a good read. I've done well . . .

Saturday 30 March

Me and Lady Weir attend the Spring Ball at Prestonfield House Hotel. There were wild and speculative rumours that Kathy had been dancing on the chairs. This I cannot confirm or deny. But ask me about the tables . . .

APRIL 2019

Monday 1 April

The date should have been a warning, but it would be for real. For a while my diary had carried the date of the Hong Kong Sevens. (I won't tell you which one of my friends asked, 'And where are they held?')

I'd been out there as far back as the early 1990s as a player, and twelve months earlier had attended the inaugural dinner – although I'm not sure it was even referred to as the inaugural gathering, either in terms of there being another to follow it, or another that I would be at. Always a risk when MND is involved.

However, I knew what an experience it would be. Hong Kong is bigger, shinier, brighter and taller than way back then, but fundamentally the whole atmosphere of the place hadn't changed, especially around the rugby community. Additionally, the attraction of an even grander dinner on behalf of me and the Foundation was a reason not to miss the trip and, normally, there wouldn't have been a second's hesitation in confirming my involvement. Normally.

We are, however, still tender after my tumble in February. Health wise, there are a few lasting effects from what even Humpty

Dumpty would have called a big fall, even if I had made light of it at the time and while recovering. I still have discomfort with my ribs, especially when I get tired. My main concern is spending so long on a flight halfway around the world. I could be fine, or at least feel that way climbing aboard the flight. At 33,000 feet and four hours into a journey, it's tricky saying you are uncomfortable, or you've made a mistake and could they maybe let you off at the next stop.

Maybe I was over-thinking things, which has to have been better than not thinking about it at all. I also had to weigh up the not too insignificant factor of where I was on this MND trip – trip, as in journey, not fall. If I said 'no', would I ever get another opportunity to attend?

Having weighed everything up, I had decided that such a big journey was possibly beyond me, and I'd mentioned that to Jill, Gary, Scott and a few others. Basically, thanks but no thanks. Instead, my eldest son Hamish would go in my place, along with the brother-in-law Dougie Mundell and brother Christopher. Dougie had been going across as my minder, but now he could chaperone Hamish, or at least that was the plan. It might have been the other way around. Chris could take care of himself.

However, when it became known that I might not travel, my very good friend, and a fantastic supporter of the Foundation, Martin Murray, who is very high up in Cathay Pacific – even higher than the pilots – sorted it out that I could travel business class. My sneaky plan had worked! Seriously, that offer changed my mind, as did finding out that Sir Billy Connolly had said yes to the invite extended to him, and he'd be there to support the cause. How good was that?

I will make a confession now. There was no way I was having Billy flying halfway across the globe, with the issues he has personally, just to lend his support, while I was staying at home. No way.

Martin worked it that I could fly out on Monday, stay in Hong Kong for two nights, then fly home to arrive back on the Friday, so I could go and watch Ben playing in the Duns Sevens. You need to support your kids. You never know when they might have to support you.

A bit of a hectic schedule, absolutely, but what else would you expect from an international jet setter. The plan was sound, less so the execution, entirely down to the Weirs jinxing it.

Hamish and myself were club class for the trip, Chris and Mundell at the other end of the plane. However, younger brother's protestations that 'forty minutes would be long enough to get through Heathrow' proved optimistic and ultimately incorrect. We missed our flight to HK. 'There will be another one,' Dougie chipped in, as if he was waiting on the Doddie bus to Gala.

There was, and we managed to get aboard; the moral of this tale being never listen to international 'time' travellers like this pair of jokers who showed no remorse for their cock-up. Still, Hong Kong here we come. What could possibly go wrong?

Well, for starters, try going to the bank to lift some cash with Hamish, then celebrate your ability to draw the local currency, but leave your credit card in the machine too long and have it swallowed up. I couldn't possibly apportion blame; however, if you work out my levels of dexterity, ATMs are a bit beyond me. I'll leave it for you to work out who got it wrong. Thankfully, we eventually retrieved it. Phew.

Once again we cast aside adversity and settled back to enjoy the adventure. There was a lot to cram in, but the mixture of excitement, jet lag, adrenalin and the odd Guinness – a heady cocktail – kept me fully charged.

Also out on the trip was the artist Gerard M. Burns, who had been commissioned by Hong Kong Scottish to do a portrait of me. Gerard, who had recently completed his portrait, was not taking a fee for his work, on the understanding that all monies raised from the sale of the picture would go to the My Name'5 Doddie Foundation. A very spirited gesture. I couldn't help think what a good guy he was – especially after I'd made him paint all that tartan.

The evening before the banquet, we went out on the water for a cruise around the harbour, a slightly surreal experience. Me and Billy Connolly on a yacht. So too was the chat between Scott and Hamish. 'Wooh!' and 'Wow!' and 'Look at that!' was all you could hear from them. I wasn't sure which one was the teenager as they pointed at the buildings and lights. But Hong Kong really is a sight to behold.

I got the chance to chat with Sir Billy who was lovely, everything you look for in one of your heroes, as was Lady Pam. It was then Billy revealed that his own mother had died of MND. I'd never known that, but you could see it had been an experience that still moved him greatly.

It wasn't all about the touristy things. There was some great rugby chat, Gavin (Hastings) and Geech (Sir Ian McGeechan) loving the moment as well. If ever I get a yacht, Hong Kong is the place to moor it, although I fancy North Berwick would be more my scene.

When it came, the big night was just that: utterly superb, with lots of money raised and, above all else, people enjoyed themselves. It was great that Tom Smith was there, Michael Johnson (who we'd met at the Sports Personality of the Year awards in Liverpool), and Andy Nicol and Scott – apart from his spotty tie – were great MCs. Jonny Gould was, as ever, brilliant as the auctioneer, managing to charm a few extra dollars out of those who have always been such great supporters of our cause, not just at these gala events, but throughout the year.

There was though, for me, and I'd imagine those who have

schemed, planned and plotted to make it happen, one part of the evening that I will never forget. A mix of the euphoric and emotional; the unveiling of my portrait. Heading up onto the stage, I was holding in the tears – and nothing had happened yet!

Gerard's sales pitch was awesome, a game changer, crowd-funding on the hoof, asking people to become partners and buy a stake in his work that would be donated to the National Portrait Gallery in Edinburgh, with their name attached to it in perpetuity. He said some in the thousand-strong audience might be asking what they were getting for their money, and someone shouted, 'Nothing!' The thing was, that was about the sum total of it. And they still hadn't seen the painting, hidden by a Saltire draped over it.

Gerard and Jonny did the honours, and then it was on to raising some cash, allowing people to pledge money at diamond level, and tiers beneath that. In total, the portrait raised £100,000, the entire dinner nearly half a million – sterling, not HK dollars. I was blown away. I think Gerard was as well. Such big-heartedness, I will forever be in their debt – and on an art gallery wall in Edinburgh.

I cannot sing the praises of Gerard enough. Hugely gifted, but someone who, let's be fair, was willing to put his reputation on the line, just to enable our Foundation to profit. His generosity, in terms of his time both in the studio and in Hong Kong, I can only applaud.

The night carried on into the wee sma' hours, and a few hours after that I was on board a flight, winging my way back to London, then on to home.

I returned, and as scheduled, made it to Duns to see Ben and Melrose win. What a great week. And, to make it even better, Hamish and Dougie didn't manage to lose each other, or Christopher, and made it back safely, maybe the worse for wear but definitely happy at having experienced one of the greatest events in rugby.

Monday 8 April

Hamish's body clock must have been all over the place, but, like the athlete he is, was ready to leave with us as we headed up to Knockhill for a day of rallying. This had been a gift for the boys' Christmas in 2017 – remember the mad Christmas when I didn't know how long I'd be around and they got everything they wanted plus a ton more? Aye, that Christmas.

However, because of everything that had been happening, putting a ring around a date on the calendar when we were all available – and that included my dad – was easier said than done. Indeed, if it hadn't been for Stuart Gray at Knockhill reminding us that we still had a day to claim – and extending the deadline by which we could take it – we might have lost the experience. But here we were, albeit missing Old Jock who had market to attend. Or so he said.

All I'll say is that the boys had a whale of a time, all dressed up in the race gear, in proper rally cars and with instructors who were not only great teachers, but brave as hell just to sit next to these three eejits. And when the times were in and the scores calculated the winner was – BEN! The only one who didn't have a driving licence.

Having seen him put a car through its paces up and down the hills around Knockhill, I'm not sure I want him on the road – or off-road.

Saturday 13 April

Ah, the Melrose Sevens, a tournament that is dear to my heart. Amazing that a wee place like this in the Scottish Borders could have given a sport to the world which has now become a multimillion-pound industry with a World Tour – it's even an Olympic event.

When I played, playing at Walkerburn was an adventure, and a pie and a pint was seen by some as the ultimate prize. Of course, that was for those who never won the Ladies Cup at the Greenyards.

Few settings in rugby match this ground when the spring sun shines. It is a beautiful setting, although many who frequent it on 'Sports Day' never lift their head from looking at the top of their next can. Yes, we were all young once.

There is a general warmth – not just because it's a lovely day – from all those I bump into and meet around the ground. I'm nearly late for my commentary on one occasion because so many just wanted to speak to me. The hospitality wasn't half bad either.

The beauty of Sevens rugby is that if you don't like one game, another will be along in a matter of minutes. It is non-stop stuff, hence why you need as many commentators and experts as you can muster. I'm in the box with John Beattie who I've been seeing quite a bit of lately, as we are working on a documentary together.

Beattie is a big laddie, but when doing comms he likes to stand on the bar of his seat. Don't ask me why he needs to be any taller when he's already up in the air. Maybe it's a Glasgow thing. As luck would have it though, he got a wee bit too excited during the match and slipped, grabbing hold of me to keep upright, but never missed a beat in his observations. Good job he clung on to me, because I had nothing to catch him with.

Now, that really would have made the Christmas out-takes DVD.

Friday 19 April

Easter weekend. I do like chocolate eggs and have stashed mine away, hidden from the gannets who frequent Bluecairn. Holidays like this are a welcome break, because most people are busy with family and friends around this time, which means I get a wee rest, out of the limelight. I never thought I'd say that.

MAY 2019

Thursday 2 May

Thanks to the success of the previous one, and because Black &
White Publishing are so full of great ideas, I'm in the middle of
writing another book. Car journeys are a great way to talk ideas
through, or come up with content, so Stewart joins me as I head for
the Angel of the North and a filming assignment with BT Sport.

'It's only twenty metres high,' he says. He should get out more.

On arrival, we go through the running order of what BT Sport
need from me, which includes various pieces to camera, some
background shots (they've even requisitioned two rugby teams
to run around for some views), and of course using the large
and instantly identifiable Angel as a prop. As in film prop, not a
tight-head.

'What is twenty metres in feet?' I ask, being clever.

'Sixty-five and a half.' He shouldn't be let out.

I do the same walk and words about six or seven times. Each
time they ask, 'Can we do it one more time?' I forget more of the
words. We could be here a while. I'm also aware that certain people
have stopped walking their dogs to watch me. A couple and their
daughter have now walked into shot.

They are dunted to one side but want to meet me as I must be famous. The usual pleasantries are exchanged, and I find out they are on holiday from Wales. The director needs me again, urgently.

Five minutes, more words forgotten, but the sun through the clouds has made it all atmospheric and arty and they are happy. Job done.

'Where did my fans go?' I jest.

'They wanted to know who you were. I told them you were Scott Quinnell. They said, "He didn't sound very Welsh?" I told them you were practising the accent for the new James Bond movie.'

No wonder I get a bad name in Wales.

The journey back is spent with me and Stewart talking some absolute drivel, interspersed with some comedy genius from me. We talk more about the new book – yes, another book – *The World According to Doddie: An A–Z of Life and How to Live It*. It's full of my one-liners, witticisms and observations.

We touch upon the Hong Kong trip and who was there and who I'd met. 'Wiki' Weir (who knows so much I'm sure he makes it up) informs me that Lady Pam (Billy Connolly's wife) had appeared in *The Professionals*, which was my favourite TV programme as a kid. You couldn't beat a bit of Bodie and Doyle on a Saturday night.

I'll know the next time if I watch the repeats on ITV4.

Friday 3 May

I pull into the petrol station. Kathy is in the car and we're headed south.

'Where are you goin' the day?' I'm asked by the woman behind the counter.

'Badminton.'

'Oh, I'm surprised you can still play . . .'

Several hours later, we have arrived in Gloucestershire, for the horse trials.

Wednesday 8 May

A year after they'd handed over a couple of cheques – the proceeds of the Tartan Giraffe Ball totalling over £300,000 – me and members of the Foundation, as well as a few invited guests, once more enjoy the hospitality of Stewart 'Benzo' Bennet, David Baird and Dougie Stevens, this time at Kelso Races.

This was to be a relaxing, good-humoured day – but when was that ever the end product when money was being lost! It became obvious from the first race that some present couldn't tip rubbish. You know when you hear 'that's my favourite colour' or 'that's my lucky number' that desperation has set in.

There were a few to profit, but only on individual races, merely making the loss column not look quite as bad. Scotland coach Gregor Townsend dropped a few quid on one nag he'd reckoned he could have given a start to. But the food and the refreshments, and especially the banter, made up for any losses.

Of course, you couldn't have a day out centring on rugby folk without there being a few games and activities taking place, in particular the oft-dreaded forfeits. These took many shapes and guises, but probably the best was saved to last when JJ, John Jeffrey, had to sprint the final furlong, on what was by now heavy going.

The big fella started off at a good lick before fatigue set in, but stumbling towards the line there was a noticeable leap in the air. Showing off? Nah, more that sensation you sense when your groin goes. Ouch! He should be fine in a matter of months.

A cracking day out and another huge thank you to this intrepid trio and everything they've done.

Saturday 11 May

Newcastle will always have a place in my heart and this weekend I'm back in the Toon with Kathy, Hamish, Angus and Ben for the Heineken Champions Cup Final.

All of what has been planned for this weekend has been around the work done by the EPCR (European Professional Club Rugby) and Jill, who is also broadcasting. I don't know how she juggles everything. Must have a well-organised man behind her.

It is a hugely successful day and our Foundation will benefit to the not insubstantial sum of £50,000 – one pound for every seat filled in the sold-out St James's Park. Ahead of the final between Saracens and Leinster, and accompanied by Jill – who more than once has been mistaken for my wife (she's not that lucky) – I have the great honour of bringing out the famous trophy the two sides will contest. In the end it's Saracens, who I once almost signed for, who triumph.

This was a cup I never managed to get my hands on as a player. The year Newcastle Falcons were the Premiership winners, the English clubs boycotted the competition because of a fallout between European Rugby and the RFU, so we were denied the chance to compete.

I've not lost a load of sleep over it, but I have no doubt we'd have won it that year had we been allowed to play. We were the best team in England and, to my mind, the best in Europe as well. Sorry, Ulster.

Sunday 12 May

One of the problems I have – among others – is that there is only one of me, and I'm in demand. This weekend, while we were in Newcastle, the Porsche Club were having a day in Edinburgh on the Saturday, which Stewart covered, and then yesterday it was the Boswell Book Festival where I should have been waxing lyrical about my book, again alongside Stuey.

We had to call someone off the bench as this was a two-man job, so who better than my old Scotland teammate and former Lion, Peter Wright.

By all accounts the pair of them had a very enjoyable day in the Ayrshire sunshine, while reports – that'll mean reading up on Facebook and Twitter – say they were hugely entertaining and, indeed, among the best performers that weekend. I don't always trust social media, therefore I consider this to be fake news.

Tuesday 21 May

We're very fortunate because we've been invited to stay the evening in the Palace of Holyroodhouse. Richard Scott, Duke of Buccleuch, was deputising for the Queen while the General Assembly of the Church of Scotland was taking place. The rooms are beautiful, although there's a queue for the bathroom. Richard has become a real friend of late, in terms of his support and in providing facilities for many of our meetings between the Foundation and members of the scientific community.

We've had a few double-takes with invites, where the name of a stately home he had kindly given us access to for various gatherings, Boughton House, has some invitees believing we are meeting at a local pub!

Tuesday 28 May

This morning, you can feel summer may be just around the corner. The weather in May can be changeable, but the sun is shining when I pull up at the Borders General Hospital. Mother, 'Nanny' as she is known to the world, is in the Margaret Kerr Unit, the BGH's specialist palliative care facility. She's been in here since last week, when living at home became impossible.

Mum and I were diagnosed with ailments around the same time; me with MND, her with cancer. Trust me, it hadn't been a competition to see who could outdo one another, although in terms of our respective prognoses, and updates along the way, it could be said she lasted a lot longer than we first believed. She's made of tough stuff, and though I've never said it to her – or felt I needed to – she was quite inspiring to me, a lesson in how to get up and get on with it.

We never went into big, deep, meaningful conversations or debates. Asking how she was, and vice versa, was enough. In all of this, in many ways she's been the one who really knew how I felt, what I had to live for, and what I had to lose, because she was going through exactly the same episode. With four kids and thirteen grandchildren, and the love of her life in old Jock, she had kept herself going when it would have been easy – and understandable – to give up.

She had been up for the fight until now, and she would not give in easily.

The facilities at the hospital were lovely; comfortable, light and spacious. I did think this wasn't a bad place to see out your days, and yes, that applies to me as well. But Mum is looking tired, and is in more pain than we'd seen previously. She was, however, still here, still planning, still worrying about others. Then, while in full flow, she unexpectedly drops into the conversation, 'Oh, and I've given Alex [my niece and Mum's eldest granddaughter] my engagement ring.'

There are certain things that will be significant to you, or within your family, that may be an insignificance to those outside your circle. My mum always cherished that ring, and cherished even more what it meant to her because of who she had received it from all those years ago.

She would never be without it. Unless, that is, she wasn't here.

In essence, my mum had told me, nicely, discreetly, indirectly, that her battle, her fight, her stay, was over. The relevance of that one line hit home, and hit home hard.

There was no point in asking if she meant it, or telling her not to talk like that. The obstinacy I possess came with the DNA she passed on to me. She'd made up her mind. That was it. Just a case of waiting.

I said I'd see her again later in the week but couldn't be sure if that would really happen. Under a different set of circumstances, I wonder if I, or she, or we, would have been quite as strong. Both of us have had a long time to think about our issues, but she appeared to have reconciled herself to the fact that her race was run. Me, I'll jog on for a bit longer, thank you very much.

Driving home there is a sadness, that she had battled long enough, was tired and just wanted peace to go. Yet I couldn't be too upset. What comfort there was at that moment was in the fact that she was getting to choose the time and the place. We should be happy with that.

I thought about her ring again, for Alex. It was a lovely and fitting gesture. It made me wonder what I might give away, or leave to my sons. The wife and some debts, probably. I better not say that . . .

JUNE 2019

Saturday 1 June

On Friday, Mother was ill but didn't want any fuss. Saturday, Thomas and Christopher were going to stay at the hospital while the rest of us – with motors and a horsebox – headed for the show jumping that Tori and Will Dodd had organised, where Alex was competing. Dad convinced my brothers that nothing was imminent and that they should go to the rugby, which they did. We were all now occupied, meaning that Dad would go to the hospice to be with Mum. Just the pair of them.

Kirsty took the call. Time to go home.

We all arrived back at the hospice, horsebox and all. Not sure what people might have thought, not that I cared. I couldn't be compelled to go into the room. The next time I see her will be soon enough. But I did wryly smile to myself. Even though Mum was unconscious, a combination of weakness and drugs, you knew somehow she'd engineered it that way, that she subconsciously knew it was just her and Dad there, Nanny and Jock together, alone, no one but them, and now it was time to run no more . . .

I came away, numbed I'd say. You prepare for this time, and

you've prepared for nothing. Mentally, it's time to pick yourself up and go again, one more effort, for Mum.

Sunday 2 June

But, as she would be the first to say, life is for the living, not just in terms of enjoying yourself, but that it was those who were still here that matter. Being mournful isn't in our way as a family. Respectful yes, but we all had things to do.

I had an engagement at Thirlestane Castle with the Borders Vintage Automobile Club, for their annual show, the highlight being – for me anyway – handing over the keys to a restored Mini Cooper to a chap from Bothwell who had won it in a raffle, the proceeds of which – a very tidy five-figure sum – were being donated to MN5DF.

A worthwhile day. It stopped me thinking about other things. What would fill my thoughts in the coming week would be recording another podcast – I'm getting good at these things – a Pro-Am golf day at the Renaissance on behalf of the Foundation, and another away day with Gazza. Time now for one last date with Mum.

Tuesday 11 June

Mum's funeral. I don't know if my emotions have become more polarised living with this condition. Before, everything was much of a muchness and just dealt with. Now I am filled with feelings at two ends of the scale: apprehension that we are saying goodbye to someone I have known every day of my life; sadness that this will be farewell; or anticipation that today will be a celebration of her life, who she was and everything that she gave to Dad, her family and others.

This is a day you have to see through. You can't just do the parts you want to do, or say, 'Okay, see ya,' halfway through. It's hard to explain, that there is a rawness to some emotions, but absolute calm around others. Is this the new me, because I can't recall the old one getting caught up with these sort of feelings?

Ever the organiser, Mum knew what she wanted today. Her funeral, her call. She didn't want black ties, she wanted colour and light. The immediate family laid her to rest before we had a church service to remember. A proper celebration, one where the tears were from laughter. There was plenty of material to go on, as Jim McDougall and another close friend, Andrew Lorraine-Smith, captured her fun, her spirit and her legendary scattiness. The grandchildren – one of whom threw a couple of pound coins into the grave so Nanny 'could buy some fags' – gave a wonderful rendition of a poem written by Kirsty, Anne and Stewart, again, one full of 'Nannyisms' which had the church congregation, all four hundred of them, in raptures.

As her oldest child, I should have said a few words. But, I don't mind saying, I just couldn't. That rawness I spoke about just overtook me. I think it was the first time my own illness, my own susceptibility, caught up with me and stopped me in my tracks. Again, I'm having to deal with that mix of emotions. I didn't want to let her down by not saying something, but I didn't want to let her down by saying something badly. I just didn't feel I could do her justice with the eulogy.

Where we did her justice was with the gathering afterwards. We toasted her memory, as we had at the grave, and told tales and anecdotes of her exploits and definitely at her expense. She would not have wanted it any other way.

If you were going to have a good funeral – assuming first of all that there is such a thing – then I doubt they'd come much better than this, with the possible exception of mine, it goes without saying. Let's just say I'm at the rehearsal stage ...

Saturday 22 June

You win, you lose; occasionally you draw. Results in rugby are never a banker, but what is a guarantee is that you will make friendships and associations that will last long after you've been a better player than you thought you were. It goes without saying that when the proposition of joining in with a Border Reivers reunion was suggested, my arm didn't need to be twisted. Would others turn up in numbers?

When you need a double decker bus to transport your 'squad' around, it tells you this was a good idea that became a great one, and one of the best days out I've had, ever.

Any chance of journeying around the Borders, incognito, was blown from the off. Having gathered at Tweedbank railway station, we boarded the bus. Not any bus, but the Doddie Bus, clad in the My Name'5 Doddie tartan, a regular sight around the Borders, though on this day there were some highly irregular customers aboard as we took a route where most of the stops were adjacent to rugby clubs and pubs. Amazing that.

The older members sat downstairs, the younger fellas up on the top deck. Health & Safety was a key factor on the day. We didn't want anyone falling down the stairs, not when they could do enough damage falling up them.

We started out with clay pigeon shooting at Bisley, near Selkirk. This was first on the agenda, entirely for safety reasons as later in the day coordination may have been difficult owing to excess alcohol. And we didn't want anyone being rushed to hospital, or worse. The rules were that if you missed all your clays, your next two shots had to be taken with your trousers around your ankles. Well done to Kelly Brown for winning that challenge. I don't think anyone noticed, perhaps with the exception of the female instructor in the next booth who really didn't know what was going on or where to look.

At Reivers we had a fitness instructor by the name of Val Houston. She missed the first four shots, but winged the next bird, just. Someone saw a puff of dust. A huge cheer went up as she saved her blushes.

While we were on the move, we had some right good choral sessions, led by Kelly, a rare singer in his own right. The CD comes out for Christmas.

From the shootin' we headed to Jedburgh and the bowling club there, where we caught up with local and national rugby legend Roy Laidlaw, who was in fine fettle, better than some of those who'd just stepped off the charabanc, then on to Kelso Cricket Club for another light refreshment before taking on some nourishment at the pizza parlour in Hawick. So far so good although Gary, who was the chief judge, a status he declared on himself, was busy tallying up fines and forfeits.

On one occasion, Gary gave everyone a time to be back on the bus, and then wound his watch forward by five minutes. Everyone who turned up on the hour was in effect five minutes late. The judge was always right. The only way you could gain passage to the next stop on the journey was to down a wee whisky, although for a few they were not so wee.

We were all given caps – childish stuff, which we lapped up – and Gary would give the command 'caps on' and you had to wear them. Except in the mayhem, Gazza had been circulating, lifting some of the headgear that had been mislaid or left on tables. The fine for non-compliance? A tenner. One individual lost his cap three times. Thirty quid. No names, no pack drill. But he looked like the Scotland coach.

Our journey wound its way eventually to the Buccleuch Arms in St Boswells, where things got a tad hairy when Gary held court and the penalties had to be repaid, in the form of nips of my own-label whisky. How can I put it? Some handled that part of the day better than others. It must have been the only time in history when people sought sanctuary in Galashiels rather than stay at the Buccleuch where the official going had become 'messy'.

I bid my farewell, but somehow reaching the door of the pub proved to be an issue, and I didn't escape until eleven bells. What a shift, but what a special day, made by the cracking company.

It was a real mix of players: Scotland caps, Lions, legends of the Border game, all bonded by the fact we were all either South representatives or latter-day Reivers. In addition to me, Gaz, Toony and Kelly, there was Graeme Aitchison, Stewart 'Benzo' Bennet, Vincent Brotherstone, Geoff Cross, Simon Danielli, Michael Dods, Bruce Douglas, Ross Ford, Iain Fullarton, Jim Hay, Gav Kerr, Ronnie Kirkpatrick, Neil McIlroy, Calum MacRae, Andrew Mower, Mark Moncreiff, Scott McColm, Adam Roxburgh, Colin Stewart, Gordon Sim, Jono Stuart, Matt Taylor, Kevin Utterson, Peter Wright and Scott Welsh, not forgetting the medics, Val Houston and Dan Pullman. They all deserve a mention, if only because they might buy this book knowing their names are in it.

No one was any better than anyone else. In meeting up like that, we were trying to keep the traditions of the South, or Borders, or Reivers, alive – because they don't really exist like the entities they once were. I don't think our livers would allow it to happen every year, but for me it would be a great custom to uphold.

We all belonged to the same club, with equal membership. Apart from Gary as he was the judge, and Toony, as he was now poorer than everyone else.

I keep saying about living the dream. This was more like a living wake for me. Yes, you are permitted to see the funny side of that. However, I was meeting up with boys I hadn't seen in such a long time, five, ten, maybe fifteen years, and in some cases, through choice. The craic was great, never ending, but so was finding out what they'd been up to, some of which cannot be disclosed owing to legal reasons.

That union between us is almost like a living history in today's rugby world. How many of today's top professionals can say they got to play for, or represent, the part of the country they lived in or grew up around? Not many, I'd guess. But many of us were of an age where the next representative level after playing for your club was your district, where you were playing on behalf of your club, who you didn't want to let down, but also for the wider community. It meant a great deal then. And those friendships mean even more now.

JULY 2019

Wednesday 3 July

The big day had arrived. I was going to be officially inaugurated, or installed, or investitured (I don't know if that is the official description or even a word), as an Officer of the Most Excellent Order of the British Empire. OBE to make it easy.

After nearly not getting it, having not returned the relevant paperwork months ago, now I would be receiving my honour from Her Majesty, The Queen. I had the opportunity to go to Buckingham Palace, which would have been nice, but the option to have the ceremony at Holyrood Palace seemed to make more sense given the complications a longer journey may have thrown up, and also that I wanted the wife and boys to be able to savour what was a special occasion.

When the date comes in, it's almost as if a countdown clock begins leading up to the day. It goes without saying that first on the agenda was what to wear. Not for me, you understand. Tartan suit would be the order of the day. No, Mary Doll wanted to look at her best and she didn't disappoint. The boys as well were suited and booted. Fingernails clean, washed behind the ears. You get the picture. The experience of being able to take the kids along gave them a memory for all time.

This was going to be a day for all the family to enjoy, because all the family had been with me on this journey.

If you recall – and I have no problem hailing another fantastic afternoon – I had met Her Majesty before, almost two years to the day, when we were kindly invited to her garden party at Holyrood, not necessarily to meet her, but we were very kindly introduced to her by Richard Scott, Duke of Buccleuch. We got a very nice photograph for the mantelpiece that day. That was when I commented that it was so nice of her to put all of this on for my birthday. I think I got away with it, hence why I'd been invited back.

That day in 2017 proved how topsy-turvy my life was becoming: in the afternoon I was having a drink on the lawn at Holyrood and blethering with Her Majesty, and on the way back home on the train, drinking white wine out of plastic cups, I had to take a call from someone whose sewage system had gone on the bung. Oh, the life of an international jet setter.

This time around, things were far more reserved and sedate. In the morning, we get a run-through of all the protocols, the dos and don'ts if you like, about what will happen during the ceremony. This is when I met with John Davidson, another Borderer, who has been awarded an MBE for what he's achieved as a campaigner, raising awareness around Tourette's Syndrome. I knew he would be there and looked out for him. This was as much so I'd have someone to talk to, if I'm honest.

John had lived with this issue all of his life. He first came to prominence thirty years before when the BBC made a documentary called *John's Not Mad*, which gave an insight into what he had to endure on a daily basis. What happened to him as a school kid was just horrendous.

Yet, here we were, having lived just miles apart most of our lives, now at Holyrood, with the Church of Scotland's first female Moderator, the Lord Lieutenant of Perth & Kinross, various other famous names, and of course the Queen. It only proves that there are many roads you can travel in life to reach the same destination.

John is a right nice lad, like a lot of folk are from Galashiels, and I can't help but think that while I've been confronted by my condition for just a few years, John has been challenged by Tourette's since he was a child. I genuinely feel, and I mean genuinely, like some Johnny Come Lately, who hasn't had a fraction of the battles John has met head on while just trying to lead his daily life. A remarkable man, a brave man.

He was nervous about being nervous and what effect that might have on him. I was just nervous, but everyone behind the scenes tried to make meeting the Queen seem a normal, everyday event. Then we were called into the room, waited our turn until the citation was announced, and then went forward to accept our awards.

My choice of cloth for my new suit (you didn't think everyone else was getting dolled up and I'd miss out, did you?) was the Holyrood Diamond Jubilee Tartan. I think it suited the occasion. I was still thinking about those dos and don'ts as I approached Her Majesty. I felt ginormous next to her and tried ever so slightly to stoop forward so she wasn't straining her neck looking up at me.

We were told about the protocols of shaking hands, but my issues meant I had trouble lifting my arm up. So we met halfway. And once you've shaken hands, you're on your way. I could have chatted for a good bit longer. But other people were waiting for their big moment. I'm glad it was captured on video. It was all a bit surreal to be fair.

Later in the day – which, being completely honest, was a once in a lifetime experience for this farmer boy and sewage specialist – me and the family went to a nice restaurant for a bite to eat, just to extend the moment. Earlier, John had said that because of his problems, eating out wasn't that simple, so he'd just be having a picnic instead.

I thought about him when I was having my steak. Sometimes, you don't know how lucky you are just to have bad luck . . .

Thursday 4 July

My birthday. I know that there are times when you try to ignore the passing of time, but I am more than happy to see another year out – particularly when the predictions were I might not be seeing too many of them. I must be one of the few people to welcome a forty-ninth birthday with open arms. Roll on fifty.

Tuesday 23 July

Kenny and Gabby Logan come to see us at Bluecairn. The trip proves a huge distraction for the boys, especially Hamish. And it has nothing to do with seeing Kenny . . .

AUGUST 2019

Friday 2 August

After everything he has done for me, it's only right that I should attend the Three 9s dinner in Jedburgh being staged to honour Greig Laidlaw, Roy Laidlaw and Gary Armstrong. Amazing that one town could produce three such influential scrum-halves, including the one I think was the best ever. But then, I'm biased, having played with Gary for Scotland and Newcastle so many times. I take great pride in telling people that – and just how good the line-out ball was I presented to him on a plate.

Sunday 11 August

Peter Winterbottom has worked wonders again in attracting great numbers for Doddie'5 Ride, the fundraising bike run organised on behalf of the Foundation. Unfortunately, while Peter is extremely good at rustling up support, he hasn't quite made contact with the heavenly powers in charge of the weather. It is lashing down, but unperturbed, the intrepid bikers head out from the Greenyards, taking in Earlsfield, Kelso, Coldstream, Jedburgh and Hawick (it just happened to be on the route), before returning to Melrose.

I have my electric bike fitted with some stabilisers, not to keep me upright but to prevent me from pulling wheelies. I don't want to show off too much.

But despite the conditions, a great, if soggy, time was had by all. Maybe I'll get an easy-boy tricycle for next year. With a bar...

Wednesday 21 August

Places and things I never thought I'd be part of No. 394 – the Edinburgh International Book Festival.

I honestly have thoroughly loved doing the book festival rounds and this has to be the highlight. Who'd have thought, when Stuey and I were lying exhausted in the blazing sun, cutting back and replanting foliage around a sewage treatment plant up at Lanark four years ago, dreaming about the book we'd never quite got around to writing for the last decade and more, that we would now be prize-nominated and bestselling authors (although my name always comes first).

Tonight in the capital, we'll be interviewed by Ian Robertson, former Scotland stand-off, best known as the voice of rugby on BBC radio, and who himself had a book, *Talking A Good Game*, nominated for the Heineken Rugby Book of the Year. And so did we, which is why we are in Edinburgh.

The marquee we are in is packed, a full house, and the hottest ticket in town by all accounts. What is nice to see is that there are people who are genuinely interested in what went into the book, and those who are interested in rugby. In other words, the former listen to Stewart, the latter listen to me – and there were more of them on the night.

Robbo is a lovely man and we give him his place to ask the first couple of questions. After that, we'll do our own thing. It's worked everywhere we've been, and this is no different.

The night flies in, indeed I think we might have overrun slightly – no surprise there. We were enjoying ourselves, with plenty of banter and audience participation. It's not every show you attend where randomly selected members of the audience are invited onto the stage to be kicked and punched. Still, they lapped it up.

There might have been one moment I went slightly off-piste. I can't recall what it was for, but it will come back to me. What came back in our direction at the end of the show was a standing ovation. According to the organisers, I think they said only a handful of people had ever received that. I must admit, I was good – but you are only as good as your stooges. So thanks, Robbo and Stuey.

Thursday 22 August

Ah, it came back to me. I said something about the NHS apparently, which was spread over the front pages of the *Scotsman* and the *Edinburgh Evening News*. No one spoke to me, just took it from a live feed of the event. I remember when proper journalists would ask for an interview . . .

SEPTEMBER 2019

Friday 6 September

Friday night and back at Murrayfield for Scotland versus Georgia, the last of our warm-up games ahead of the World Cup. The Foundation has the use of a hospitality box again and we have several old friends and teammates along for the night, among them around the world cyclist Mark Beaumont and my former Scotland squad colleague Cameron Glasgow.

The Georgians are not the Barbarians, so it takes a while for this one to catch fire. Being honest, I'm so engrossed in the craic that before I know it the final whistle has sounded and we've won 36–9. That's the effect good chat and company has sometimes. Gregor will be satisfied, but he has a bigger date ahead – and I don't mean in Japan.

Sunday 8 September

With this entire Foundation malarkey, there are some individuals who have come up with the most outrageously bizarre ideas to raise cash and support MN5DF. I played long enough with Gregor Townsend to know that you don't always know what is going on in his head, or what he is thinking. I suppose that's what made him such a fantastic player.

However, I think he has surpassed himself this time. Just a couple of days before he jets out to Japan with Scotland for the World Cup, Gregor has taken it upon himself to play one hole of golf at each of the Border courses. And there are twenty-one of them; Newcastleton, Langholm, Hawick, Minto, The Woll, Selkirk, Innerleithen, Cardrona, Peebles, Galashiels, Torwoodlee, Lauder, Duns, Eyemouth, Hirsel, Kelso, Roxburghe, Jedburgh, Lilliardsedge, Melrose and St Boswells.

No wonder we teed off on Gregor's Border Golf Challenge at 6.40 a.m., with an estimated finishing time of 8.30 p.m., in other words, nearly a fourteen-hour shift for Toony.

We had some great crew to make sure everything ran like clockwork, brother Thomas was behind the wheel of the people carrier, with Iain Stoddard of Bounce Sports management on the stopwatch. But timing between courses was tight, while on the course – between teeing off and holing out – everything had to be kept to within some very tight parameters. Not easy when at virtually every course we were stopped for autographs, selfies and the handover of pin flags and cheques. And that was just the 'normal' things.

Beginning with a par-3 at Newcastleton, we start with a couple of bacon rolls, conjured up by Jen Pass, the official keeper of the Dodgy's diary (among other things), a prized position within Team Weir. And we're off and running. A bunch of mini Doddies – complete with Foundation headbands – celebrated our arrival at Langholm. Legendary Scotland centre Jim Renwick was awaiting our arrival at Hawick, with Greig Laidlaw and Stuart Hogg playing the next hole at Minto.

Then, '84 Grand Slam hero John Rutherford was on hand to give Toony some guidance around Selkirk, while St Ronan's Silver Band added a musical accompaniment at Innerleithen.

We had a pipe band providing a guard of honour at Peebles, where we also had a gallery watching; a full-scale crowd turned up at Kelso before 1984 Grand Slam winning scrum-half Roy Laidlaw partnered Gregor at Jedburgh.

At every course, we, and especially Gregor, were greeted like heroes by supporters of all ages. Toony actually played quite well most of the day, until he was penalised for the first double bogey – which became another double bogey, or two. That maybe owed something to him having to sink a can of gin and tonic every time he went two over on a hole. Amazing the effect that can have on an athlete. Me, I was fine.

We were a bit over the clock, and I think for a moment Gregor thought I was going to come out with some R&A rule that said he needed to sink another can for every minute over, but I couldn't have done that to him. Actually I could, but was talked out of it. It was just a fantastic day out and once again all thanks to my old South, Scotland and Lions partner. Tomorrow I get a lie in. Him, he's away to win the World Cup. No pressure.

Tuesday 10 September

Jam-packed week ahead starting with a golf day on behalf of the Foundation at the Renaissance. I can't play golf these days, but, as Hoggy reminded me, 'even when you could you couldn't'.

Usual meeting and greeting (or greetin' if you've had a bad round), and buggy driving and prize giving. Then I jump on a train to London, meeting up with Kathy who'll be at Berwick-upon-Tweed station. Why does rendezvousing aboard a train feel more difficult than astronauts linking with the International Space Station?

Wednesday 11 September

In London, at Sunrise Brokers and BCG Traders for their charity trading day with Kenny and Gabby and a few others. Quite incredibly, Kenny has found something he's quite good at, although I keep watching for the FTSE 100 to suddenly vanish entirely.

Today has been set up and organised by Simon Brennan, himself diagnosed with MND, but who has become such an incredible champion battling this disease and working on behalf of MN5DF. What a guy.

Thursday 12 September

Fly straight to Dublin for the MND Charity Gala Ball. Thought I'd bring Kathy. Well, she's here now. Our good friends Jack and Gemma Clark have joined us too. As does Craig Doyle, who is MC on the night, along with Lions legends Keith Wood and Paul Wallace. Of course, we were just slipping into the boozer for a quiet one. So much for a quiet evening.

I also have the opportunity to speak with Professor Orla Hardiman from Trinity College Dublin and consultant neurologist at the National Neuroscience Centre. A title and a half, but the kind you only get with being very clever. Always good to chat MND with great people. Networking is so important. Also thirsty work.

We get that chance to talk with a couple of MND sufferers, all in the same boat, but every one of us going in a different direction, if you catch my drift; one of them being Roy Taylor, who sang in the 1988 Eurovision song contest with his band, Jump the Gun. They didn't win. Someone called Celine Dion did that.

Roy was diagnosed in 2018 and told he may never sing again. Undaunted, he and son Terence set up 'Watch Your Back MND' to raise awareness and funds for MND research, with Roy and his band 'The MND Assassins' releasing a couple of tracks, one of them, 'My New Dream' – the initials of the song being MND – hitting No. 1 in the iTunes chart in Ireland.

Another amazing example of how people, from all walks of life, have joined forces to conquer MND.

Friday 13 September

Now that we are here, and Kathy is here, we might as well stay a couple of days in Dublin. A little R&R. Ah, like the good old days.

Sunday 15 September

Back in time to start the 2019 Kiltwalk with Sir Tom Hunter, such a wonderful benefactor to so many great causes. Glad I've been at training camp for the last few days.

Monday 16 September

It isn't all about bright lights, big events and celebrities. A great many people want a piece of me at various times, for various things, and today it's the turn of the pupils from Coldingham Primary, in particular the P7s, and Anna Campbell, Nikki Wright, Sophie Mahon and Lulu Kendrick who wrote 'Standing With Doddie'.

They made my day, I hope I made theirs.

Tuesday 17 September

Today, I'm back in Edinburgh. No, not looking for my own travel lane – but looking for answers.

Myself and Sean McGrath are at Holyrood to have a meeting with Cabinet Secretary for Health Jeane Freeman to discuss the lack of care pathway and research for MND.

Thus far, we've had a couple of meetings with politicians in the Scottish Government about the treatment of MND patients. The issue I have with politicians is that they are very good at nodding and not so good at dipping their hand into the public purse.

I don't expect anyone to turn up for a meeting with a swag bag full of cash, however – and this applies to Westminster and in Scotland too – you are looking for someone to come back to you if the answer is no, and at least explain why. Instead, you are left hanging.

The problem is, MND sufferers hang around for less time than most. If you initiate something, or approach with a proposition, there is a chance it won't apply to a percentage of sufferers because they plain and simple won't be here.

Imagine thinking an issue, as bleak and stark as MND, can be left in a filing tray for another day. The sad thing – the absolutely frustrating thing – is that those who fight the hardest and are the most determined are the ones who have bigger things to struggle with, like life itself and facing up to a terminal illness.

As I say, frustrating.

Thursday 19 September

I'm in Glasgow, doing a motivational speaking engagement for JP Morgan as part of their Colleague Appreciation week of events. I don't feel rusty, or anything like that, but it feels ages since I did something like this. Anyhow, my chat is well received. I haven't lost the touch.

Friday 20 September

Today I'm at the BBC studio in Edinburgh to record a show with Ricky Ross for his Sunday morning slot. Ricky has been a great supporter of the Foundation along the way and it's always nice just to have a blether with folk you like, and about things other than rugby and illness. I've always quite fancied doing *Desert Island Discs*, though my choice of music would have people looking at their radio in a strange way.

Tuesday 24 September

BBC Scotland are tonight showing a documentary about the life of Fernando Ricksen, the former Rangers player who died from Motor Neuron Disease last week aged just forty-three. I'm not sure what to expect.

Those I've spoken with or met haven't mentioned 'The Final Battle'. Not really football parts around here, or it could be that folk are uneasy mentioning Fernando's passing in my presence.

To be honest, I never gave it a second thought about not watching it. I know, some will find that strange, to say the least. Why watch some else suffering and ultimately succumbing to something that has a 99.9% chance of doing the same to me. But this documentary was about him, someone who, apart from having the same condition, I wouldn't have seen play or know too much about during his career.

Indeed, it was only after my own diagnosis that I learned of him. Why was that? Did he shun the publicity, or had he decided against raising awareness of the disease, preferring to keep his life private? Or was it impossible trying to gain publicity or make a difference around a subject many would shy away from, something too difficult to accept or understand, which others would just turn into sensational headlines? The latter part could be hurtful to him and those closest to him.

I watch the programme, somewhat dispassionately. It is about someone else, not me. There is an association, and there are parts of it that do have me pondering things. But this is Fernando's story, about how he coped with MND, and how he battled against it for so long.

That part of his story did get me thinking. He was diagnosed in 2013, six years ago. For an illness that can take life so swiftly within a year, why was it that here was another sportsman – rather like Joost van der Westhuizen – who defied the odds and convention by living on several years beyond the norm. Was it something to do with an inherent fitness? Or was it a will to win, single-mindedness against adversity? No doubt someone, somewhere in a laboratory, will be running the checks on that theory.

It is obvious that his plight tugged at the hearts of Rangers fans, and those who had supported him back in the Netherlands. Again, and this is looking at it from the path I've taken, the charitable aims he and those around him tried to pursue came late in the day, when the disease had really taken hold. This is not a criticism. People are entitled to live their life – and, particularly, live out their lives – however they see fit.

But so much of the battle against MND has been about awareness. So, for me, this is perhaps a missed opportunity, especially given how ardent Rangers fans are in supporting one of their own. It is, nevertheless, not for me to reason why, simply mourn someone else who gave it his best against a relentless opponent.

Tuesday 24 September

Stewart and Campbell from Black & White are at Bluecairn to talk about our latest book idea. I afford myself a chuckle as I am now a recognised author. Well, at least I put my name on the front cover. Others do some of the hard work.

Friday 27 September

I quite like invites to do motivational speaking engagements. I wouldn't say I'm grateful for having MND, but it has certainly given me some new material when it comes to facing adversity, coping with disappointment and relying on teammates. The folk at GSK have kindly sought my services for their own team gathering at Barnard Castle, and like Glasgow last week, my chat is well received. I haven't lost my touch.

Thankfully, I haven't lost the script I used in Glasgow either . . .

OCTOBER 2019

Tuesday 1 October

Part of being a recognised – and, indeed, award-nominated – author is doing the round of book festivals around the country. Stewart and me today find ourselves at the Wigtown Book Festival, the place famously known as Scotland's Book Town. I ask Stewarty Boy, 'Scotland's book town, does this mean we've made it?'

'Aye, again,' was his to-the-point reply.

The people at these events could not be nicer, even if there is a business side to the occasion which means keeping to the schedule and, generally, keeping to the script. Or at least, that is the theory. Whether it's me and Stewart, or me and Gary, we do like to go off-piste when it comes to the formulated procedure. The look of fear in the faces of hosts and compères is a source of great merriment – although probably not to them.

The hour – plus a few minutes – fly past and we receive a standing ovation at the end. I'm not sure how much the locals or visitors wanted to know about what goes into a successful book, or what styles you have to employ to get your tale over, but I don't think anyone had any complaints by the end.

But speaking for an hour – particularly when Stewart doesn't say much – is extremely thirsty work. It's just as well some members of the local farming and rugby community are at hand to steer us in the direction of a local hostelry where we can grab a glass of water – black, Irish water, with a head on it.

Tuesday 8 October

Gary Armstrong and Doddie Weir, for one night only, York Race Course. No, we were neither runners nor riders on this occasion, but speaking at the Persimmon Homes Building Futures Awards. The wee man is funny. Not as funny as he looks, but funny nevertheless.

Wednesday 9 October

The postman – arguably the fittest on the planet given how heavy the load has become since the summer of 2017 – arrives at Bluecairn with a special delivery, except I think I know what it is. And it is!

The World According to Doddie: An A–Z of Life and How to Live It, my newest book – the most recent out of two in other words – has just been published. It's an amusing mix – though I say so myself – of things I have said over the past twenty-five years, collated by Stewart (Weir) and wonderfully illustrated by Jonty Clark. There's something for everyone there and anyone who buys it will be a better and wiser person after reading it – honest!

Thursday 10 October

The Logan Invitational Golf Day at Stoke Park gives me a chance to meet a whole bunch of people who have assisted our Foundation, but also allows me to say thanks and give support to Kenny and Gabby on one of their big days. The day ends with a late flight to Newcastle from Heathrow. I am shattered.

Friday 11 October

An early alarm call. Not what was needed, but I am more than happy to lift my head off the pillow this morning. The Weirs are on the 06.00 a.m. to Mallorca. Phone off, feet up. Oh, and toast well buttered!

Sunday 13 October

Oh, well. Scotland tumble out of the World Cup, beaten by hosts Japan. It wasn't the best tournament for the Scots and, to be honest, they were pushing water uphill from losing that first game against Ireland. All told, it was a disappointing venture.

But in going down 28–21 to Japan, there was one crumb of comfort. At least it wasn't New Zealand . . .

Tuesday 22 October

A day after coming back from our autumn break, me and the missus are back on it, letting the train take the strain as we speed down to London to take part in the Just Giving awards ceremony. We then speed back north again the next day to take part in a couple of photo shoots, one for Scotrail, the other with the Perth Rotary Club. It is all go.

Sunday 27 October

Gary and me are headed upcountry to Musselburgh for a very special day for an equally special man. Scotland's finest after-dinner speakers along with hundreds of guests will be paying tribute to Scotty Glynn MBE, charity fundraiser, comic, actor and would-be prop. Scott isn't well with cancer. Today is a chance to show support for him, but also likely to be a farewell visit too.

We can have a laugh – black humour at its best – as to which one of the pair of us would see off the other. Not the kind of win you'd celebrate, but certainly, given our precarious welfare, something that is inevitable, and sooner than planned.

I have shared a stage, an evening and a microphone with Scott, his totally irreverent style making him a huge favourite within the rugby fraternity across the country. Not for the faint hearted. His material was rich to say the least, but hugely funny. But there are few kinder individuals than Scott, going out of his way to help his Tranent community and beyond, and assist others, when he himself was very poorly.

When he was in hospital in October 2017 after a liver transplant, I went to visit him, unannounced, still kitted out in overalls and work boots, and planked myself on his bed in the high dependency unit just a few days after his operation – so incurring the wrath of the unit nurse. Boy, she went to town. All we could do was laugh like stupid laddies.

After an initial improvement in his health, the dreaded disease struck again, forcing his retirement from performing, although today he gave one final recitation of his 'Weegie Budgie' joke. Heard it? Where have you been if you haven't, more to the point. Go look it up on YouTube.

I must have heard it a few dozen times, and always laughed. This grand finale was no different. I had a photo taken with me, Scott and his laddie Gareth, them in their outrageous Hawaiian shirts, me tartaned up. It looked like a fireworks display had scored a direct hit on a paint factory. Then we said cheerio.

While it's nice to say it in person, you can't help but think about the finality of it, or wished you'd said something else, just to confirm how special he was. Blah. Another instance of being in the company of someone who knows exactly where you've been, where you are, or where you are headed.

It was a brilliant day. Gary brought me home, but I was bursting for a pee. You've got to go when you've got to go, so as he nipped in for a cup of tea, I did what I had to do out on the drive, and did a good job, not even getting my shoes wet. In my rush, however, I hadn't closed the car door so tried to do so with my bum.

Unfortunately, the door closed quicker than I expected and I fell, on my back, at the side of the house, stuck like a turtle. Not ideal, and having wriggled around for a few minutes – longer probably – help eventually arrived when Gary noticed I hadn't yet come in. Oh, how we laughed – no, we didn't. He got the fright of his life, I was duly chastened for drinking so much wine, getting in that state and ultimately that position.

It could have been serious, but thankfully wasn't. Others did not see the funny side, but I bet you big Scott certainly would have laughed.

Still, out of bad comes good. I got an iWatch so if that happened again, I could at least phone for help.

Wednesday 30 October

John Beattie and the BBC Scotland crew check into Bluecairn for what, I am assured, is the last batch of filming for the documentary they have been making about me and MND. There are not too many re-takes. They want the spontaneity and the emotion to be natural. The latter comes easier these days. And not just because I'm talking to Beattie.

It has never been too far away, always close to bubbling over, but I have until now kept a lid on it. However, that could be because I try and park certain issues, which John, because he is only doing his job, brings back to the front of the rank.

I am looking forward to seeing the end result. How I feel afterwards, time will tell.

NOVEMBER 2019

Saturday 2 November

The rugby World Cup feels like it has been going on forever. Today, however, we finally get a winner. Either England or South Africa will take the spoils, though you almost know in advance this will hardly be an advert for flowing, thrilling rugby. A fraction of my family are really willing England to win. The remaining percentages are rather nonplussed by the title decider. In the end, England lose. No celebrations, only commiserations. I'm looking at the long game. This means the Lions will be meeting the World Champion Springboks in 2021. It could not be any better.

And, this afternoon, I am honoured to be given the duties of opening the new 3G pitch at the Greenyards which has been laid – at considerable cost – to benefit not only the rugby club but all of the various sporting teams and clubs in the town. It is, as they say, changing times and in a place like Melrose, and mirrored around the country, communities are entitled access to the best sporting facilities possible.

I'm a traditionalist – and I loved playing on grass – but then I'm old. Maybe I need to move with the times. What I did have moved for me was a good few feet of the original Greenyards turf. Many a happy day spent playing on that, and many a winning one as well. I will get the grass transplanted into my garden so I will always have a bit of the Greenyards with me – although I probably already have some of it in me as I'm pretty sure I swallowed bits of it during my playing days.

Saturday 9 November

The Assembly Rooms in Edinburgh welcomes me and Stewart for the latest exciting instalment of our literary sales campaign, this time talking up the wealth of information, comical genius, and other lifestyle tips included within the covers of *The World According to Doddie*. A full house gives us a rousing welcome, and laughs at all the various tall stories, jokes and anecdotes we treat them to, even those delivered by Stewarty. Bless him.

The meet and greet at the end was, as ever, entertaining in itself. Maybe I should record the audience's best one-liners. Campbell from Black & White Publishing will be getting a call on Monday with this latest brainwave.

Wednesday 20 November

'Scotland will be the first side to face newly crowned World Champions South Africa on next year's summer tour and will also play New Zealand, Scottish Rugby has confirmed,' according to the BBC Sport website.

'Gregor Townsend's side will attempt to defeat the Springboks in two Tests on 4 and 11 July. They will then visit Dunedin to take on the All Blacks in the first of two scheduled meetings next year.'

Mmmm . . . food for thought. What's for dinner?

If I didn't know what was for dinner, then lunch would be steak pies (and beans) delivered by Stewart, as we would be joined for lunch by Rob Robertson from the *Mail on Sunday*, Mark Palmer from the *Sunday Times*, and photographer Craig Watson, who would be working on a feature for this Sunday's papers.

Where possible I like to accommodate the press guys for, on the whole, they've been good to me and given that I have a story to tell and something to sell – namely the world of the Foundation – it's good to keep in with them.

I think the steak pies are a clincher – and definitely in the plural for Rob, who can make food evaporate. Craig appears to be the one doing the real work, outdoors on a chilly day, taking photos of me on my quad, in the fields and hanging over that most famous of farming props, the five-bar gate.

A cup of tea thaws us out and the lads are soon on their way, but not before Rob's had a Tunnock's Caramel Wafer. Well, we didn't want him getting hungry on the way back to Edinburgh.

DECEMBER 2019

Thursday 5 December

Rugby is a fantastic sport, but an equally great way of life. You form friendships, you form rivalries that become friendships, you make enemies who become friends. There is a bond and a camaraderie that endures through the years. Today that theory is tested when the Class of '99, the Scotland team which won the Five Nations Championship, the last ever played, comes together again at Gaucho in Edinburgh.

I'm not sure whether this was a reunion lunch that morphed into a fundraiser for our Foundation, or the opposite way around. Anyway, we're here, although the emphasis has shifted to another one of our own, Tom Smith. 'Tammy Troot' as I christened him (after the author Lavinia Derwent's character which Thomas hadn't the foggiest about) is pretty ill. Monies raised today will also go to him and his family as he battles cancer.

He is in our thoughts in everything we do today, including getting drunk. It would be rude not to. Occasionally, get-togethers and gatherings like this can be quite cliquey, but this was no such example. From the off, you were never sure who was where, who was talking to this one or that one, or who was sitting next to who at the table. A lot of these guys hadn't seen one another in years, plenty of years in the case of a couple.

I'm feeling a bit of a fraud to be honest, joining in the celebrations for the winning of a title when I only played forty minutes, crocked in the final line-out of the first half against Wales. Then I spot Chick Chalmers who was only on the bench and my place at the table is more than justified.

Chambo was drafted in as cover for Duncan Hodge who broke his leg just after the turnaround. Where was Hodgy? As a coach with Edinburgh, he arrived late. Always leave a space for the workers. Many forget that it was Duncan who quite literally set the ball rolling that season with his kick-off that landed straight in the arms of John Leslie, and the rest was history. A try in nine seconds? Usain Bolt doesn't move that fast.

Both the Leslie boys were there, Martin as well, but most of us hadn't seen John since the early noughties. My old Falcons teammate looked amazing. What had he been eating and drinking? Different stuff to us, evidently.

John and Alan Tait were deep in conversation, probably less about their devastating partnership at centre, more likely for 'Victor' reminding his co-collaborator that he still owed him eleven pence from a round of drinks in 2001. Taity invented copper wire fighting over a penny, didn't you know?

And if John Leslie looked swell, Glenn Metcalfe appeared fit to play. 'Snowy' was another 'Kilted Kiwi' and had travelled over for the gathering. If you want to look healthy and ageless, New Zealand's obviously the place to be. I'll get in the queue – behind Peter Walton, Paul Burnell, Stuart Reid, Stuart Grimes ... only right they go first.

There was only a handful of the troops missing who had made up that team, but the captain and my companion Gary Armstrong was there. No show without Punch, and his schoolboy antics were still to the fore, covering the reverse side of people's cutlery with salt – imagine what their first mouthful would have tasted like – and hiding Taity's bottle of whisky, which he was desperately searching for. Well, he'd got it for nothing after all.

Some were definitely on their way to partying like it was 1999. And why not.

Jill (Douglas) and Andrew Cotter kept the afternoon entertaining, and Kenny Logan gave a masterful display as auctioneer. If only he'd been as talented as a place-kicker. Did I say that?

My big mate, Danny Sawrij from the Leo Group, had taken a table, by the sound of things populated mostly by English voices. Danny, though, was determined to 'Jockify' them, purchasing ten tartan scarves from the wee lassie from the Scotland Shop – a great store for all things tartan and touristy (tell them Doddie sent you) – and spending a fortune on signed prints and memorabilia. A generous man is our Danny, and a great supporter to me and the Foundation.

It was nice to see so many old faces, particularly the double act who looked after this bunch of eejits in every sense of the phrase – Jim Telfer who was coach and his sidekick and team manager Arthur Hastie.

There wasn't much – make that there wasn't anything – that these two didn't know about rugby and players. Ours was a team that was given its head on the pitch, because they knew how to keep us in check off-field. Or at least we allowed them to think that. If it hadn't been for the England game, and we should have won that (and probably would if me and Hodgy hadn't been injured – tongue-in-cheek there, folks), it would have been a Grand Slam and Triple Crown year.

As it was, and as luck would have it, what we did win was an even bigger prize that we still hold as the last Five Nations Champions, reigning and undefeated, a trophy retained for ever. Well, unless anything untoward happens with the Italians, and even then we'd just invite Georgia to take their place.

Aye, we are that desperate when it comes to keeping hold of that crown, but we have to safeguard the 'Class of 99' brand. I mean, we might need another reunion dinner for them.

Friday 6 December

Always read the small print, or if you can't, get someone to read it to you. Somewhere in the paperwork from Black & White Publishing, there is a clause that says you will assist, as an author, in promotional work around any titles you are involved in. Thus far, we've appeared at town halls, in tents, book festivals, stately homes, shops, theatres, store signings, and even co-opted Peter Wright in as a body double when I was predisposed. But a garden centre?

Today, we are at Mortonhall on the outskirts of Edinburgh. It's not what I would call trepidation or anxiety, but do they sell books among the potted plants and wreaths? Take that as a given. In fact, there are as many people there as we've seen at some shops, and the coffee is so much nicer as well.

Harking back to my rugby days, it was always nice to meet the general public and supporters. If you think about it, they pay your wages. Being an author it's no different. If people are willing to take time out of their lives to come and see you, then you can spend a few minutes while they throw curve ball questions, pose for selfies and get the obligatory signature. What is distinct, compared to the rugby spectators, are their reasons for turning up and buying books. Some liked me as a player, one liked someone else but couldn't remember his name. I concluded that must have been Stuart Reid or Gordon Simpson. There were those who were collectors of books by Scottish authors, or by sportsmen, or rugby players, or who just wanted a day out. I ticked a few of those boxes.

We are into December, Santa territory, and Stewart is busily transcribing various messages in books for the Christmas gift market. Me, I just smile, say thank you, and add my Zorro-like moniker.

We are bobbing along quite merrily when a gentleman is wheeled in by a younger woman to meet me. You can just tell he is an MND sufferer. He motions that I'm bigger than he expected. I quip I hadn't noticed which raises a silent laugh. His daughter tells Stewart what message she'd like in the book, adding that her dad was only diagnosed in September and cannot now walk or talk. To the eye, however, he looks absolutely normal. MND is so utterly indiscriminate, so utterly brutal. We wish them a Merry Christmas when it comes. Who knows what 2020 will hold for them, but dwelling on such things saps your own energy, selfish as that sounds.

The queue has dwindled until there is only one man left. He looks up. 'A-ha!' It is none other than former Scotland coach Richie Dixon, one of the nice men of rugby, who in his first season in charge so nearly steered us to the Grand Slam, only to lose out to England (again) in the decider at Murrayfield. That was a great year because post-World Cup, and the retirement of Gavin Hastings, not too many expected us to do a great deal. But we silenced them and shocked ourselves into the bargain.

Richie was a good coach, and almost Telfer-esque with his quotations, like 'too high, you die' and 'bump and burl'. However he communicated it, he got the message through.

I must admit there is a bit of guilt on my behalf that I was maybe one of the players who meant Richie's tenure with Scotland didn't last longer. However, he appears to have let bygones be bygones – not that he has ever raised the matter – and has become a bit of a global ambassador for the game, currently helping Georgia – with their juggernaut pack – steamroller teams at international level.

Wee surprises like this are just so nice and it is great to have a good long talk with someone so well liked in the game – and that has nothing to do with his generous donation to the Foundation. It really cheered me up.

Before we leave the venue, there is time for a coffee with Ian Watt, chief executive of Fosroc, who are terrific supporters of the Foundation and Scottish Rugby. What a lovely day.

Back in the car, and now in darkness, I wish there was autopilot to get me home. Driving is one of my one remaining pleasures in life that I can do, unaided, maintaining my independence status. That means a great deal to me. And after today, and a reminder of the cruelty MND can exact, all the more precious.

I head away from Edinburgh and back to the Borders. The journey doesn't take too long, nor is too stressful, despite it being winter, rush hour and dark. The reality is it doesn't take any less or more time than usual. It just appeared quicker, probably because my mind has been elsewhere.

At seven o'clock, on BBC One Scotland, a documentary about me and my condition, *One Last Try*, will air. It has been shot over the last year and a bit, the Beeb turning up at various events to get some footage, while John Beattie has been a regular visitor down at Bluecairn, and local boy Cameron Buttle has popped in occasionally as well.

The one thing I've noticed – rather like having a book pieced together – is that you are never quite sure of the context, or the sequencing, or the chronology that will go into the end product.

Given that they know what they are talking about, and I trust them, Jill, from a TV perspective, and Stewart, with his editorial hat on (although it could belong to someone else), were sent off a few weeks ago to watch the final cut. Jill thought 'it was beautifully produced' and found herself getting 'quite teary and emotional'. Stuey said it was, 'Aye, good,' which is straight out of the Gary

Armstrong playbook of compliments, which probably rates as an 8/10.

Whatever their take, they went to the Candleriggs in Glasgow city centre afterwards and got hammered, as part of the debrief. Total pros. Well done you. It's why you're part of the team.

It wasn't quite popcorn and sodas around the telly at Bluecairn. You are never sure what you'll see or how you might react to it. I know I'd watched a similar programme about the Rangers player Fernando Ricksen a few weeks back, but that was about a fellow sufferer who in some ways had endured the same journey as I was now taking. I knew what that was like. But I had steeled myself to expect the unexpected. Maybe I had readied myself too well.

All in, it told my story pretty well. There would have been parts I might have expanded upon and made more of, some bits I thought were irrelevant, but the large majority of it was what I'd expected, or had come to expect. I did wonder, however, where and when my mother had found her politeness and accent.

It was quite strange initially; ultimately though it was just quite nice to see and hear her again. Also, if I ever contemplate selling the farm, do you have any out-takes I might use for the sales pitch? It looked really nice on camera.

What I hadn't banked on, and this was either naïve or just entirely silly of me – probably the latter – was the wave of support that gushed in my direction through social media. Having at first heard just a few alerts, it then just became a constant tinging, so much so that I had to reduce the volume to zero, and then stick the phone on the charger because the battery had begun to drain.

If I wasn't too touched or overly emotional at what I'd viewed, then some of the messages were heart-rending, both at what people's view of me was or had become, or just how many people had been touched or hurt by what Motor Neuron Disease had done to loved ones or people close to them, or what it was doing to sufferers, slowly but surely.

That side of it was very real for me. I'm sure those who contacted me, or any of my team when the show was over, had the very best intentions, either as a show of support or affection. And I thank them for taking the time to message me and the Foundation. But it wasn't easy, oh no.

And that was just from around Scotland . . .

Tuesday 10 December

Behind the scenes Stewart has been working on a wee thing with BBC Radio 5 Live for about a month now and today it comes together. Olympic gold medallist Darren Campbell is coming to interview me for *The Inside Track* show, to be broadcast on Thursday. Joining us will be former footballer Stephen Darby, who had previously been with Liverpool and Bradford City before joining Bolton Wanderers where he was a player when his career was cut short in September 2018 after being diagnosed with MND.

Darren will no doubt have lots of questions to ask, but I have a few myself for Stephen. While my playing days were long gone when I was given the news, I am interested to know how Stephen – married to England Women's captain Steph Houghton – handled a career-ending and probably life-ending condition.

News like that is hard enough to accept or deal with on an individual basis, but this was a double-whammy of devastating proportions. Like me, there was no easy pathway to finding out why. First, he had started losing the feeling in his hands when he was driving, before all the testing revealed the inevitable conclusion, that he had MND.

From my own experience, and as I detailed in *My Name'5 Doddie* (my first book, nominated for various awards, which I am always loath to talk about), I knew – thanks to the interweb-thingy – that

I had MND before Kathy and I took that fateful trip to Edinburgh before Christmas 2016.

Stephen, by coincidence, by chance or by luck, thinks he first saw signs of an issue something like three years prior. It shows the randomness of this disease, firstly in having the misfortune to be diagnosed with it, but secondly – and here Stephen and me might be exceptions – how long you can continue, if not unscathed, but certainly fit enough to continue some kind of normal functionality and life. But we are the exceptions.

Darren seems to have enough material to make a show, and make us sound good. Time then for lunch. Stewart supplies mini-steak pies from his local butcher in Stonehouse, and the beans to accompany them. It's the quietest we've been all day as we munch into them. I have Mr Campbell down as a two-pie man and he doesn't disappoint. Stewart's daughter Zara, a bit of an athlete herself, is totally transfixed by Darren, who delivers a psychological masterclass on sprinting, training and running, as well as a few dos and don'ts for life in general. She has two pies as well. The Campbell effect.

Over lunch, Stephen explains his plans for his foundation, the Darby Rimmer Foundation, set up with former British Forces veteran Chris Rimmer, a friend of Stephen's brother, who had shown symptoms of MND during a tour of Afghanistan in 2014. Their aims and targets are not dissimilar to MN5DF. We belong to a select club and there is no doubt we will work together again going forward. It is, after all, in both of our interests.

Sunday 15 December

There is nothing spontaneous about awards. Firstly, you may have been nominated a while ago, but that aside it's a certainty that you will be contacted well in advance, to forewarn you and to ask, if offered, would you accept.

I've already given a few interviews and am on my way to Aberdeen on Saturday 14 December when the news breaks that at the BBC Sports Personality of the Year 2019, I am to receive the Helen Rollason Award, named after the BBC sports presenter who sadly succumbed to cancer in 1999. It's a very special award, presented for outstanding achievement in the face of adversity. There are some amazing names on the roll of honour but am I worthy of mention alongside these men and women, because to my mind, they are right up there with the best and bravest? This news will come as a huge surprise to so many people, even those who know me. That's it, I didn't tell anyone about this either.

But what I wasn't really aware of was that *One More Try* went out on BBC1 network on Saturday afternoon throughout the UK. And what a response. If my profile gained a boost, then the entire story around MND had just been given a massive lift.

Having had a blether with Gary Armstrong, my wingman throughout everything, we've decided it's best to arrive in Aberdeen a day in advance simply because this is going to be a pretty full-on weekend, and that's before the TV cameras start to broadcast. We want to enjoy it and do everything right.

The Weirs and friends have invaded the Granite City. Stewart is missing, brought out of retirement after thirty-five years to play tubular bells at a Christmas concert in St Mary's in Lanark. Another talent no one knew about until a recent Christmas lunch.

With so many of my ain folk there, it would be rude not to partake in a small aperitif or two. Bet you didn't know Guinness was an aperitif. Well, until recently I thought aperitif was another name for dentures. Though I'm enjoying the lovely black stuff from the Emerald Isle, I can't have too much as I need to keep my wits about me (they missed out on a clear head twenty years ago), as there is going to be a semi-rehearsal just to go over what will happen on the big night.

The engineers and scene builders are still adding finishing touches at the P&J Arena as I'm shown where I'll be sitting, my check mark on my walk-up, and where I'll be on stage. Kathy is given her orders. All straightforward. Simple. Big barn this place. But I was a move or two ahead as the mind wandered, thinking three things: one, it was good doing that training run; two, maybe time for bed; and three, maybe after more Guinness. Aye, I'm enjoying this.

'Oh, and Princess Anne will be here to do the presentation.'

Oh. Oh shhhh, sugar! It was lovely for her to give up her time and come along to the evening. But it was a measure of the importance of the occasion that she – a former winner herself of the main prize – had been asked to be there, and had wanted to be there.

I've met her a few times performing her duties with the SRU, and at other functions we'd attended supporting various enterprises around Motor Neuron Disease – she is patron of MND Scotland and has been for thirty years – where the conversation had been a bit lengthier and more informed. She's also quite friendly with Rob Wainwright. But apart from that, she's a lovely lady with a real zest to take the battle to MND. All good.

This prize giving, though, was totally away from the norm. There was a void in my stomach. Had I really been convincing myself, or kidding myself on, that I was going to breeze through this? I was starting to slip out of my comfort zone, where the quick one-liners might not work or be welcome. Oh, why me? I hadn't even asked that when diagnosed with MND. *Sugar*. Actually, shit. I'd feel better tomorrow. Of course I would.

We'd all been down to Liverpool a couple of years ago for the SPOTY, a few months after I'd announced my condition, a great experience and an amazing event, especially all the bits you don't really see on TV when people are coming and going, and the set is being changed and the like. I thought that was great. Everyone had a great old time as reflected in the number of selfies the boys and their mother took with the proper sporting celebs.

Back in the hotel, I was happier, and who wouldn't be with a beer and good company, one being Carl Doran, executive editor for the Sports Personality of the Year. Amazingly, we first met when the BBC took me and high-jumping legend Steve Smith to Lapland to meet Santa for the 'Mystery Guest' sequence in *A Question of Sport*. Fair to say, I think he's done quite well in his career!

Happy days. Well, not really. The more I speak to Carl about that trip, the more one or two memories start to drift back about getting a hammering – from the wife. I think it might have been something to do with her thinking I'd tried to kill her. Well, how was I to know that trying to do doughnuts on a ski-doo perhaps wasn't one of the cleverest thoughts I'd ever had. Put it this way, my theory never became a reality. I think I ran out of talent halfway through the manoeuvre and barrel-rolled the ski-doo – with Kathy attached – at high speed. Hence her anger. Ah, the volatility of young love.

But back to the bar. Not that I'd ever complain, well not forcibly, but in today's modern world you don't just have a beer at the bar. There are the obligatory selfies. Hey, I'd think there was something wrong if I wasn't asked. That must be how Gary feels. 'Oh, I never realised you were that height,' said one wee wifey – to Gary. That made my night. But it's lovely to be recognised. People can be so genuine with a beer in their hand. Eventually, we call it a night, or a morning.

During daylight morning, we rally ourselves. Sunday is spent lazing about, eating, only light refreshments (no, not half pints of Guinness). Not thinking too hard about it, but need to be up to this. People there to see it – see me – and there are those watching on the TV as well.

We are all dressed to kill, and on time for a change, as we make our way to the auditorium. Having seen the size of the theatre, I didn't really take into account that they'd have chosen a place that size in order to get a whole load of people in. This was going to be busy. But I'm an old pro at these things, appearing and chatting at dinners, stadiums, book festivals. You've done it before, I convinced myself, why take stage fright now?

Everyone ensconced, we went through all of the house rules to make sure everything ran smoothly and on time. Then it was sit back, relax and enjoy the show. No.

But what was I doing here? This was not down to me, but everyone else involved, the people who had cycled, climbed mountains, cycled up mountains, run marathons, half marathons, 10 kms, 5 kms, walked, swam, you name it. And to those who had dipped their hand in their pocket to sponsor individuals or buy cakes or books or raffle tickets or tables or auction prizes. Perhaps they'd all been invited, that's why it was so busy.

Leader, figurehead, call it what you will, but I had emerged as a champion of the MND cause, and a lot of good causes in general. But worthy of a prize like this? Could they not have found someone else? If it had gone to a phone vote, I'd have spent a good few quid voting for the other person, comfortable in the belief that they'd have deserved it more. But no. People had bestowed this honour on me and the Foundation, so there was no good reason to wish it away or push someone else forward.

Gabby made the announcement that I was the winner of the Helen Rollason, my cue to head for the stage. And that's when the occasion hit me. No, make that smashed me. I had no idea just how noisy it would be when the entire arena erupted and began applauding and cheering. They never said anything about this when we did our rehearsal.

That crescendo, that noise which just swelled up and filled the hall, was like walking onto a straight jab, but what nearly floored me was that in the background 'Flower of Scotland' was being played. Sixty-one times I played for Scotland, and I might have been benched for a few as well. The poignancy of that tune – I'd heard it and sang it every time I'd appeared in the thistle jersey – just took my breath away. I could feel myself welling up, I could feel the top lip tremble a bit, and if I'd been asked to say so much as a word at that point, I'd have cried like a baby. 'Come on, big fella, come on,' I said to myself, as I took a couple of real gulps of air. Fortunately, very fortunately, the big walk to the stage gave me time to compose myself. But it still wasn't easy.

I was also trying hard not to pay too much attention to who was on the stage; it was almost like a guard of honour. I think if I'd made eye contact with any of them for too long, it would just have set me off. I could see my dad, Kathy and the boys at the front, brothers and sister at the back. Then I nodded towards Stuart Grimes, my old Scotland and Newcastle teammate and that wasn't the wisest thing to do. Come on, Doddie man, keep it together. Wainwright, Andy Nic, Shawsy, Gary, Gav, Hoggy – Hoggy?, Mooro, Jill, Jim Telfer, far enough back so he cannae tell me what I'm doing wrong, Jonathan Davies hiding in there, with Stuart McInally and Jonny Gray, Toony, Kenny, Alun Wyn, Jones the Prop. Were the BBC funding a touring team or something?

It might not have shown, but I was slowly crumbling and would soon have been in bits. But thankfully, and I have never, ever been as happy to see him, I was distracted by what Scott Hastings was wearing. Obviously, he didn't get the dress code memo. For a minute I thought a Rupert the Bear tribute act had sneaked onto the stage. Scott was kitted out in a bright red Santa sweater, with the emphasis on 'sweat' under the extreme TV lights, and his tartan troosers. I fancy he was looking to land the presenter gig in *What Not To Wear*.

But oh my word. I was out of my comfort zone meeting the

Queen. But that was a one-to-one experience. She spoke to me, I replied. This was up another level, seriously. Because there was Princess Anne, with a microphone and the trophy. I was going to have to speak. No pressure – 12,000 folk all settling back into their chairs, looking to be entertained, plus the millions watching at home. I hope they have a long video to run with lots of people saying nice things about me. Actually, right now I wouldn't care if they were saying horrible things about me.

This whole episode – the MND years – has been one massive adventure and a learning curve from day one. And I have been learning, with all of my guest appearances and speeches, about what to say and what not to mention, and who not to leave out when it comes to thanking people – and there are a lot of them to thank.

As it was, the Princess Royal made it all very easy for me. Her speech was warm and touching, and what a pro. Having presented me with the trophy, she then offered to hang on to it for me. Has she done this sort of thing before?

I'll admit it, I had prepared a speech of my own, all stored upstairs. It's kind of difficult holding notes with MND. There were a few wobbles, when I thought more about those I was talking about rather than just sticking to my script. What was off-putting, in a nice way, were the sniffs and coughs coming from behind me. I think I was making one or two emotional. Not my intention, you'll understand, but my general message to the wider world was obviously getting home to those I was closest to as well.

In concluding, I thanked my boys for supporting me, and my good lady, Kathy, and hoped everyone had a good night and a good Christmas. I couldn't speak another word. Emotion, the worst opponent I'd ever faced, had got the better of me. Looking out into the vast audience, all I could see were hankies!

Actually, I didn't know until later, but the microphones picked up on me saying, 'Right, the bar. Where do we go?' This was a general question, not specifically directed towards the Princess Royal, but even so it seemed a good idea.

Gary and I exited stage left. I'd done my bit. I wasn't ignoring the rest of the proceedings, or the other individuals for whom this would be their big night as well. But I was shattered, spent. I think the nervous energy I'd been burning had left nowt in the tank. We'd find a quiet corner, have a sit down and rehydrate with a Guinness. Good plan, badly executed.

There is no such thing as picking up an award like that then aiming to keep a low profile or hide. As soon as we entered reception, a huge cheer went up, another explosion of sound, feeling even louder because we were in a more confined space. I was man-handled, and woman-handled as we pushed on through the crowd, people shaking my hand, patting me on the back and offering up kisses. Particularly enjoyable from the ladies in attendance.

It became very busy, but one who joined our party – when she was invited by Gazza to come with us for a drink – was none other than super-athlete Katarina Johnson-Thompson, the heptathlon world champion and one of the contenders for the top prize. She was made very welcome, as was Chris Hoy and his wife Sarra, and Gabby who was there with her husband.

It all felt very familiar, because it was like what we used to get in the old amateur days after international games, crowded bars, people aiming to enjoy themselves, plenty of chat and good company. Like the seasoned professional he is, Simon Shaw decided he was peckish, headed off into the night and arrived back with a McDonald's. Once a Lions tourist.

Katarina left us briefly, only to return with her mum, once she'd slipped into something a bit more comfortable – but intent on trying a Guinness for size. Good girl. I have a house rule that you have to finish your drinks. She'd about half a glass of Guinness left as she was going to leave. No, finish that first. So she just skulled it. She can come out with us any time she wants. I think she left a real impression on those who met her, just being so down to earth and, as someone who, having put all the hard yards in that year, was now out to enjoy that moment. What it's all about.

I could see my eldest laddie Hamish taking more than a passing interest in young Miss Johnson-Thompson, although that didn't last very long once my brother, Thomas, got in on the act, identifying Katarina as 'Dina'. You really can't take them anywhere beyond Gala.

But a great time was had. And if you didn't enjoy it, there was only one person to blame. Rather like wondering the next morning how you woke up with a hangover.

Monday 16 December

Monday would be very leisurely. We were in no hurry to head home. Have a bit of breakfast and square up any outstanding bills. The manager on reception asked if everything had been to our satisfaction. It had. Have you noticed, they always ask that question before they pass you the bill?

I glanced at it, blinked, refocused, and the numbers still didn't look any better. Who was I to argue? Drink had been taken. A lot of it.

Heading back down the motorway, I broached the subject of the bar tab and how it was a bit steep. 'Oh, that might have been me,' came the voice from the back. Hamish, blaming the lofty total on the cocktails and coffee liqueurs he'd been drinking with Ben. And yes, it was *that* Ben – Stokes – winner of the 2019 SPOTY.

Nearing our journey's end, Stewart rings. 'Do you want to carry on to Newcastle to do a live TV piece? I'm sorry if you did because I've already said no . . .'

He was looking after my wellbeing. But it confirms my long-held belief that some media folk think I sit around all day waiting on them calling. Wrong. That's every other day.

Back at Bluecairn, I don't think it will ever not be a relief to see this place. Something to eat and then a quiet night after the last two we've had. But first, I have a bit of *Changing Rooms* action to participate in, rearranging my soft furnishings. I seem to have acquired some lovely SPOTY cushions from the BBC couch (that Sally Nugent slipped me them with a wee wink saying 'don't tell anyone' – so I won't).

That'll be another conversation stopper for any visitors...

Wednesday 18 December

A week until Christmas and we've got the last book signing of the year, what might be described as a 'home game' at St Boswells. You always wonder just how busy these things will be and, like so many, the official rating is 'mobbed'.

Being local we're guaranteed there will be a mix of the curious, the well-intentioned and those who have known me too long to be remotely impressed that I've written another book. The book, for them, is incidental. Whether it's from the farming fraternity or the rugby community, they've just come along to say hello, have a wee chat to see how I am, and get me to sign a couple of stocking fillers.

Invariably, chat turns to the land, tractors, Scotland performances and the occasional introduction to a youngster who I last saw in short trousers at school, and who is now a few inches off my height. Another wee wake-up to the reality that the years have just flown past. Have I made the most of them? Now is not the time to reflect.

We are a well-oiled machine when it comes to these signings. My signature has changed, entirely due to my issues, but it is still recognisable. A big 'D' at the start, a couple of spikes in the middle being smaller 'ds' and a big 'W' as a finale. Perfect, unless you happen to scrutinise them, when signature number fifty will look slightly different from the first of the day. But it's the thought that counts.

Occasionally my co-author is asked for an autograph as well. I don't think the purchasers realise just how much Stewart's name devalues the book if you ever go to sell it on eBay. However, I say this to one woman who jumps to Stewart's defence saying that, as co-author, then he is every bit as entitled to add his mark, her only disappointment being that the illustrator, Jonty Clark, wasn't there as well.

The book is well received, something a bit different, filled with 'Doddie-isms', the things I've said that I haven't realised I've said. It's not too serious. Tongue-in-cheek. The way life should be, and is, mostly.

Our publishers, Black & White, have been talking with us about possibly doing a third book, to the extent they put a contract offer in place a few weeks ago. I've chatted this through with Kathy. I'm not sure if I'd want to do another one. Apart from wondering what we'd put in another book, they are quite time consuming, even if Stewart puts the real work in (but don't tell him that).

Stewart and Campbell from B&W don't think content will be an issue. But who'd be interested on what I've got to say that I haven't already said?

I'm not sure. Stewart, though, wants to commit and explains his thinking behind it, about what the story would be, namely me living life with MND and the trials and tribulations around that, and about timescales, that this wouldn't be something you could suddenly play catch-up on. Still not convinced.

At this point, we have what could be considered the first cross words we've ever had. I'm a little stunned, but unmoved. 'Fine,' Stewart says; the offer will still be there for me, but if I change my mind, I can get someone else to write it because he'll be doing other things. Fine by me as well.

We shake hands, wish each other a Merry Christmas and Happy New Year when it comes, and go our separate ways. Cheeky b . . . boy.

He heads back to his fellow 'Weegies', as Jim Telfer has reminded him a few times (something Stuey vehemently argues he is not), and I leave St Boswells and head for Gary's place to pick him up as we are going to Carlisle to meet someone, a chap called Rob Burrow.

Rob is a rugby league player with Leeds Rhinos, and he'd contacted me off the back the Radio 5 interview. Not much was said, other than he would like to discuss a few things about MND – like, living with it, as he'd just been diagnosed.

Gary can share the driving, is good company, but above all else, he can add a bit of moral support. There isn't much on this journey (a phrase I don't like using but it ticks the box) that Gaz hasn't been part of. There isn't much of the last twenty-odd years that he hasn't been inexorably connected with. He is so often my wingman, the sort – like a few others – who would say they'd do something for me, even if they wouldn't necessarily be comfortable with it.

I don't know what to expect. There is a common belief – make that a common misconception – that because I have MND then I'm an expert counsellor, or I know how to handle circumstances. If I do, it's only through past experience. I might come across as assured and confident, but far from it. I am just as nervous, get tongue-tied about what to say, and about how I might respond or react.

The reason I'm meeting Rob is because the first language we'll talk – apart from English obviously – is rugby. We know the sacrifices and disciplines needed to take us where we've got to, which to my mind puts us on the same page from the start.

When we meet, the first thing I'm struck by is how small he is. Five-four, five-five. But he survived rugby league at the very highest level. It's not the size of the dog in the fight, and all that. This wee fella will be up for the battle. The second thing I'm aware of is that, at times, his voice wavers, slightly, not through emotion, but naturally.

We compare notes, predictably. There are many things common to us both, some incidental, others less so – a wife and kids, an incurable disease and a mixture of fear and bravery. The last one is hard to quantify. There is a saying, 'There is no such thing as bravery, only degrees of fear.' The meaning of that is that if you are not frightened, you appear, and act, courageously. Appearances can be deceptive.

There will be gains along the way, but ultimately he and I have much to lose. I have spoken to hundreds of people and addressed thousands. There can be an empathy between people coming from a different start point, but the real, deep-down knowing of what all this means, and how it will play out, that is something unique to the victims, and I include wives, husbands and partners in that.

If today took some courage for Rob, tomorrow is going to be a day for big boys when he announces to the world that he has been diagnosed with MND. I was fortunate during the summer of 2017 when I went public with the news, expertly stage managed by Stewart, Jill and a few others. Dealing with the press and media was one side of the tale; the other was the messages of support, love and affection you receive. I didn't see those straight away. In order to avoid attention, acceptable or otherwise, I had immobilised my phone by breaking the SIM card on my way to New Zealand. So, anything I saw or heard was second-hand, already filtered and monitored.

None of it was nasty, but it was like a wave of compassion, a sugar rush of sensitivity that just took my breath away and completely threw me emotionally. I asked Rob if he was ready for it. I think all he had been worrying about was getting the news out there, not the aftermath. If I'd unintentionally worried him, I tried to placate him by saying the bravest thing was convincing yourself to go public in the first place.

As we say cheerio, we both know this was only the first of many chats and meetings we'd be having. Back in the car, I asked Gary what he thought. 'Aye . . . that's another sair yin.' The man of few words summed it up perfectly.

Thursday 19 December

Rob's news is out there. I hope he's okay? He will be. There will be no shortage of camaraderie for him. I hope he'll feel relief as well, that he has told everyone, and now he doesn't need to hide anything, or as I had thought on occasions, living a lie when someone asked how you were and the only answer you could give was 'fine'.

I have a call to make. Stewart answers immediately, unusual for him. We share the usual platitudes, speak about how the book signing had gone, shared a story about the gents of the 'country set' (his words, not mine) that we'd met in the pub car park the previous day. The real intention of my call wasn't about any of the above.

I wasn't angry or upset, maybe peed off, but I wasn't happy with the ultimatum he had left me with yesterday. Stewart said it wasn't an ultimatum. Had it been, he says he'd have told me to f**k off. Being honest, that did sound about right.

It hadn't been my intention to have an argument on the phone, but Stuey Boy was quite heated in making his case, saying that if I didn't see the bigger picture, fine, but to countless sufferers and their carers, I had, to paraphrase him, become a trailblazer, cheerleader, flag-waver, spearhead, leader, talisman, voice, mascot and spokesman in the battle against Motor Neuron Disease for those who hadn't had a trailblazer, cheerleader, flag-waver, spearhead, leader, talisman, voice, mascot and spokesman in their battle against MND. And that if I didn't want to put my thoughts, concerns, worries, upsets, fears, ideas, and unique insight and understanding on how to deal with a disease that will kill you down on paper, fine.

He was quite good with words, I grudgingly thought.

Had I heard about Rob Burrow?

Not only had I heard about it today, I informed him, but I'd learned about it last night when I met Rob. Stewart only knew I was meeting someone. I hadn't said who, other than Gary was going with me, not through secrecy, but because I wasn't sure how things or the situation would pan out between me and Rob.

'And why did he want to meet you?' enquired Stewart. Was it anything to do with me being a trailblazer, cheerleader, flag-waver, spearhead, leader, talisman, voice, mascot and spokesman in people's battle against MND, who had his own thoughts, concerns, worries, upsets, fears, ideas, and unique insight and understanding on how to deal with a disease that will kill you 'but couldn't be arsed writing about it'?

Hmmm . . .

Friday 20 December

And that as they say is that for 2019. Closed – for official purposes anyway – until 2020. From here until the New Year it's all about me time, doing what I want, when I want – and when Kathy tells me it's okay to do it.

Jen, Jill, Scott, Gary and Stewart, sometimes saying the same thing, sometimes offering their take on events, reckon I'm done in. Between them, they have put a line through my diary. I am not offering up any argument. This has been a busy month and a busy year. I haven't stopped.

I cannot think of a period where I wasn't doing something or other. It is all very well saying it's good to stay busy, stay active, keep moving, but it feels as if the batteries are drained. Not something I'd offer up publicly, but internally, I can sense it. I'm not sure if I am plain tired, plain crabbit, plain crabbit because I'm tired, or if my condition is working busily underneath the surface. Two out of the three ain't bad, as Meatloaf once sang, and I can do something about that, namely, go into hibernation for a couple of weeks over the holiday period, going nowhere, speaking to no one outside of family.

A bit of Ho Ho Ho, Hamish's birthday – and that of my nephew Graham Dun on the same day – and then let's see what the New Year brings. Drink will be involved.

Wednesday 25 December

Merry Christmas! A day that means so many things to people. For me, a time to eat, drink and be merry. Also a time to reflect, and although I don't dwell too much on thoughts of Christmas past, there is one in particular that cannot be ignored.

Christmas Eve marked the third anniversary of me being told I had Motor Neuron Disease. Three years that I didn't even know I would see when we had that life-changing news broken to us. Three years of change, three years of trying to make change in a positive way.

I haven't really been one for over-exuberance, even during my playing career. But, if there is one day when I've allowed myself to punch the air, it is today. When I was diagnosed, the professor predicted that in a year I wouldn't be walking in to see him. And he was right. But for health and safety issues, I'd be galloping up the corridor to see him, performing a neat spin turn, a jig and taking a bow on one knee, just to show him he'd got it wrong, with me anyway, and reminding him of the score: Doddie 3 – MND 0. While that is the running score, I know that my opponent only needs to get one to win. Still, I didn't get here by being pessimistic now, did I?

That first year, now I've had a bit more time to reflect on it, was so difficult. Everyone was happy, enjoying the moment, and Kathy and I had to join in twenty-four hours after someone put a wrecking ball through our dreams, our plans, our future.

Brave? We had to be, because Mum was quite sick with her cancer. We didn't know whether this would be her last Christmas – even if, given what she'd been told, she was predicting with some confidence that it would be – so we weren't going to say anything that would take away from a day she deserved to enjoy.

Brave? We had to be, but maybe we were also overcome by shock. Once or twice, Kathy and I had a glance at one another, only a glance. Any longer and we might have crumbled. It showed what a strong-willed, determined person she is, that she could put on a happy face, when inside there could only have been turmoil. I won't say it too loud, but she has made hard times easier, because she has been an absolute rock holding things together. If she reads this, I'll deny everything and blame Stewart for making it up.

Every year thereafter from his 'you'll be in a wheelchair' prognosis, I let out a big scream of 'ya beauty', albeit in my head rather than physically, just to celebrate that this big galoot is still stomping about the planet, still seeing Santa Claus, still singing Jingle Bells, and still stuffing my face with all the seasonal fare, still being with those I love the most.

Once Mum and I had made it past our 'sell-by' dates, we were never not going to have a party.

It is a big family occasion, because I'm from a biggish family, as is Kathy, and our siblings have kids of their own which all adds up and means we need a bit of space if we are to celebrate properly. There is one space empty this time, so there was a tinge of sadness and reflection. But I can hear Mum's 'life is for the living' mantra, and intend to keep doing that today with my nearest and dearest.

My kids might have noticed that they didn't quite get as much as they have the last few years. That was because Kathy and me treated each Christmas as if it was my last, and treated them to everything that they wanted – game consoles, motorbikes, phones, the lot – and quite a few things they didn't expect. But, I'm still here, so bollocks to them. I hope they like their chocolate rabbit and shiny new pound coin. It's time to hold the annual spending spree in check a little bit.

Still, there isn't anything they want for, which, I have to say, is what it was also like for me growing up.

This year's celebration was at my brother Tom's place. Christmas dinner is a huge ask and can be really demanding for the 'cook', so we all took various items and bits to make the workload less daunting. My sister was in charge of procurement and organising who would do what, all terribly organised and clockwork. Funnily enough, having been in charge of the schedule, she didn't appear to have done very much herself. Can't imagine that, but that's what it looked like to me, and to those I may have mentioned it to.

If there was anything left over, it all went into Tom's dog, a muckle big Great Dane. It's more like a pony than a dog. It must have thought all its Christmases had come at once with the amount of leftovers it had to eat – on top of what it helped itself to. Christopher's wee one Lucinda was in the highchair, and every time the pooch walked past, it would snaffle whatever she'd been given before she could get her hands on it. Never perform with animals or children.

Thursday 26 December

I check my phone. It looks like we might be on the bestsellers table again given the number of folk who have received *The World According To Doddie* from Santa, and some – after seeing the Beeb documentary and the Sports Personality of the Year Awards – have got a double stocking filler with a copy of the first book as well. How do they work out sales commission?

There was a stack of stuff left over from Christmas dinner, and the plan was to have a buffet for lunch on Boxing Day when we all went back for the cars. That was the plan. Unfortunately, under cover of darkness, Tom's precious pup felt a bit peckish in the wee small hours and devoured anything within range. Lunch therefore was cancelled. And I was really looking forward to some of the things Kirsty had taken time over, which looked like not just any food, but Marks & Spencer top of the range food. Well, I suppose she wouldn't be her mother's daughter without passing M&S stuff off as her own ...

Saturday 28 December

Hamish's birthday and a big day for me as well. Heading off to Newcastle as a family to see the Falcons take on the Southern Knights for the inaugural Doddie's Club Trophy, played off between the two clubs that mean most to me. A day to meet old friends, hopefully be entertained on the field, maybe sign a few books, and then do the cup presentation.

This has the potential to get messy as a) we have a bus booked (thanks to Austin Travel and sorry if your insurance policy is double for the next twelve months), and b) that bus may contain the odd refreshment and/or libation. Put it this way, we were in good fettle when we arrived.

The hosts score a thumping 57–10 victory over the visitors from the Borders, and Hamish does the honours in presenting the trophy to the Falcons skipper for the day, Tom Waldouck. It was Newcastle's biggest home crowd of the season (yes, I am such an attraction), and that was reflected in the sizeable donations and collections gathered. There was even a cheque for £2,500.01 from the Durham County RFU Referees Society, although no one could answer me as to what miserable bugger donated a penny! As they say, though, it takes a lot of crumbs to make a big cake and it's the thought that counts.

I even have time to share a pint of Guinness with Scott McLeod, another one of the handsome second-row club. You'll notice how that is in lower case as it isn't an official club, and unlikely ever to be – although the Gray boys have raised the bar on that one.

And then it's time for home. Our good friends, the McConchies from Mossyard, have somehow managed to miss their train back to Dumfries from Newcastle. I don't think there ever was a train or a line that ran that route. Whatever, they did get home, by taxi, stung for just 150 quid. Ouch. The bus was a bit quieter on the way back. The fresh air had taken its toll. But as Wallace and Gromit might call it, a grand day out.

Sunday 29 December

Another day on the rowing machine. Get it up you, MND. Still here, still fighting. Just feeling a bit bloated. A Guinness would help, I'd imagine.

And where better to sample one, or several, than Kelso Racecourse where I meet up with some of the chaps from the London Scots consortium who own the racing horse Behindthelines, which they – Kenny Godsman, Patrick Bryceland, Colin Bryce, Malcolm Offord, Colin Dempster, Neil Watson, Fergus Loudon and David Morgan – will run on behalf of the Foundation, with any prize monies going to MN5DF.

The first four lads I've mentioned there all grew up in Greenock within four hundred yards of each other; Neil Watson is son of Bobby Watson (the former footballer and manager who many will remember from his time at Rangers, Motherwell and Airdrie); Fergus Loudon, meanwhile, is the man who makes sure your

Tunnock's Tea Cakes and Caramel Wafers always taste the same. Not sure how much they know about horses.

Thankfully, Colin Dempster might be better informed as his better half Deborah Thomson co-owned Grand National winner One for Arthur. One lady who certainly knows her stuff is trainer Lucinda Russell.

My Guinness becomes a couple as, first time out, Behindthelines is placed. A great day for all concerned. Happy New Year.

2020

Me and advice have never been great bedfellows. I'm always happy to listen, or at least give the impression that I'm all ears (no laughing at the back), but I usually have an opinion on most things.

JANUARY 2020

Wednesday 1 January

A Happy New Year. A big one for me. I'm fifty in July. All about pacing myself to what should be a magnificent climax, God willing. I'm not really one for New Year resolutions, but I think after everything I've packed into the previous twelve months it will be more about quality than quantity in the appearances and events I undertake.

Still, I'm not thinking about that as we hear the New Year bells. I'm thankful for that, and the great family I have and the good company I keep – or who keep me. But what the hell. It's party time.

The day, and 2020, is but a few hours old when I'm told that big Scotty Glynn MBE has died. My wingman at times, my confidante often, my pal forever. Life picks you up, then drops you. If you are lucky, that's the worst of it. Other times, it batters you, shakes you up, and hammers you down. That was Scotty's experience. But did it get him down? Never enough not to come back with a great one-liner or an even better gag.

I'm sad he has gone, but I can hear his reply to that: 'Ah couldnae gi' a f*ck whit you think.' Walk on, big fella, walk on.

Friday 10 January

Getting out and about is magic, and as long as I'm able to, nothing is going to stop me. But while there are a lot of events on, and I feel the need to support them, those who support me, in whatever form that takes, will matter more. I know in my heart of hearts I can't keep up with what some weeks feels like a tartan treadmill. I sincerely hope people can see that.

I've been making a slow return to normality, in terms of my daily business and extracurricular activities. The batteries are fully charged, I'm re-booted, re-configured and re-focused on the year ahead.

Wednesday 29 January

Much of today is spent in the Scottish National Portrait Gallery in Edinburgh with the big 'home' unveiling of the fantastic oil painting crafted by artist Gerard M. Burns. Kathy has often said I'm no oil painting, but I'd beg to differ now.

We arrive during the afternoon, the idea being that we can get any newspaper, radio and TV interviews out of the way before the main event that evening. This also means the obligatory photographs as well. What is the collective noun for a group of snappers? Some (Stewart especially) have their own ideas. I quite liked the suggestion of 'a persistence of photographers' – 'just one more please, and another, and another.' Why take one shot when forty-odd will suffice?

Gerard and I are all smiles for the cameras, only because we are talking about them. He particularly likes the request to 'just act naturally' when the TV people are doing some cutaway shots (see how I slipped the technical term in there?) and the fateful line, 'Now, can we just try that again but this time . . .' from the stills operatives.

Ach, I shouldn't be too critical. They are there to do a job, and they do a great job in promoting various activities, whether it's Gerard's genius or our Foundation. They have, for the most part, always done me a turn and latterly several have donated their services free of charge to help the Foundation. If I haven't said it before, thank you for that.

The same applies to Gerard. This unique canvas started out as a handful of still photographs, taken down at the farm a year ago, me posing against a white or neutral background. To see what he started out with and what he achieved is stunning. Basically, in two-and-a-bit months he'd gone from meeting me for the first time to completing the portrait in time for the Hong Kong dinner. Utterly remarkable.

Stewart took three and a half months to write my first book. Lazy so and so. Mentioning this to him, he shrugs his shoulders. 'There's probably a painting by numbers drawing underneath and he's just stuck your heid on it.' Sensitive, these artists.

Those who have seen it in all its glory keep asking how long it took me to sit for it. I string some along by saying a few weeks, and they then marvel at how patient I must have been. The cold, up on the hills, was the real issue, I add. They nod, a mixture of concern and knowing what sacrifices I must have gone through.

Where I think I made it difficult for my artist-in-residence was by wearing a tartan suit. He asked what I'd be comfortable in. Gerard, a lesson. Never ask people who wear tartan suits for all occasions what they are comfortable in. It is a trademark, I know. But I think most folk would recognise me whatever I wore (apart from a Gala kit). Making life laborious and arduous for Gerard wasn't my intention. No, it wasn't – no tongue-in-cheek either. I bet his first question now when he's doing portraits is, 'Please tell me you don't have a tartan suit?'

The process and the backstory of how all this came about is, in itself, quite incredible. Gerard contacted Sir Jim McDonald, principal of Strathclyde University, about getting an 'in' out in Hong Kong, and he set up a meeting with Gerard and Stewart Saunders, president of Hong Kong Scottish – in a garden centre coffee shop in Perth – and they formulated the idea. Stewart passed on his thoughts to Martin Murray, another of the HK stalwarts, who knew Scott Hastings, which brought the concept to the Foundation, who immediately said yes. I do love a plan. I may have delayed it slightly, by an hour or maybe a month, but Scott was on the case and really got the proposal. If I love a plan coming to fruition, then I also love the end product.

For me, Gerard absolutely captured the moment: me, how I was maybe feeling, and a few other things that weren't entirely obvious. During the photoshoot, he took a load of pictures – what did I say about photographers – but then said, 'No, I'm not getting it.' What *I* was getting was slightly hypothermic and, to be fair, Gerard realised that. 'I need you to look serious. You are in a dark place,' or words akin to that. I wasn't. The sunlight and the snow made it very bright, too bright for the artist. But I learned a long time ago that if you want something done in a hurry, just do as you are told.

'Look straight into the camera.' So I did. All he said was, 'That's it.' And here was me thinking I'd be lying back on the couch, or looking mysterious and thoughtful in the chair. None of it. We actually spent more time blethering and drinking tea than we did taking snaps. But he got what he wanted, so too ultimately did the people in Hong Kong, and so did me and the family.

However, all he had was the image of me. Where would the bigger picture be set. Murrayfield was mentioned. Too obvious. Edinburgh Castle? Too twee. The Greenyards? We were just on a road trip of possible locations. I maybe said the Seychelles. Then Kathy and I mentioned the Eildons. 'The whats?' said Gerard. As soon as I explained their importance, that they overlooked where

I'd played, where I was schooled, how people from the area in general felt about them, and that I could see them from the farm, it was like a big penny dropped.

And about capturing what isn't immediate to the eye?

The landscape was fine, but Gerard decided that this picture wasn't all about fun and happiness. He'd got the serious look, what now? This was where his artistic licence came in, although I only saw this when presented with the complete article.

Gerard had painted in some black rain clouds, in the background, but very noticeable nevertheless, in the moment but also depicting impending darkness. I could see that. But what I also saw was the sunlight coming through. If the clouds were for me, those rays from the sun streaming through were my sons. I never thought that observation would tug at so many heart strings and make folk quite tearful. Sorry about that.

There were also tears, this time of joy, the first time the assembled guests that night got to see the painting revealed for about the fourth or fifth time. That was lovely to see, because it meant so much to so many. I think Gerard was quite taken by that as well. I'm writing this with stoor in my eye.

Getting around to speak to everyone at these gatherings is never easy, although I've simplified the technique by letting the masses, audience, guests or gatecrashers come to me. Leave the walking to others. And the pro that I am, by positioning myself strategically in front of my image on the wall, I make posing for selfies and happy snaps that bit easier as well.

This was a great night and the culmination of a great chapter on this busy adventure. I really do marvel at Gerard's genius. And he's a nice guy with it. Sometimes, you can just be too talented. I have the same failings myself . . .

FEBRUARY 2020

Saturday 1 February

Ah, the Six Nations. A break to the winter gloom, a wee chink of sunlight that signals springtime is near, even if the thermometer, the weather forecast and the sleet and hailstones battering the windows at Bluecairn tell a different story. It's like four seasons in one hour, let alone a day. Still, it might keep away the Corona-thingy that's flared up in China and seems to be spreading.

Despite an awful World Cup, which included a bit of a battering from the Irish, hopes are high that Scotland are going in the right direction under my pal Gregor. Eighty minutes in, Dublin and the drawing board is being revisited. As with all who support the various Scottish national teams across different sports, it's the hope that kills you. Did we expect too much considering we'd been walloped in Japan a few months prior? Maybe. Maybe we were just hoping – and dreaming – for a wee bit too much. Like a miracle, for instance. And maybe more than one miracle at a time...

Saturday 8 February

The news is full of this thing called coronavirus. Unfortunately, some people across the planet appear to be full of it as well and it isn't pleasant. Not wishing ill luck on anyone, but from a self-preservation viewpoint, and for once being terribly selfish, those countries who have it can keep it to themselves. What makes it more ominous is that they don't seem to know much about how it spreads – a bit like flu I suppose – or how far it can carry. Not expecting a visit soon in the Borders, though.

Big day today, meeting the Auld Enemy, England, at Murrayfield. But before the game, I've got all sorts of ceremonial duties to perform, the main one being collecting the match ball which is being delivered by my old captain and big pal Rob Wainwright, who on his latest Doddie Gump challenge just decided wouldn't it be a great idea to pedal from Twickenham to Edinburgh with the game ball. As you do!

Under the 'Wounded Lions' banner, Rob, Russell Kesley, another ex-Scotland captain John Barclay and their usual two-wheeled cohorts have been raising funds and awareness for the Foundation, and also for Tom Smith's battle with cancer, hence the 'Wounded Lions' label, as there is now more than one of us toiling. I met up with the pack at Carfraemill, a well-known local watering hole, where by chance we've enjoyed several trustees meetings over the months. The crew took one last breather before their big push into the capital, and they all seemed quite fresh given the absolutely horrendous weather. According to Rob, they'd encountered 'horizontal ice' coming up over the border so when I say 'fresh', it was probably a mix of being freeze-dried and the adrenalin kicking in.

Just so no one missed out, the same weather, buckets of rain and gale force winds, welcomed the fans and players at Murrayfield. I don't have any happy memories of Scotland–England games as a player, other than the post-match drowning of sorrows. But this game was enough to drive you to drink twenty minutes in. It was dreadful, the kind of game that just sapped you of enthusiasm. England won, but even those who were sporting the red rose found it impossible to get too overjoyed. Sanctuary was sought in the public hostelries and inns across Edinburgh, each and all drinking to forget. Rob & Co. raised a right few quid – and raised quite a few glasses, purely for medicinal purposes and to help them thaw out. Honest.

Monday 10 February

There is no such thing as a free dinner. I now understand why Sally Nugent from the BBC slipped me those highly desirable Sports Personality of the Year cushions when we were up in Aberdeen. Of course, I'm only joking, but as a good journalist friend of mine would tell you, having seen me with Stephen Darby, then seeing me in person, and then seeing Rob Burrow and his membership application for this most exclusive of clubs, Sally did what any decent journalist would do, namely join up the dots and make a bigger story out of what was already there.

After discussions with her editor and producer, she was given the green light to put all three of us together, same place, same time. I think herding squirrels would be an easier assignment than tying this trio down. But manage it she did and we all met up at Dalmahoy, a place I am not unfamiliar with as it was one of the many bases and gathering points we had with the Scotland team.

You can never be entirely sure how these things will turn out, but Sally went route one (I think that's the soccerball expression) and came with a simple game plan: throw in the first question and see where it took us.

Where we went after that was revealing. Other than standing under the same MND umbrella, each of us was battling MND in a different way, with differing priorities, owing mostly to the varied ways the condition was afflicting us and our daily lives. There were all the usual symptoms, but each of us was at a different stage of how the disease was impacting on us.

Master of all I survey – and a gate.

What is the collective noun for
giraffes – a line-out?

The Doddie mobile gets its
'brand messaging'.

Me, Stewart and Iain Robertson at the Edinburgh Book Festival.
Who'd have thought?

'The wheels on the bus go round and round' – and so did a few
heads after the Border boys reunion day out.

Wow! But enough about what Scott Hastings is wearing.
SPOTY and all the trimmings.

My new Guinness partner, the immensely talented
Katarina Johnson-Thompson.

Meeting the Big Yin, Billy Connolly, in Hong Kong, with Andy Nicol.

The Doddie Gump ahead of the Springboks game and me in
the noisiest Land Rover in the world.

Kathy and me with Oor Wullie.
He's bigger than I expected.

An amazing day of golf with the
Scotland and Lions legend. Toony was
there as well with a cheque.

Doddie the Great meets
Doddiethegreat.

The then Celtic manager Neil Lennon
helped launch the Lions' Roar game –
until Covid took a hand.

Two with big lugs and tartan. Me and the
Doddie Weir Cup with Mary Doll.

A sizeable contribution from the SRU and WRU –
and I don't mean Al Kellock.

© Chris Johnson

Above
PD Doddie, off duty. One pint, gone . . .

Left
Making the podium with 'Team MND' members Stephen Darby and big Rob Burrow.

Bottom left
Welcome visitors to Bluecairn – Scott Quinnell and Will Greenwood.

Bottom right
Not much to say, other than 'ouch . . .'

© Sean McGrath

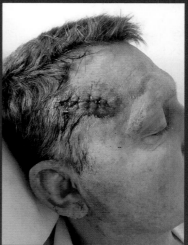

A grand day for Paw OBE, Maw and the weans with
a wee something from Her Majesty.

Say hello to Zena, the Princess Pup
– my nemesis.

Merry Christmas – although
I should have had someone famous
to turn them on.

It was like comparing notes and experiences, something akin to going through a tick box exercise. One of us had this worse than the others, someone else was experiencing something the other pair hadn't felt or seen. But when you placed all the bits in the lid of this medical jigsaw, the message that appeared was clear, concise. We all wanted to stay alive.

I think, speaking for myself, that if there is a deterioration, physically, for a spell or period of time, but you knew that you would still be here in ten years, I think I could almost live with that. The 'not knowing' part of MND, meaning just not knowing how long you have left, is an imponderable, and I'd say again, unhelpful.

We chatted for ages. I wasn't sure if this was a piece for news or had suddenly become an eight-part series. But it was enjoyable and enlightening. I can only imagine how long we could have been there had Sally brought more than one question!

If I was left with any lasting impressions or thoughts from that initial joint meeting it would be that there are a couple of battlers, showing all the spirit and traits that made them professional sportsmen, and that we should do this again. Indeed, I took so much from meeting these guys, in terms of how they were adapting and coping, and how we were able to take strength and positivity from one another.

I admit, I'd been a bit sceptical in terms of what fellow sufferers could glean from each other. Might it become too sombre, or upsetting, a bitching session about our misfortune or a gathering that may fill us full of pessimism. Far from it. If anything, I headed home refreshed and optimistic. There were some pretty tough laddies involved in this fight now, and they weren't for coming second.

Saturday 15 February

For all my involvement in sport – through rugby, equestrianism, trying to whack a golf ball occasionally, watching football, the darts and pool I played all those years ago when I was supposed to be selling beer, and not to forget participating in *BBC Superstars* (the resurrected version, not the peak-viewing '70s and '80s variety) – I have never actually attended a proper athletics meeting. I knew a few of the quick guys who had run on the Borders sports circuit but have never watched an entire track day until today.

We are Glasgow-bound, headed for the Emirates Arena when Kathy, Hamish and I – minus his uncle Tom – are going to see our drinking partner from Aberdeen, Katarina Johnson-Thompson compete at the Glasgow Indoor Grand Prix.

It's a fascinating spectacle. There are races on the track, but in the infield there are other events taking place, various jumps and sprints. No hammer throwing, though, which is probably why I haven't seen my pal Chris. Katarina is participating in the long-jump as part of her preparations for the Tokyo Olympics. It really is relentless for these athletes.

Sprint legend Shelly-Ann Fraser-Pryce is there, winning the 60 metres field event; Mondo Duplantis breaks the world record in the pole vault, a performance that has you desperate to watch the replay just to prove your eyes haven't been deceived when you see how high he jumped; and the local fans have plenty to cheer about when Laura Muir wins the 1,000 metres.

We don't get a chance to meet up with KJT to thank her for the super tickets she'd sorted out for us, but during the events I sat beside someone who obviously recognised me. She was Irish, and I really only caught her name as being 'Dame Mary'. I didn't want to boast I was an OBE and a doctor. We had a right old chinwag and a great time. Lovely to talk to and very knowledgeable about athletics and what Katarina excelled in. Fair play, she knew her stuff. And then I found out why! Taking our only gold medal at the 1972 Olympics in Munich in the pentathlon gave Lady Mary Peters a bit of a head start in our athletics chat.

And who else should I bump into, but a man who I'd seen a wee while before at Holyrood, Professor Jason Leitch. He was out for the day, like us, enjoying the sport. Small world.

All in all, a great day out. I could get to enjoy this athletics caper. This could be my new sport for 2020 . . .

Sunday 16 February

Today I'm jumping around doing odds and sods when I notice the front page of the *Sunday Post* smiling at me. Actually, the smiling was being done by Lucy Lintott, pictured holding her baby LJ. I'd recently got to know Lucy, who was diagnosed at the age of nineteen and is Scotland's youngest MND sufferer. I'll admit, even in February, there was a bit of stoor blawin' aboot. Made me a wee bit sniffy.

Right at the outset of my journey, when I was trying to glean advice and knowledge from everywhere and anyone, about drugs, diet, you name it, I spoke to Pieter van der Westhuizen, brother of Joost, who really forced home the message of positive thinking, maintaining your happiness, and keeping the focus on living. Without a real alternative in terms of treatment or drugs, Pieter said positivity was key. If you wanted to go on holiday, go. If you wanted to eat steak for breakfast, have it. If you wanted a glass of wine or a pint of Guinness, drink it. That cure especially appealed to me! But, I have to say, he was right.

It is about maintaining a focus on what will take you into tomorrow, or the next week or months; it's about setting a target and achieving goals. It was becoming a bit difficult to punch the air in celebration, but mentally I did that every time I did something my body or brain was telling me I wasn't capable of, be it driving my buggy, or the tractor, or signing another book. It was an effort and while I couldn't gesture that emotion, I would always mutter 'get in there'.

Don't get me wrong. All the optimism in the world won't halt the onset of this dreadful condition. It may, however, stall it, and give you a better quality of what life you have left. Looking at the photographs of Lucy, I do think being pregnant and making sure she did everything in her power to make sure baby was going to be fine, gave her a different perspective, maybe a different determination, not to be beaten and not to dwell on her predicament. It is hard to tell by a photograph alone, but I don't think she looked any different to when I'd seen her several months ago.

I'll have a crack at anything, but having a baby might be beyond me – although, looking at the belly I've put on, it appears I've been eating for two!

Seeing Lucy and her baby son on the front page of a national newspaper has certainly cheered me up, and I'm sure a great many others would be delighted to see her radiate such joy.

Saturday 22 February

A couple of years ago, Rome was the setting for another Wainwright brainchild, the Doddie Gump march on the Italian capital with five thousand Scotland fans in tow. He is a clever guy, but sometimes I think he has too much time and space up on Coll for his own good, scheming and planning his mad plans and ideas. Not that anything which raises as much money for the Foundation could be considered as hare-brained.

This time around, there was another gathering planned in Rome, although I wouldn't be attending, much as I would have wanted to be there. Social media is a great way to stay informed, however, and I've become a dab hand at Twitter, Facebook and a few other platforms, although I'm much more of an observer than a participant.

Still, there are enough Scotland fans – and enough of the Doddie tartan – to make it a terrific day, made all the more memorable thanks to a Scotland win, 17–0, with the 'H-Factor' to the fore, with tries from Stuart Hogg, Chris Harris and Adam Hastings. I'm in front of my big telly, with the heating turned up and Peroni in hand. Well, you've got to make it as realistic as possible, haven't you?

Wednesday 26 February

I first met John Davidson when he approached me after I'd talked at his son's school. He gave me a magnificent bottle of SAS whisky, and I gave him my business card. A fair exchange I thought at the time.

The next I heard from him was in 2017. He had heard my announcement about being diagnosed with MND and wanted to do something about it. I suggested various things he might want to do or try but said that probably the best person to speak to was Jill (Douglas) who was right across all the various activities people had participated in to raise awareness and money.

I spoke to Jill and it came up in conversation about John. She'd tried to steer him in the direction of others, who had run marathons, cycled miles or climbed hills, but John wanted to do something different and unique. He then came back and told us he'd been to see a friend who had organised Row For Heroes and off the back of that he had decided to row the Atlantic!

For a man who had done many things in his life, and who had a wide and varied skillset, oarsmanship wasn't one of them, possibly because he'd never sat in a boat before. John, however, had decided that if I was a unique character then he had to do something equally unique, and so had signed up for the Talisker Whisky Atlantic Challenge.

That meant purchasing his own boat, funding his venture and then seeking out sponsorship. He gave himself just five months to achieve all of that, an impossible deadline. So, December 2019 became his target, and in the intervening twelve months, he went overboard (see what I did there) in terms of appearances – towing his boat, bedecked in the MN5DF tartan – around the country chasing backers and raising awareness of himself and the cause.

All this time, John was speaking to Jill, who was telling him that even if he was to fail, he would still have done a magnificent job for the charity. Failure, however, isn't really in the vocabulary of anyone who belonged to the Special Air Service.

What Jill was really concerned about, ultimately, was John's welfare. A fifty-something man who had carbed-up instead of training (he wanted to feel how I had felt when, with no preparation, I was told about MND and had to overcome that mountain) was giving himself a mighty ocean to cross.

Jill also had the not inconsiderable concern – and spoke to me and John about it – that, should he go missing, it might not make great PR for the charity! Again, John's philosophy was there's no such thing as bad publicity, and 'just think of the exposure'. Jill still wasn't seeing it that way when John lined up at the start in early December, and set out from San Sebastián de La Gomera, Canary Islands, headed for Nelson's Dockyard, English Harbour, in Antigua. I just hoped he'd remembered his passport.

Seventy-five days, 23 hours and 56 minutes have since elapsed, three thousand miles of sea have been navigated, and John – looking rather more hirsute facially than when he departed – has made it, alive, to be greeted by his wife and children.

He will have his own tales to tell about this epic effort. For me this is a story of what others have done for a common cause – that being me and my Foundation. And I will be eternally grateful, if still thinking he is completely bonkers!

Thursday 27 February

Our Foundation is very fortunate, both in terms of the individuals we have working on our behalf, but also with those who are thinking about how they might assist us. Not many come as big as Celtic Football Club, so it was rather exciting to find out that their own Foundation had been in contact with the idea of hosting an all-stars game, 'The Lions' Roar', probably near the end of the season.

Celtic's awareness in Motor Neuron Disease is, sadly, through their experiences around one of their own, Jimmy Johnstone. Stewart knew the backstory and the history intimately (being an old fella, he'd seen Jinky play before I'd been born – absolutely true), and had been involved in a couple of meetings with Tony Hamilton, chief executive of the Celtic Foundation, who had come up with the idea. Tony very kindly invited the pair of us, plus my nominated driver (a certain Mr Armstrong) along to Celtic's Europa League tie against FC Copenhagen, who come from, well, Copenhagen.

Having been a successful goalkeeper in my time – although I seldom talk about my record of played one, won one, and with a clean sheet while keeping goal for Stow – I've always had more than a passing interest in fitba, and I loved mixing with the football players at Newcastle United during my time at Newcastle Falcons. This was a great chance to get to know the Celtic folk better, and to sample what is one of the most legendary atmospheres in European football. There can't be much that beats a full Celtic Park on a European night.

Before the match, we had a wee feed (and a wee drink) and got to meet all the movers and shakers at the club, with the usual introductions and pleasantries. Stewart seemed to know most of them, some of them quite well. Again, an old man in that particular sphere for a while. The chat was, of course, about how Celtic would get on. They had drawn 1–1 in Denmark and most were tipping them to finish the job off in front of their own fans – although Stewart did say the Danes were 'quick and dangerous on the break' and 'would take a bit of watching'. But what did he know . . .

We take our seats in the stand, directly in front of former Celtic player John Collins, a fellow Borderer, who only played football for Scotland and scored at a World Cup because he couldn't play rugby. Immediately, thanks to Garry's negotiating skills – 'you'll dae whit yir telt' – we sign him up for our team for the Lions' Roar game, which he was pretty happy to do, with not so much as a hint of coercion or menace or threat to his good looks if he didn't. This football management caper is easy.

John knows his stuff as an ex-player and manager and tells us that Celtic should win, but adds that Copenhagen are 'quick and dangerous on the break'. I'd heard that before.

In front of us, Stewart is greeted heartily by someone who is obviously an old acquaintance and introduces me to 'Robert'. 'Christ, big yin, yir even bigger close up,' he laughs as he shakes my hand, a gesture which while not unusual, was very revealing. While others would wait on me swinging my arm up or around so we could shake hands, Robert sought my arm, lifted it, and then took my hand. Innocent, meaningless, natural to probably the vast majority of those watching, but for me it was a tell-tale sign that he knew, or had confronted and identified the difficulties that face MND sufferers. 'Hing in, big yin, hing in. You're a champion,' he says kindly.

'Robert' is, of course, better known to Celtic fans and a different generation as Bertie Auld, a Lisbon Lion and a Celtic legend. Stewart gives me his history, and highlights his closeness to wee Jimmy, which explained everything around his welcome. Stewart adds that 'Robert' is now in his eighties, but that he still wouldn't trust him in a 50–50 tackle. What, that nice wee man?

At half-time, Stewart, the walking version of Wikipedia when it comes to sport, gives us his anecdote about Bertie, and what he did to England's World Cup winning 'enforcer' Nobby Stiles when Hibs played Middlesborough in a pre-season friendly. Stiles smashed Bertie and broke his collar bone, but Bertie played on until revenge was exacted – and Nobby left on a stretcher. Seriously, that nice wee man?

Forty-five minutes to go and it could have gone better for Celtic, but at 0–0 they had a toe in the next round thanks to away goals. Gary is none the wiser. Celtic have the ball in the net, but while Gary and I jump up and down in celebration, John Collins and Stewart sit, unmoved. They spotted the foul on the Danish keeper. Aye, these boys do pay attention.

Celtic go a goal behind on the night, but Odsonne Edouard is the coolest man in Glasgow as he slots a penalty late on to square the tie. The joy doesn't last; Copenhagen score another two in the closing minutes, all three of their goals coming on the break. I hate clever folk.

The Celtic boardroom is like a morgue at the end. There isn't really much anyone can say. Defeat in sport, whether it's rugby or football, is so deflating. I say my thanks and farewells with Gary and beat a hasty retreat. Don't want anyone thinking we'd jinxed them!

MARCH 2020

Monday 2 March

My good lady is driver – I think the official title is chauffeurette – for the day as we head up to Glasgow and back to Celtic Park to formally launch the Lions' Roar game.

There is a very real empathy with what our Foundation is trying to achieve, much of it a legacy from the passing of Jimmy Johnstone, a club legend, adjudged by many as their greatest-ever player. I only know him through what I've seen online, but Stewart raved about his skill and bravery, something required in equal measures for wingers back in those days when kicking your talented opponent repeatedly was par for the course.

Like all of these functions, there are new people to meet, and today that includes Celtic manager Neil Lennon. Because of when the game is scheduled for – the night before the Scottish Cup final – much of what happens revolves around Neil's plans, especially because the final takes place a few weeks from the end of the normal season. That makes him a big player in this project and I had better be on my best behaviour then, but I needn't have worried.

Neil, who is chasing an unprecedented quadruple Treble (that's the league title, and both cup competitions) in domestic football, couldn't be nicer and says he will do whatever he can to help. The mood is better, with normal service resumed the previous day with a Scottish Cup win over St Johnstone. Then Neil asks if we enjoyed the Copenhagen game the other night, not the easiest question to answer.

'The atmosphere was great, maybe not the result,' I reply, being the ultimate diplomat.

'Aye, that's about right,' Neil concedes. Phew.

Everything is set up: TV, radio, newspapers. All we need is the Celtic manager, Neil Lennon, who is fitting this in between training, other team business and meeting the press to preview another league game on Wednesday. It's interesting seeing him going about his business close up and you get a taste of just how intense the job of a football manager is. That is probably multiplied three or four-fold at a club the size of Celtic.

Because of the reasons I've explained, there is a bit of meat to put on the bones, but provisionally we have a date in the almanac. I'm getting quite excited at the prospect of this game and I'm wondering if I should give Sir Alex (Ferguson) a call for a few tips. Stewart suggests that if I'm going to make the call, why not just ask him to manage 'Doddie's Dynamos'.

'Is that our name?' I ask Stewart.

'No, but it's better than Doddie's Diddies.' As club owner, manager, assistant manager, coach or whatever capacity I'm involved in, I've decided Stewart won't be playing. The cheek.

Neil is quite relaxed. Domestically, his side are on target for more trophies, including a ninth successive title. 'Can you make it ten?' I ask.

'That's the plan – but don't let them boys hear you,' he adds, giving a nod in the direction of the hacks.

After the general press conference, there are some individual sit downs for TV, radio, newspapers and Celtic's extensive media operation. Sometimes you feel as if you are just repeating yourself, but having fitba to talk about makes a pleasant change.

And once they've had their fill of us, it's the photographers' turn, the ones who can never just take one photograph.

It might not seem much, but even holding up a rugby ball is quite tiring. It is all for a good cause, yes. But I can't help but feel that while I'm walking, talking, standing and breathing, in the eyes of some, I'm one hundred per cent fit. Thanks for still thinking that way, but the reality is that I can feel my energy levels wane.

Another cup of tea – rude not to accept the hospitality – a cheerio to Neil and Tony, and Kathy and me can head back to life on the farm, but only once I've had a word with Martin Brown, an old acquaintance from the car hire and leasing world who I know through Martin Wilson at Thrifty. Life must be good. He has a Ferrari. I do say that, if I had one, I'd be getting one without a dent in the bonnet. It wasn't, as you might have thought, an optional extra but man made. Even Italian supercars come off second best to an overhanging wall in a multi-storey car park. Ouch.

Sunday 8 March

I am back in more familiar surroundings again today, Murrayfield, for the Six Nations game against France. These contests have, in my experience, always been entertaining affairs, with plenty of tries the norm.

The only thing I need to do today is to sit back in the comfy seats and enjoy the afternoon, made all the easier because of the company I'm keeping, namely John Jeffrey who, given his lofty status within international rugby, can get me a decent seat with added legroom. I don't think the bodyguard was particularly happy at being asked to shift, but never mind.

Dominic McKay, Scottish Rugby Union's chief executive, has kindly made us his guests for the day. For our day at Murrayfield,

I am accompanied by my niece, Alex, who likes her rugby (but seems to like Charles Ollivon even more) and the pre-match food. As I might have mentioned, she isn't her mother's daughter for nothing.

Rugby, particularly at this level, is full-on, high-impact stuff, especially around the breakdown where rucks have to be cleared out, basically, by wiping – I mean clearing – out any opposition players who happen to be lying around, making the place look untidy, especially when there is a ball to be won.

In my day, you removed any unwanted obstacles – let's call them bodies – by rucking over the top of them. Occasionally, your inch-long steel studs might accidentally snag on an opponent's jersey as you attempted to hurdle them in order to keep possession of the ball, but that was quite accidental, because what you were really trying to do was rake those who were intent on stopping the ball from being played, away from the ruck. Again, ever so accidentally, your boot may meet human flesh. However, it meant those killing the ball were less likely to hang around on the floor if there was a herd of stampeding forwards headed their way. You needed to be persuasive at times, but eventually the message got through.

That, however, in someone's book, was considered dangerous. Better now, it has been deemed, to have guys charging into stationary objects – again, let's call them bodies for the purposes of this explanation – to keep that ball moving. So, what you have is often inanimate and defenceless players being clattered by fifteen, sixteen, seventeen stone opponents, regularly travelling at a rate of knots. It is brutal, and collision damage can be severe. Yet, standing on someone was considered more dangerous? Are you sure? Make your own mind up.

Back in the old days, JJ was especially good at making sure his opposite numbers didn't go to sleep on the ball. But today, he is a rule maker, having once been a rule breaker, but only accidentally.

In the Scotland–France game, one particular pile-up has JJ and me glancing at each other, wincing. The TV cameras caught the moment. Given my previous big screen moments, I was worried they would come back and expect to see a kiss. Not this time, BBC.

John is passionate about rugby. He was as a player and now as an administrator, he desperately wants to get it right. There is an honesty about him, he's a straight-talker, with less of the diplomatic speak. How that goes down with those on-high, time will tell. But he is quite near the top himself. The classic case of poacher turned gamekeeper.

When the ball did move, Scotland made better use of it and scored three tries – a brace for Sean Maitland – in a comfortable, but hard-fought 28–17 win. Time for a celebratory beer.

My popularity is showing no signs of waning, and long may it continue. People are only too pleased to see me – and me them – and tell me what they've bought or ventured to assist the Foundation. Several had been in Italy and registered their disappointment, nicely of course, that I hadn't been in Rome a few weeks earlier.

There wasn't anyone making a huge song and dance about it, but there are mentions of one or two not feeling great – a bit flu-ey – once they'd came back from Italy, and people saying, 'Hope it isn't anything to do with this Chinese thingy that's going about.'

Monday 9 March

Me and advice have never been great bedfellows. I'm always happy to listen, or at least give the impression that I'm all ears (no laughing at the back), but I usually have an opinion on most things, which I've arrived at without anyone's help, so my mind is made up before the debate begins. Once my decision is made, I am not easily swayed. Kathy has said I can be a tad obstinate – 'a big pig-headed *****' has been mentioned on occasions – and I can see why that stubbornness has caused frustrations and friction for others over the years, not just at home but also while a player, even a farmer or businessman. But that's the way I am. At the end of the day, if I've made the wrong call, I need to live with it.

When Annabel Howell said that she didn't think travelling to Cardiff for the Wales–Scotland Six Nations game would be such a great idea, you can imagine that was not how I was seeing things.

Annabel is one of those looking after me, but so impressed was I with her and how she went about her business with patients, that she started working more closely with the Foundation and is now one of the real drivers in what we do. She knows what she is talking about. Which made it awfully hard to disagree with her when she said I shouldn't be going to Cardiff.

Air intake is crucial for my wellbeing. Pointless then using it up in an argument I ain't going to win.

This was a big sporting week. There was an offer – as there had been in previous years – for a trip to Cheltenham for the Festival. The fact was that it led straight into the Six Nations weekend in Wales and the Doddie Cup game, so geographically it wouldn't have been too challenging, and there was always a bed at Chateau Hoggy, which made it quite appealing. Others would and could do it, but the realities of the situation were that even just going to Cardiff was a bit of an undertaking, never mind what would be a beer-filled stopover in the West Country.

Not having the normal creature comforts around me was, at times, making trips and visits a bit of a chore, although Cheltenham, Cardiff, and the chance to see my Welsh friends – and Hoggy – and see Scotland win the trophy that bears my name (that's that confidence for you) meant Cardiff was always in the diary.

Until Annabel put a line through it. The pen is mightier than the sword I was taught at school. And here was the proof.

I wasn't just going to give in, but even I was beginning to appreciate that this virus 'thingy' was something none of us had encountered before, and there were already stories of people being taken down by it, specifically in the rugby community, most of them with some kind of link back to that Italian game.

Annabel's caution was based around numbers, how many thousands would be at Cheltenham, at the game and quite probably how many tens, dozens, even hundreds I would have direct contact with. There is a time and a place to be popular and Cardiff would really not be one of them.

Her case was forceful; however, she really was pushing at an open door. I'd had my doubts, and they'd been growing. You couldn't ignore what you were hearing on TV, or on radio. Like rain, or someone from Kelso, this thing was headed in our direction and there wasn't much, it appeared, anyone could do about it. All Annabel had done was confirm my thinking, rather than me having a complete change of heart.

Disappointing, given the boys were playing for a trophy in my honour. But needs must.

Friday 13 March

If there was a day that brought home to me what strange times we were moving towards, then it was this Friday – Friday the 13th. If that day was unlucky for some then it was doubly unlucky for me.

The Six Nations games involving England in Rome and Ireland away in Paris have already fallen by the wayside owing to precautions over foreign travel, given what was happening with the spread of the virus over the continent. But we'd been assured that Wales–Scotland would go ahead as normal. After all, the Cheltenham Festival had just about run its course, what with around quarter of a million folk there for its duration, and there had been Champions League and Europa League matches played in front of full houses that week, even with fans from abroad in attendance from Spain in Liverpool, and in Glasgow, from Leverkusen in Germany.

I wouldn't be travelling. I was already making arrangements to, once more, be planked in front of the telly, but others I knew were already headed for Cardiff, and might even have been in the pub, when news broke that the game was to be called off. At the same time, all domestic football – remembering that less than twenty-four hours prior there had been 50,000 at Anfield and Ibrox – had been halted with immediate effect, until the end of the month at least. Serious stuff.

The consequences of that meant there would be no homecoming for the Doddie Cup, that it would stay in Wales. Ho hum. More pertinent, however, was that there would be none of the various lunches, hospitality and appearances taking place as fundraisers for the My Name'5 Doddie Foundation, in Cardiff or anywhere else for that matter. Bugger. A missed opportunity, but the reasoning and the decision making appeared sound, to keep people safe and to prevent spread of this dangerous bug.

Just after lunch, and my mobile lights up. It's Stewart. He's quite chirpy. His daughter, Zara – the sprinter – has just won team gold . . . at the Lanarkshire Schools Cross-Country champion-ships. That's the effect a tutorial from Darren Campbell can have on you!

'See the Scotland game is off?' I said.

'Eh . . .'

I wasn't sure what was coming, but words were being picked carefully. I'll admit, it didn't spring immediately to mind, but the cancellation of domestic football in Scotland meant that he'd taken a call from Tony Hamilton at the Celtic Foundation. Unfortunately, but understandably in the circumstances, Celtic couldn't commit to staging the Lions' Roar game in May, when the reality of the situation was that no one knew when clubs would be able to fulfil their scheduled games, let alone postponed and cancelled fixtures, meaning it was impossible to plan for a charity exhibition game and everything that would have to be in place around it, including travel and accommodation.

Celtic had said this was a postponement, not a cancellation. But, for the second time that morning, 'bugger' sums up the complete helplessness of the situation. I ask Stewart to pass on my thanks and regards to everyone at Celtic who had tried so hard to help us. There wasn't anything anyone could do about the unfolding scenario. It was what it was.

I sat back and looked out the window, and laughed. Not many people – who are alive and kicking – have a game of rugby played and a trophy named after them which two Test-playing nations will contest. There are not that many either who see a great institution like Celtic create an event to benefit our charities and raise awareness.

But I had both – or at least I did up until a few hours ago. What were the chances of that happening? The laugh is one of bemusement, but I can't help but ponder at where this virus, and the consequences of it, are taking us. Somewhere we'd never been before by the sound of things.

Monday 23 March

After various warning signs over the previous few days, we are warned that whatever Prime Minister Boris Johnson says this evening is going to be a game-changer in terms of how we lead our daily lives.

Occasionally, a good movie or a rugby match will have the Weir household facing the telly at the same time. When Boris appears, all eyes are on him, in complete silence. It's pointless the kids asking us about Covid, pandemics or the likes, because Kathy and I have never witnessed anything like this before either. That, if you reverse the argument, means it's pointless us offering an opinion, again because we just don't know what the future holds. It is an almost eerie atmosphere tonight.

There are some sighs, some sharp intakes of breath as to what the next twenty-one days will hold. But, effectively, we've been told – like the rest of the population – to shut the doors and don't let anyone in or out.

'What about training?' says a junior Weir.

It might take a wee while, methinks, before the message and this unique set of circumstances hit home.

Friday 27 March

We're a few days in now, but I could get used to this lockdown. It's still March and we are sitting in the garden, in the sun, having steak. Does it get any better? It does.

The boys have mucked out a couple of sheds and spruced them up. It was needing done, but with sod all else to do, now is as good a time as any. I sincerely hope they haven't peaked too soon. Time will tell, I suppose.

Ben was missing school. It doesn't matter that he is off. He is young and wants to play rugby with his pals. Hamish is on the prowl, looking for things to do, other than work for me, and Ben gets on with the things that interest him, but ultimately looks as fed up and confused as the other two.

Kathy says nothing has changed for her: sheep, horses, washing, cooking, chasing four men (one less so than the other three), shopping, tidying up, caring for me. So, no complaints then.

I could be the only person saying this, but lockdown has been a great time so far.

APRIL 2020

Wednesday 1 April

When we were out in New Zealand in 2017 on the Lions tour, we came across an aircraft museum owned by the *Lord of the Rings* director Peter Jackson, full of planes of all ages, shapes and sizes. No, don't look at the date thinking this is a long-winded way of pulling you into an April Fools gag. It ain't.

I couldn't have told you what went over our land of a day, other maybe than one of the RAF's fast jets making a hellish racket. Then I'd look around and try and spot it, just because it was something different.

Right now, the skies are clear of clouds and aeroplanes. For the first time in ages, I find myself looking into the air and thinking how peaceful, tranquil almost, it is. I laugh. Of everything I thought might happen over the coming months and hopefully years, this was not even on the agenda. Another of life's great surprises.

Wednesday 8 April

Where possible, which is almost always, I try to steer clear of politics. I don't have to become involved. I had a taste of it during the

2014 Independence Referendum when a bunch of Scottish rugby players – most of them Lions – pinned our colours to the mast. Put it this way, we were on the winning side that day, but I'm not one to rub people's noses in it.

I will happily run with the foxes and the hounds so to speak, if it improves my lot and those of other MND sufferers.

For instance, I did an interview with former First Minister of Scotland, Alex Salmond, on Russia Today, not because of any political leanings, but because the opportunity arose to let folk know what I was about and what I was campaigning for.

In November last year, Annabel, Sean McGrath and I met Jason Leitch, the National Clinical Advisor to the Scottish Government, who is becoming one of the best-known faces of the pandemic north of the border. Who'd have thought it? Nice guy as well.

I had also met Catherine Calderwood at one of the rugby matches at Murrayfield. Again, very nice, but unfortunately she didn't last long when she became the story. And just last week, Jeane Freeman, the Cabinet Secretary for Health and Sport, sent me an email just to keep in touch. Always nice when people are thinking about you.

That doesn't mean to say that if I have a gripe, or a concern, or feel things aren't moving speedily enough, I won't train my sights on them. This week, Matt Hancock, the Secretary of State for Health and Social Care is the one I'm asking questions of. We may be in the midst of a pandemic, but that doesn't mean they are in for an easy time of it.

Bewilderingly, MND sufferers are not – that's correct, NOT – on the list of extremely vulnerable persons laid out by the government. What would coronavirus do to a person who is struggling for air, because they cannot fully expand their diaphragm, or because their resistance is low, or because they are weak beyond the point of fighting flu never mind this strange and deadly virus? It does not bear pondering.

Not a decision I arrived at with any degree of spontaneity, but, needs must, especially when you are living – or existing as some would be – in an environment of fear. I felt the need, therefore, to put the message out there, to direct it to Matt Hancock, but to let others be the adjudicators, that one in every three hundred men has the chance of being diagnosed with MND.

On video, I ask: 'Mr Matt Hancock, Secretary of State. Firstly, I'd like to thank you, your team, and all at the NHS and everyone else involved in trying to fight the coronavirus.

'My name is Doddie Weir and I have MND, Motor Neuron Disease, a terminal illness with horrific short and long term issues. I need your help.

'So, I ask you: why is MND not on the very vulnerable persons list? Would it be possible for you and your team to work with the MND Association and MND Scotland to change this?

'People with MND have a hard life in itself, never mind trying to fight the coronavirus. Please help us stay alive as long as possible. Thank you.'

Short, sharp and to the point, I felt. Not quite Robert De Niro. It took two takes. Not because I fluffed my lines, not because I couldn't read my idiot boards. Because after I'd nailed it, Mary Doll ruefully admitted that she hadn't set the video running. But she did get a cracking photograph of me looking as if I was about to say something meaningful and important. Should I sack her? I couldn't really. It was only me and her. I had to sit for five minutes, compose myself, and talk myself into another performance.

If the video you saw was good, the first one had been even better. Like the fish that got away. Will the message get through?

Mr Hancock is a busy man, but hopefully someone points this out to him. We can but hope.

Thursday 9 April

To use a rugby expression, quite a few have picked the ball up and run with it after my wee video yesterday. I'm offered the chance to expand upon it, but really, I've made my point; it's hard enough fighting MND without having to fight on two fronts, the other being against Covid. I think most of us know what it takes but we do need a helping hand, a bit of assistance. Quickly.

Or those who need it most might not be here. The hard fact is that MND will kill us. That's been hard enough to accept. That there is a virus out there that could assist the process, even beating what MND has started, is frightening. That isn't an exaggeration. That isn't a throwaway headline. That is the truth.

The mental anguish it will cause some – sufferers, families, loved ones – is immeasurable. MND wasn't something we had seen coming. Watching Covid creep up on us is too painful to watch and experience.

Sunday 12 April

Last year, Kathy was under severe pressure when it came to lambing – quite stressful because she was having to do it on her own. But, thanks to the boys being around, they've been able to share the duties. So, one would do one shift, with the second covered by another. They are coping, but I think having to spend time with me is annoying them.

I don't mean that in a nasty way. But Kathy, Hamish, Angus and Ben have their own lives to lead, and their days should not be all about being on toilet duty for me, or making sure I'm fed, or making sure that when I am I don't leave pizza on my top lip or tomato sauce on my chin. Or, if I have sanitised. Something new every day.

Friday 17 April

There are a number of things that will never cease to amaze me. Human kindness is one, human spirit is another, and the desire to survive in adversity. The last could apply to all of us currently. Lockdown has been upon us for a few weeks now, but everyone appears to be – so far – playing to the rules, just getting on with things. Amazing to think that no generation – even those who grew up during wartime – has ever faced anything like this before. We are unique, except we don't really realise it.

The same could be said for Captain Tom Moore, unique without being aware of it. Aged just ninety-nine, he challenged himself to complete a hundred laps of his garden during the pandemic, ahead of reaching his own century, on behalf of the NHS, having set a target of reaching £1,000 for those who helped him survive cancer and breaking his hip.

I sat in awe at his efforts, and disbelief as his aim to raise a grand became £100,000, then a million. Looks like he could end up raising many more millions. Absolutely remarkable. Maybe we all feel the need to get behind such a worthy cause as, in our minds, we all know that the NHS will be there for us in our darkest times. Those vast sums of cash roll in as both a gesture of support for Captain Tom, but also an act of defiance; that if we stick together, not even Covid is going to defeat us. Remember what I mentioned earlier about human kindness and spirit?

Like most I may have been totally shocked at the total funds raised by this old soldier, but not that so many bought into his thinking or his single-mindedness, entirely based on my own experience.

When I announced that I had Motor Neuron Disease, I had no

idea that it would be the starting gun for countless thousands of people to buy into an idea I had to help fellow sufferers. That was my aim; however, I had no idea that it would snowball the way it did. Was it a need to support a good cause that might guard against a loved one being struck down by a horrible illness? Who can say?

The My Name'5 Doddie Foundation has raised awareness of MND, but has also generated donations way beyond my wildest dreams. I remember thinking £100,000 would be an amazing sum to raise, then that grew to quarter of a million. When we reached £5 million I genuinely laughed out loud. Who'd have thunk it. And all of it from the generosity of people, most of whom knew me as a rugby player and latterly as that big fella in the tartan suit that has something wrong with him.

Never question human kindness, human spirit, or the desire to survive adversity. It is there. It just takes the right cause or fight to spark it. But you should never lose sight of it.

Saturday 18 April

This must be hitting others as hard as it is hitting me. I decide to send a message to Rob Burrow, just to keep his pecker up.

'Hello, pal, how are things? Hope you and the family are safe and well. If the trials have been paused, get yourself into the Guinness and red wine – two pints and a bottle of red, or four pints. Does you the world of good although you are a bit of a lightweight. Best start with a couple of cans! Stay indoors and stay safe. Speak soon, Dodgy.'

Everything in moderation, but these small gestures mean a lot. I await his reply. The wee bugger doesn't. He'll have been sitting there wondering if he needs to pay for the wine and the ale, or whether I'll post it to him. Typical Yorkshire Tyke.

Thursday 23 April

One month into lockdown and the novelty is beginning to wear off, the reality now hitting home. An initial period of the country being shut down to all but essential acts has now continued into another three-week window. For so many, a window will be their only view of life, of the world. How cruel.

This was not on the agenda, for me, for anyone. These things – epidemics – happen in other places. A pandemic? We'd heard about such things, but it was like something you'd read in a sci-fi book, or see in a film. These things didn't happen in the real world. How wrong could we all be?

I was isolated from even before lockdown was officially triggered. In some respects, I was lucky, and when I say that I am not being dramatic.

So, Bluecairn, my home, has been a bit of a mini fortress. The kids still go about what business they had, and Kathy had to cut about doing various things. But the farm has become a no-go area for everyone else, be it family or friends; the sorts who would just turn up, usually unannounced, let themselves in, and expect a tea and a chat. The severity of the situation isn't lost on anyone.

I am, nevertheless, very fortunate. If I want to go for a walk, around the fields or the yard, I can. If I choose to go further afield, in my buggy, I can. Social distancing – while limited to two metres for everyone else (and if you want to know what that looks like, imagine me as your two-metre measuring stick) – could be two miles and more for me depending on where I end up while out driving.

Not for the first time in this part of my journey, I become acutely aware that even though things could be better, they're not as bad as they are for some. I can get the wellies on, go for a meander around the sheds, say hello to the animals, and get the wind – and often the rain – in my face. I could only imagine how terribly hard it must be for those confined to a bed, staring at four walls each hour of the day, only seeing one or two folk. It will be just as difficult for those who might have a couple of kids, but no garden to let them run wild in, or worse still, living in a high-rise flat in a big city.

When you view your lot against others, sometimes – despite the circumstances – I've still got it quite easy. Lockdown it might be, but I'm determined not to get down. There is a message I want to send to MND – and to me – that I'm not giving up the fight, even just to have a bit of normality in my life, even in circumstances that are entirely abnormal.

My wee buggy is paying for itself during lockdown, taking me into parts of the countryside you sometimes forget are there. I can also get out in the tractor and do a bit of harrowing in the field. When I say I can get out in the tractor, I can only do that if someone gives me a helping hand, which usually means my beloved wife. To be honest, I think it suits her to put the effort in, because once she has loaded me aboard, I'll happily work away for a good few hours. A win-win for both of us, you could say. But they're not the only toys I had to play with.

Saturday 25 April

Anniversaries always bring back happy memories, and even if from a perspective of something sad or upsetting, you tend to end up smiling. I had plenty to smile about when I found out BBC Scotland were showing a rerun of the 1995 France–Scotland Five Nations match. Twenty-five years ago? I demand a recount.

My memories of that match were nowhere to be found. Nothing to do with my condition or anything like that. All I remember, really, was replacing Damian Cronin at half-time after he'd done his elbow, and thinking we are losing and it has nothing to do with me for a change. Forty minutes later and the rest, as they say, is history. That night after the game, though, was more of a blur.

I have seldom seen such silliness from grown men, all of the high jinks and unbridled delight spilling over – unlike the alcohol that was poured. Vintage champagne and quality brandy. You can acquire a taste for these things when someone else is paying for it.

It had been twenty-six years since Scotland had won over in France, so long ago they'd moved stadium, and the pictures were black and white. What made rectifying that barren spell all the more important was that for nearly thirty years we'd had to watch Jim Telfer scoring the winning try. He never spoke about that, much.

On this repeat of the '95 game, the winning score came from captain fantastic, big Gav (Gavin Hastings), played in by some magic by Toony, with his now infamous back-of-the-hand pass. It was great to sit back and watch the highlights, even though I was wondering nearing the end if we were actually going to win the game. I thought we were going to run out of time. I didn't realise it was so close to full-time that we'd won it.

Gavin will tell you he had to get up following his sprint to the line and compose himself to land the winning conversion. Between touching down and kicking, he took nearly a minute. Compose himself? He could have had a cup of tea.

Watching that game, you appreciate just how good some of those I got to play with actually were. Basil and Chick at half-back, Toony was like a magician with what he could do, Gavin also kicked a ginormous penalty in the first half, Eric Peters had just emerged in the team, Wainwright and my big pal Stewart Campbell packing down beside me. That was a team.

One thing, among a dozen other things I had to remind myself of, was that we were all still amateur then. Ian Jardine cracked his cheek, which was fixed when he got home, but that meant he was off work because of that. Amazing to think.

Harking back to what I said earlier, that game in some respects was the making of me. I got back in the team through big Del

Boy's misfortune (having previously replaced him on sheer talent), I got a move to Newcastle off the back of that, and then on to a Lions tour. Fate, luck, chance? Who knows? Whatever it was, it conspired in my favour, that time.

Of course, playing in France, Damian was the natural choice for Gavin to seek him out to help with his captain's speech for the post-match dinner, a sermon which has subsequently become part of Scottish rugby folklore. How can I put it: the French may have thought he was a wonderful player and leader, but Gavin's honesty around what he'd been up to in the shower with his wife, that he was wearing her knickers and how he occupied himself of an afternoon left our hosts aghast. All told in perfect French.

Today, we'd have had sensational headlines and a social media storm. Then? It was just one more excuse for folk to buy Gavin another drink. Changed days. Thank goodness I played back then. It all brought back some lovely recollections and, near the end, a sad one or two when Dougie Morgan appeared.

Sadly, Dougie passed away at the start of April. A legend of Stewart's Melville, he played for and coached Scotland, and was also a British Lion in 1977. His passing should have been commemorated for everything he achieved in rugby. Instead, because of this damned Covid that is floating around, no one could attend his funeral, when the reality was hundreds would have been there to show their respects and celebrate a great life within the game.

This pandemic disrespects everyone. Dougie was greatly respected and well liked and should have had a great send off. He was deserving of that. I hope sometime soon we are able to show what he meant to a great many of us.

Sunday 26 April

London Marathon Day. That's right, I'm not doing it, but then neither is anyone else. While I hugely admire those who dedicate themselves to completing 26 miles 385 yards, long-distance running has never been for me; even a full-fit Dodster wouldn't have tackled that. It might well all be in the mind, and I could see myself failing after just a handful of miles. Even when I was at my fittest, the prospects of doing laps around a pitch or a track filled me with dread. Many a time I had to clutch a precautionary hamstring.

However, this year, Covid has forced the cancellation of the big race. In the past, I might have watched the marathon on the telly – not today – for a bit, but something else has grabbed my attention instead. While having breakfast with my lovely wife, a couple of kids came on telly to say that they would be doing something inspiring for charity. An alternative to the marathon has surfaced and it involves doing a tenth of the distance – 2.6 miles – by whatever means you see fit. I just said, 'I'm doing that.'

Kathy is very supportive, but she let out a 'huh' in a kinda jokey way. It was no joke, I'm joining in. I chose by tractor, until it was pointed out to me that it had to be within a sporting context. Running wasn't an option, walking perhaps? But if I took to the home gym I could either pedal the distance or row it. I chose the latter, because the first option, I thought, was just a bit too easy – although easier in my outhouse than at Strathclyde Park, and certainly a safer option. Swimming might be a bit of an issue.

It was an experience that left me exhilarated, because I'd joined in with the rest of the nation, and completely knackered because two and a half miles is longer than you think. That last third of a mile was almost too much. The body started shaking, the knees began knocking, the gasps for air became deeper and longer, and the tiredness meant I lost grip on the bar. But I made it, just. The good part was, of course, that I didn't have to turn around and get back to where I started out from!

I had done a wee bit, but it made me appreciate all the more those who had run 5 kms and 10 kms, and further, for the Foundation, or who had climbed mountains or got on bikes and cycled hundreds of miles.

I recall years ago playing in a golf day up at Gleneagles. Chris Hoy was there, except he didn't play golf. So he just took his bike out and went for a ride – eighty miles. Basically that day, he went to Edinburgh and back. A 'ride'. I've not gone that far on holiday some years. Hence why I'm in awe of these people.

Still, I'm proud of my 2.6 miles . . . Then, I found out I'd done 2.6 kilometres instead. No difference. The tide would have taken me home anyway.

Monday 27 April

I try, but there is so much happening within the Foundation that it is impossible to keep up with everything. There are times, scanning emails and the likes, or receiving direct messages, when things just stop you in your tracks, and you feel the full, brutal force of how bad things can get around MND. People dropping you a line to say thanks for all the help you have given my parent or sibling, but sadly they are no longer here, MND claiming another warrior, changing the lives of families irrevocably.

A multitude of thoughts cross my mind at such times. Is there more I can do, more the Foundation can do, more the professors should be doing, more the MND Association could be doing? What about governments? Then you rerun that thought process, and even taking Covid out of the equation, is it just a case of we are where we are?

People don't see this side of my life, the mental anxiety. People won't see this side of a great many lives. No one looks for praise or sympathy. Understanding would be enough. I think where we are in the world right now, the awareness on that front is heightened. So are the senses.

Having noticed problems with his speech in October 2018 – just months after completing an Iron Man challenge in Norway – and putting some of that down to the stresses of working in the City, Simon Brennan was eventually diagnosed with Motor Neuron Disease in May 2019.

From that moment on, he was a committed champion for our Foundation, raising fortunes – hundreds of thousands of pounds – through his adversity, so that we might help others. In July last year he took part in Doddie'5 Ride having already ridden from Cornwall to London with his son Freddie and brothers Mark and Paul to raise cash and awareness.

We also spent a day in the City last October, working as traders, raising funds for the Foundation. A remarkable man.

Last month, while we were in London for Tom Smith's dinner, Kathy and I met Simon at his home. He could do very little, the reality of progressive MND.

Today, Jill passes on the news that Simon has passed away, aged fifty-three. Heart-breaking, made more so by the fact that his 87-year-old mother Kitty will be unable to travel from Wicklow to attend her son's funeral, and neither can his two brothers out in the States, or his sister Katherine living in Kent.

Motor Neuron Disease has no pity for individuals or their families. Those who are left now, however, are often confronted with a doubly bad scenario because of this pandemic, unable to see sufferers in their final days, unable to mourn them on their final journey.

Stories like Simon's leave you upset, but determined to do better in their memory and for those still ravaged by this disease. The hollow sensation, however, lasts longer, a void you take a while to fill. Imagine then, how the families feel?

Thursday 30 April

What do they say about boys and toys?

I got myself an industrial log breaker and can manage – with a bit of ingenuity – to load it up with wood, without loading myself up with the wood. There is now a healthy supply of timber, dried out, ready for winter. We also knocked some fence posts in and repaired some fencing around the farm, assisted by my apprentice, Alice, aged somewhere north of seventy. We'll leave it there as it's never nice to discuss a lady's age.

But other than Alice, Mary Doll and the boys, the only people we see now are the postman and the vet, who could chap the window to tell us they had been and leave it at that, although the vet emailed his bills. The obligatory DHL and Parcelforce delivery drivers seemed to be making regular – make that daily – visits. Just what was Kathy buying online?

In terms of family, my brother Tom would arrive with animal feed every now and again, for the cattle and the horses. But he leaves it at a safe working distance before departing. I'll agree, I'm quite impressed with how disciplined everyone was in staying away. While I could speak on the phone, and use Skype and Zoom, not having contact with 'outsiders' is tough going at times. Who'd have thought it; missing folk I'd tried to miss for all those years!

The seriousness of the situation meant that no one was going to break the embargo or quarantine guidelines. I'm living in splendid near-isolation, although after several weeks of it, there is little splendid about it. Aside from the unusually warm weather.

All the boys and girls had steered clear of me and the farm, although I soon realised why they had been so disciplined, playing to the letter of the law. Nobody wants to be the one who visited me, and then got the blame for evermore as the one who killed me! Yes, I am laughing as I write this. But, ultimately, that is what the risks entail. The odds are stacked against me should I even catch a glancing blow from coronavirus. And while it is hard going, I am eternally grateful for each and every person adhering to the law.

On a Thursday night, I make the effort to clap for the NHS staff.

I might not be very good at it now, but it's the thought that counts. Out in the middle of nowhere, clapping. The madness has set in . . .

There are some horror stories flying around regarding PPE for frontline carers and workers. How are these people supposed to do the job they are asked to do, and stay safe, if they don't have proper gear? It's like asking someone to play rugby without boots or a gumshield. You only get away with it for so long before you get found out, or worse still, get hurt.

But whether it's tractors, buggies and the likes, I can get out and about. My thoughts are still drawn to those who are stuck in flats, stuck in their home. How much is this draining them of their fight, of their will to live, of their battle to exist?

It saddens me, truly it does.

MAY 2020

Sunday 31 May

For obvious reasons, May has been a pretty quiet month this year. No running around attending events, no visitors, not a lot going on. Tomorrow is June: summertime, out and about, visit the pub, have people bring the pub to me ... Not this year, it's not 2020's style. For a word that I don't think existed prior to this pandemic or lockdown, 'shielding' has become a way of life now. I can sit in the garden and people can shout abuse at me from the drive or the gate. This, though, as they said on *Star Trek*, is life, but not as we know it.

Every time I think I've had enough and it is time to escape, up pops another set of numbers on TV, cases versus victims, coldly delivered figures that tell you nothing of the suffering people or families have gone through this year. Amazing, my itchy feet are suddenly itchy no more. The possibility of becoming a number, a statistic, soon calms the wanderlust.

If at any time I've come close to ignoring the risks or dismissing the danger signs, there is a number I can call.

I ring up and say, 'Can I go out?' and the voice at the other end says, 'No.'

That's Annabel Howell for you. To be honest, if it hadn't been for her dire warnings back in February, I might not still be here. So, I thank her for the reply and say cheerio until the next time, when her response will likely be the same again. She should just set up an answering service.

I have a confession to make, however. A week or so ago, I went out in the car with Kathy who had to pick up a prescription from the chemist. Of course, I stayed in the car, but it was a strange world I ventured into. Very quiet, very peaceful and, above all else, very good when it came to parking spaces.

JUNE 2020

Thursday 4 June

Today I'm in pain, agony. I don't mind saying so. I'm suffering from what Robert Burns described as 'thee-thou hell o' a' diseases'. In addition to MND, I have toothache. I have never really had any problems with my teeth over the years. However, of late, I think that I've started grinding them and clenching them tightly while asleep, hence the issues. I will survive.

What it has made me consider, as just about every eventuality in life does these days, is that even with MND, I don't really suffer acute pain, unless self-inflicted by taking a tumble. But, on a day-to-day basis I am relatively untroubled, other than bits not working properly or at all.

That is in comparison to other unfortunate souls who might have cancer and suffer incessant pain, or a skin condition that irritates nonstop. That must be a nightmare, when your body keeps throbbing. What must that be like, being constantly distressed, when what little relief you might get is through medication but knowing that the effects of that will soon wear off.

Toothache lasts a few hours. Imagine what it would be like

twenty-four hours a day, every day of every week? I can't imagine what that must be like.

My teeth are playing up, but this whole scenario has also meant that I haven't seen the dietician, or the speech and language specialist, although, in a way, I wonder what would they do?

In contrast, my issues are small beer compared to some. Again, another example of being lucky even when you are unlucky. Not that I'd say having sore teeth is a blessing.

The biggest problem is trying to get a dentist during lockdown and this pandemic. Not easy. The vet is due later today. I might get her to give me a quick once over.

Friday 5 June

Everyone is telling me Amazon is a great place to shop.

Let's give it a try.

Garden furniture? Computer says no.

A bingo machine? Computer says no.

A new BBQ? Computer says no.

A better camera for my Zoom calls? Computer says no.

Great place to shop? I say that's nonsense.

Saturday 20 June

This caper is dragging out now. We've all missed something during this lockdown; family and friends, work and travel, or simply being out and about. I'm counting the cost, though, of the things I've missed.

Because of the pandemic, and the rules and regulations applied to everyone, I haven't been getting the one-to-one care I require. There has been no medical personnel available, unless it's been an absolute emergency. Thankfully, something I've avoided.

So, there has been no input from the speech and language specialist, and nothing from the dieticians either. When I have seen them previously, I haven't always liked what they've told me. It is, however, for my own good. Right now, I would settle for whatever they told me to practise or eat. I feel like I need them, but I'm just as aware that right now I don't know what they would do.

I've been doing sleep tests, which is a piece of kit that tests your CO_2 levels when you are at rest. It's just to make sure you don't go into too deep a sleep. Maybe Jim Telfer should have put one on me at lineouts twenty-five years ago. Again, if that came out with poor results, or dangerous readings, where would that leave me? Unfortunately, on one of the tests, I'd decided to have a wee drink to help me nod off as I hadn't been sleeping too well. Needless to say, I had to do the test twice. They were very concerned at my comatose state.

Being honest, I feel a wee bit down, but then I correct myself. Feeling sorry has never been my way. No point in starting now.

I feel blessed that I have the constitution I do, never beaten, certainly never one to accept the norm or what others accept as being the only option. I want to challenge convention, and when you are challenged or put to the test, you find a way. I'll give you an example.

Lockdown has given me a chance to play in my tractor, doing some grass harrowing out on the fields. But when you come to the end of a row, you need to turn and go back the way you came to do the next line. Now, it takes me pulling on the lever with two arms to lift the plough, but when I'm tired that isn't always easy – a roundabout way of saying impossible. There are buttons which mean you can operate it electrically but that was just too footery, trying to get your hands into the right place, and then hit the right button. So, unable to lift the till, all I did then was spin the tractor around, but between the stones you've gathered and yanking the harrower around in a tight turning circle, all that did was trash the blades. Not what you want.

To alleviate that issue, I got the buttons – one up, one down – moved onto the floor, the handiwork done by Alistair Hogg at Thomas Sherriff, the John Deere dealer, so with a bit of tap dancing – it's easier to use my feet and be more accurate with it as well – I'm able to turn the unit around and keep it in fine working fettle. Because of those improvisations, I – on my own, working about two hours a day – was able to top and roll all the fields. There is always a way. It challenged me mentally to come up with a solution to a problem, and then fix it. Physical dexterity is important. But you have to keep your brain healthy as well. Doddie 2 – MND 0. Or 30–0, if you like your tennis.

MND, to use another sporting analogy, has bowled me out when it comes to clothing myself. And washing myself. And keeping my appearance model-like. Kathy is my official dresser. When we are being sweet to each other, I get nice clothes to wear. If I'm cheeky, she dresses me like she did it in the dark. Let's just say some days my attire is rather bright, and not always matching.

I have a really fancy shower, more akin to a car wash, which can do all sorts of fancy things. Every home should have one, while as for shaving and doing my hair, again that's one of Kathy's chores. What would she do without me?

She neatifies my hair, and I trust her. I cannot say the same of Hamish, Angus and Ben, who seem intent on giving me the most outrageous styling on a daily basis. One day my hair is clapped down flat, then next spiked up like a punk rocker. I am not buying their chat that it is fashionable. For them, aye. For a nearly fifty-something, naw. If we happen to see anyone, I'm never sure now if people are looking at me because I'm Doddie Weir or they can't believe I'd appear looking like that. I'll tell you now, folks, I don't have an option. I cannot get my arms up to change it. Perhaps I should just run my head up and down the side of a coo?

JULY 2020

Wednesday 1 July

The farm gives me the bit of escapism I'm fortunate to have. I pootle about doing various odds and sods. Nothing too exuberant, only what I can manage. But again, it means that when I sit down to watch the TV, I have a feeling of accomplishment, a feeling that I've contributed and done something for the day-to-day working of the farm, even if it is making a mess for someone else to clear up.

Simple pleasures and chores, yes. But oh so beneficial and crucial to my general wellbeing and mindfulness. Especially at my age.

Yes, the countdown has begun. Reaching forty, or fifty, is usually accompanied by a major celebration, but often taken for granted, assumed that you'll reach that date on the calendar, that big day. In my case, nothing could be assumed. When I was told I had MND, seeing fifty, given the hard facts about this condition, looked distant, almost a dream. If I didn't reach it, how much would I miss it by? If I did get there, what condition would I be in, and would I be able to experience the celebrations? As I say, assume nothing.

I've never been able to work out if time has gone very quickly, or very slowly. Most folk reading this will know what I mean. Something that feels like yesterday in reality was actually two years ago, and so much seems to have happened over the last twelve months. Maybe it's keeping busy that acts as a distraction.

Lockdown mirrors those dilemmas about time and where it's gone. Have we been doing nothing for more than three months? Yet it seems like Boris was only on the telly a few weeks back.

Setting targets has spurred me on, giving me an incentive, in particular those of a chronological nature. I was determined, whatever happened, to celebrate Hamish's eighteenth, and any other birthdays of significance Angus and Ben might have. Is celebrating my fiftieth, then, wishful thinking, kidology, bluff, and clutching at anything that would give me a bit of belief and hope?

Despite the obstructions, the odd hurdle, the odd hoop to be jumped through, some of which were ablaze, we made it. To repeat myself, positive thinking. It has gone a long way.

Now I need something else to reach for. I don't think I've quite found it yet. But I won't sit around, waiting for it to arrive. I'll go hunting for it. Of course, I'm meaning long term – Kathy has her fiftieth in October. I will not miss that!

Thursday 2 July

When I was first diagnosed, I had in my head a plan of what my fiftieth would be like. You are only fifty once, and for the reasons I've detailed, I was going to make the most of it, making it a birthday party that I, and everyone else in attendance, wouldn't forget.

I'd started out with plans to have it in the garden, but given what I wanted to do, it didn't take long before that appeared rather confined. What we needed was an expanse that could take a couple of hundred guests, comfortably. To hell with that. Make it five hundred.

The Borders Events Centre – where the Mad Giraffe Dinner was held – would be ideal. It's in Kelso, but that aside, it had plenty of scope for what I wanted to do.

I wanted, in addition to the main hall, to set up a games room, with Xboxes and PlayStations for the kids and the bigger kids, and have a whisky room, a gin palace and a cocktail lounge. You could even have a fun fair outside. I wanted this to be the biggest and best . . . And then I didn't.

Having such a spectacular party would have been awesome, and I'd be able to invite so many to the big day. However, the more I thought about it, why have all those folk there when I might see them only once, briefly, during the day? What did I really want from that day? It was to celebrate, especially with those closest to me – and that meant Kathy and the boys.

As time passed, and we got further away from when I was diagnosed and closer to my fiftieth year, the more the appeal of going away for my birthday grew. Then in November last year, Scottish Rugby announced they were going to take part in a two-Test series against the World Champions. A little lightbulb moment.

It had always been my intention to take Kathy and the kids on a Lions Tour to South Africa in 2021, but when MND came on the scene, that plan was hastily revamped to take in the Lions out in New Zealand in the summer of 2017.

But here was an opportunity to finally get them to South Africa, a place I'd fallen in love with having played there with the Lions in 1997, and two years earlier with Scotland in the World Cup.

It could be a goer; it was only eight months away, and the First Test, the Springboks versus Scotland, would be on my birthday, and I would probably have sobered up for the Second Test a week later. Interesting? It certainly was.

Friday 3 July

Everything is set for the weekend. The cow shed has been power washed (I steered well clear of any hoses), freshened and spruced up, the decking is up, the tables are set, dressed and distanced.

All I need is some guests. Welcome to my birthday celebrations.

Bluecairn replaced Cape Town and Durban. Rumours in April that the Scots wouldn't be touring were confirmed in May once the full effect of travel restrictions due to the Covid pandemic took hold. Being honest, I'd put any thoughts of going anywhere on hold even before Boris Johnson quarantined us in March.

For me, in my condition, the risks were just too great. And as luck would have it, even my ideas for Kelso wouldn't have survived the complete shutdown of the hospitality industry. Bluecairn then it is, but even that has been curtailed.

Today, I'm expecting a couple of passers-by and neighbours. Martin Wilson of Thrifty and his wife and kids pop in, as does Stewart and Nicola with Callum and Zara. We are so socially distanced we literally have to shout across the tables. Then some neighbours appear and the Wilsons and Weirs take their leave. It's like some kind of weird family speed dating event.

An utterly weird set of circumstances is just becoming all the more bizarre. Talking of which, another early birthday present has arrived, and it is very welcome. I have been inducted into Scottish Rugby's Hall of Fame. Me, the man Jim Telfer shouted at (daily on occasions), me, the man who came good after failing as a No. 8, and me, the man Bill McLaren christened 'a mad giraffe'. Yes, me, as of today, I take my place alongside legends of the Scottish game – Gordon Brown, Sir Ian McGeechan, Andy Irvine and Ned Haig – in the game's exclusive club. It is an honour and a privilege, my work on MND extending on from anything I managed as a rugby player for my country.

There is a downside, however. Not enough for me to contact Murrayfield and hand back this magnificent achievement, hell no. I lost too many times to England not to accept accolades when they are being handed out.

But glancing down the list of other Hall of Famers, there are the names of Armstrong, Finlay Calder, Hastings (G) and Chris Paterson. It may be a trivial matter, but in recent times, I have slated and berated these guys for being anywhere near this list. Are the SRU so desperate for me to rewrite my after-dinner routine they have now made me part of this club?

Her Majesty, in presenting me with my OBE (which I seldom mention, or wear), forced me into overhauling my award-winning speech because I couldn't poke fun at Armstrong, Calder, Hastings and Jeffrey (he's a JP when he's not doing several other things at once), for having letters behind their names.

I keep it quiet about me having letters in front of my name (i.e. Dr). But then none of them do much after-dinner stuff as they aren't very good.

Nevertheless, I could have been doing without yet another edit on my material. I mean, it's only a matter of time before I attend another lunch or dinner – at this rate, I have this time next year underlined.

Saturday 4 July

Sing everyone! I've made it. I'm not sure if I feel relieved or old, but I am fifty, officially. I thought I might get half a telegram from Her Majesty. Perhaps it's still in post. You know what things are like during this pandemic.

Today my family are coming over to join the celebrations. Tomorrow, it will be Kathy's. I think we've reached the stage now where no one is one hundred per cent certain what the rules are. Regardless, we'll continue to play it safe. But it hasn't stopped anyone from enjoying themselves.

I got a lot of nice and notable gifts. The lovely bottle of whisky the Weegie Weirs brought me gets a thumbs-up from me, but also from Thomas and Christopher. Hamish is instructed to hide it and to give them the cheap stuff. They'll hardly notice the difference.

I'd always wanted a John Deere tractor. I'd bid for one at auction, unsuccessfully, and have never quite managed to get a deal that meant I could own one. Anyone reading this who needs a John Deere taking off their mitts . . .

But having dropped enough hints, lo and behold, on my fiftieth I get a John Deere all of my own – in the form of a birthday cake. It's the thought that counts, but someone had put a lot of work in either coming up with the idea, finding someone to make it, and then having it decorated like a mini Deere, right down to the private number plate on the back. And what do you do with birthday cakes? That's it, slice them up and share them around with family and your tummy. WRONG!

This was just so nice, and I was so impressed by it, I put it to one side to keep, not eat. Boy, was that an unwise move. Kathy and the boys went mental that I wasn't eating my birthday cake. It was *my* cake and I'd do what I liked with it. Another wrong move on my part. I don't think there would have been as much hostility if I'd said I didn't like cake or that I'd gone right off John Deere.

Instead, this work will take pride of place on the sideboard, beside my BBC trophy and my Edinburgh Award. Still in one piece. And still all mine.

Gary and Chick turn up to go out on a bike ride with Kathy and a few others, but that never transpired as the champagne and Guinness was already in full flow. Remember, this is early in the morning, about eight o'clock. Now that they were here, they might as well stay. Unbeknown to Craig, he has been Gazza'd – because while we were drinking half cans, Gary has been feeding Chick full tins. And yes, it was taking effect.

Eventually, about three, I said right, Craig, you are going home. I'd only had a beer – two half cans really that I'd shared with Gazza as I wanted to pace myself, so said I'd take Chambo back to Gattonside in my buggy, chauffeured by Hamish, with Craig's bike on the back as he wasn't really in a state to pedal fifty yards let alone twelve miles.

It isn't as far as that if you cut across fields, use a bit of the Southern Upland Way and bridle paths and farm roads. He was adamant he was going to take his last can with him. We got to the top of Gattonside but I wasn't for crossing the main road, so we told him to walk down the hill and let him go – except he decided to jump back on his bike, went a few hundred yards and crashed into a wall. I hope he was okay . . .

Sunday 5 July

The third and final instalment of Doddie @ 50. Kathy's crew make it a memorable finale. This was not what we'd planned but it was the best we were going to have, given the circumstances. I had no complaints. Celebrating was great, deep down though, the best part was just seeing this day and the delight on the faces of my family and my extended family – although it was more puzzlement probably with Tom and Chris.

Where had that nice whisky gone?

Monday 13 July

I'm always a bit wary when, after a good night's sleep, I wake up to find my mobile phone full of messages and alerts. Not being blasé in any way, but I've gone, in the last few years, from wondering what have I done to what have I won! And yes, I have had another honour in my name.

I have always been a Falcon after spending such a successful time at Newcastle, but this morning I have become an osprey. No, not a Welsh rugby-playing one but the feathered variety.

Three osprey chicks have hatched at Loch Arkaig Pine Forest in Lochaber, and Woodland Trust Scotland have run a poll to see what they'd be named. One was called Vera after Dame Vera Lynn, one Captain after the fundraising exploits of the centenarian Sir Tom Moore and the other named after me. What a thrill and what an honour.

People never cease to surprise me, either with their financial generosity or in just thinking about me and the Foundation. I am honoured and humbled. I'm waiting to see some pictures of the trio just to see if my namesake is taller than the others...

Saturday 25 July

The gates are open and a version of freedom is returning to the world. We're being told that we've just got to watch what we are doing, which is a bit tricky. Where we are – and I'm being entirely self-centred here – is now a more dangerous time and place for me than where we were while in full lockdown. If some could take liberties when we were supposed not to go anywhere, what might they do now, or how might they behave with the shackles removed?

Does it worry me? Not really, in as much as I've always believed that what's for you won't go past you. It doesn't worry me, but I am concerned. I realise the dangers, but I'm not going to spend every hour of every day, watching and waiting for something that might never happen.

The big question, though, is have I had Covid? How, I hear you ask? Kathy really got quite ill around Christmas, not in a normal way. But there were so many stories of people showing all the signs of what we now know to be symptoms of Covid. In January I got the flu jab, being a vulnerable individual, and wasn't very well after it. Stewart was really ill in January, again at a time when there appeared to be so many struck down with very bad flu-like symptoms. Was Covid already here then, right back at the start of the year? The experts have said no – but they've said that about so many things around this wretched virus.

I read this week that someone may have had Covid for a second time. A one in a million chance, or did they even have it the first time, or what should everyone expect? Who knows? It makes you think – but not for too long. I'd prefer to dream about someone clever coming up with a cure. And while you're at it, take a look at MND as well.

Saturday 31 July

'Wee man, I'm bored. Get yourself round here. We are going for a drive.' We – me and the Gaz – we're off on an adventure, a wee field trip, to see my fellow MND warrior Rob Burrow.

The sun is shining, summer is well and truly here, I'd made it to fifty and the restrictions have eased to allow travel across country. We think. Scotland and England seem to be moving at different speeds. I find it confusing. Think how simple folk must feel, Gary. I hadn't seen Rob in the flesh since February and, having spoken to Kevin Sinfield, a great human to have in your corner, I just wanted to give Rob a wee lift, just to show him I was still thinking about him.

We arrived at his beautiful new house and there he was, sitting in the garden, sunning himself. And why not. We still had to play by the rules, in terms of distancing. But put it this way, two metres was a hell of a lot better than two hundred miles.

When you don't see someone in a while, you immediately reference your last get-together. We'd had a four-way Zoom call in June with Sally Nugent off the Beeb, but it's never great in gauging someone's demeanour and wellbeing by looking at a screen.

His lovely lady, Lindsey, is there, but the kids are away with relatives meaning we can indulge in some big boy chat.

He looks frail, smaller – he isn't huge anyway – but you could see he'd lost a bit of weight. His speech is proving a bit tricky. We'd spoken, what, a month before, online, so I was maybe used to it. But he is struggling. It's July, and he is straining to get out of his

219

chair. Or he was, until we stuck some chocks under the back legs, just to create a bit of an angle to make standing up simpler.

He confided in me that when he was eating, he had started to struggle a bit, in stopping his food sticking to the roof of his mouth. That is an issue I've had on occasions. But as I keep saying, if you have a problem, don't stop, find a solution. Mine? Stick a bit of mayo on your food, or gravy, or sauce, or ice cream, or custard. Don't toil, don't use up energy you don't have to. Go for the clever option.

He'd just been away for a couple of weeks, though his movement was curtailed. While he had the surrounds of his house tarmacked, during lockdown, he was really having to force himself to walk any kind of distance. I have mentioned my saying: 'If you don't use it, you lose it.' But MND sometimes takes no notice of willpower and determination, just as it takes no notice of what your brain is trying to tell your leg. It doesn't matter how nicely you ask, the message, eventually, just doesn't get through. No point in saying try harder, because as I'm experiencing, you might have an idea of what you'd like to do, but there isn't a guarantee it will be delivered.

Similarly, I have no idea what his mental state is, or what his confidence is like. If you have a fear of walking – or falling – you are not going to be as willing to make the effort. But who am I to criticise or doubt someone's intentions? I'm not. I know first-hand about trying to coax your body into functioning something like it once did. Easier said than done. Perhaps I'm just looking for signs that he is making some gains against this disease. That could be as much for my good as it is his. Any positivity has to be welcomed.

We chat about lots of things, though I know not to overstay our welcome. Exhaustion sweeps over you so easily. We give him a wee basket of bits and pieces and, obviously, some Guinness, and it comes to time to say goodbye.

All the time we'd been there, he'd been on the garden furniture.

But I wasn't for taking my leave without seeing him up on his feet. He eventually got up but was unsteady, like a new-born calf. Gary stood with him, just to steady him up. He conceded being on his feet was now a problem, his balance had gone, not helped by his two-year-old innocently running into him and tipping him over. There's not a lot you can say to that. Imagine your little one just being a normal toddler, yet being able to exact such harm on his dad, a guy who a year earlier was still at the height of his rugby league career. Bless him.

When we get back in the car, Gary admits he was shocked. He hadn't seen Rob since we met in Carlisle in the December when we had seen him before Christmas, and he had even played in a benefit game back in January. It wasn't what Gary had anticipated. He went very quiet.

The one thing Rob has got, like me, is a bunch of great people surrounding him: his wife, family, former teammates and the rugby league fraternity in general. What I call being lucky when you are unlucky. With Stephen and myself, he is one of our team and we'll always look after him because of that.

It's been a good day, but a hard one. For the first half-hour on the way back, me and Gaz are pretty much silent, keeping our thoughts well hidden.

This disease just numbs you at times, but leaves you heartbroken most of the time.

AUGUST 2020

Sunday 1 August

I officially qualify as a petrol-head, loving all things powered by the internal combustion engine, from tractors to Formula 1 cars. I like things that go fast, having sat in a few over the years, and especially like watching motor racing of all types. It's amazing how you can, after just a few laps of viewing, be completely absorbed by a race, so much so that you end up backing a driver or car you don't even recognise in some obscure race, from a circuit you've never heard of, all because you've been doing a bit of channel-hopping at two in the morning.

Imagine then, mixing my metaphors, having a horse (or horse-power) on the track that you are right behind from the off.

And that's what I found myself doing this weekend when the Mini Challenge joined the British Touring Car Championship circus as racing returned at Donington Park, all thanks to Peebles-born racer Robbie Dalgleish, racing in the Mini Challenge JCW.

His Lawrence Davey Racing team entry was bedecked and resplendent in the My Name'5 Doddie Foundation tartan, easily picked out in the field when his races were broadcast on ITV4 no less.

I won't be offering my services as a test driver any time soon – not if he wants to complete the championship – but Robbie's efforts are another amazing example of the support and promotion me and the Foundation receive from individuals, all wanting to contribute.

Sunday 16 August

Gently does it. Lockdown has meant a breakdown in keeping myself in peak shape. The rowing machine has taken a hit, as has the exercise bike. Not tokenism either. Two or three times a week, sometimes with the boys joining me, other times focused on my own. In some ways, however, you are doing what you can, in a manner that you are comfortable with, without pushing your body, or indeed your thinking, in much the way you should have been doing. You convince yourself you have done a session, where you could maybe only have done ninety per cent of one, or less.

Today, with a bit of trepidation, we are going to get back in the swimming pool, all very secure and secluded, and something I'm happy to get back into, as I consider it will improve the wellbeing element in my life, physically and mentally. Wow, the reality is, however, not what I've been expecting. Sugar.

It was quite a scary difference to when I'd last been there. As I mentioned, there is only so much that you can do on your own. But this was me finding out just how much I had lost in terms of mobility, strength and movement. I suppose it's the same as people not seeing me for a while and noticing the difference. I see myself every day, but now I was back in 'unfamiliar' familiar surroundings, a bit of a benchmark as to where I'd been before lockdown. It was a real shock, a wake-up call, to where I was in my condition. It was scary, I'll be honest.

Maybe I was in denial, that I was better than I was. I had been making small amendments, little changes in doing standard things because it wasn't as easy as before. For instance, in the pool, your balance is all to pot. I have polystyrene dumb-bells. A splash can be like a tidal wave hitting you, easy to end up off balance and taking a dive. Which is why I always work with lifeguards to hand. First time in the water, I feel hugely nervous, uncertain. It's as if I've never stood in a pool before. And that is with both feet on the bottom, before you start walking on the spot, or doing the high knees. I was wobbling like a flagpole in a hurricane. My jumps, side to side, back and forwards, no use. The message was not getting through to events under the water. Within minutes, I was knackered. I knew how long I could stay in the pool previously. I was nowhere near it.

Looking back, were the signs already there, for instance, when in standing up or getting out of a chair? You, at home, will plant your feet and push up with your legs, maybe even giving yourself, quite literally, a helping hand by pushing with your arms. My arms don't work, and the legs don't act now how they should.

You say 'right, come on, body' and go through the launch programme. I've likened it to starting a chainsaw, when you need to sequence priming it, taking off the brake, and giving the cord a pull or pressing the button. Do it the wrong away around, and it may not fire up, or will help you on your way to a nasty accident. Standing up is exactly the same.

Sometimes you get up in a oner, or you need a bit of help from a passing crane driver. Where I'm at, I give myself a gentle rock back and forward, gently mind, not too far forward and then use my extraordinary leg and abdominal strength to get upright. I may not have been entirely honest in that last sentence. Can you see where?

Problem is that if you don't get the shoogle and the upward thrust quite right, you don't go anywhere except backwards back into the chair. Irritating. Or worse still, take a flyer forwards. Irritatingly dangerous. I confess, I do have a chair that will do all of that for me. An ejector seat, as I call it, offering a wee angle to slide off the chair, not the kind of seat you'll find in a fighter jet. But there will be time enough to work that gadgetry. Just now, I'm still working under my own steam.

You can see why people might just give up, faced with a series of challenges or setbacks like this. But that isn't in my DNA.

What I know is that there is no point worrying where I was then and where I am now. Things have obviously progressed, or regressed in my case. But I have a starting point that I can gauge myself from, and improve upon. Any little will help.

Saturday 22 August

Protectionism, for someone classed as a vulnerable individual like myself, comes in many guises. I'm still participating in sleep tests, which has nothing to do with me trying to sleep, more to make sure I wake up again. They monitor my CO_2 content, making sure I'm not producing too much of the stuff during the night. So far, there has been nothing untoward with the test results. I'll sleep better for that . . .

Tuesday 26 August

I did a podcast this week with Michael Anthony over in Ireland – international broadcaster me, now, thanks to Skype and Zoom – and he was asking the question about MND and the fact there aren't a lot of people with it, so did that have a bearing on what the doctors, professors and pharmaceutical companies did in finding a cure? Firstly, the reason there are so few is that too many have died, and secondly, yes, I do think they might not spend enough time or money on developing a drug.

I'm bound to say they should. But then there are so many neurological issues today, which touch so many people and families – like Alzheimer's, dementia, Parkinson's, MND – that you would think

225

someone, somewhere, might focus in on that group of conditions, from scratch.

I appreciate it's an expensive endeavour, coming up with a brand new drug or medicine, especially one for something as rare as MND. But don't sufferers of this condition deserve a chance? Let's see how long it takes before we get a Covid jag, just like we get the flu injection. Ten years, five years. Sooner than you think is my bet. And why? Because Covid happens to create billions of potential victims.

We all need to disappear off this earth at some point in time. When is often in the hands of the chemists. I don't have an issue so much with that. I'd like to hang around for a wee while yet, but I know what the odds and chances are of that, and they are not the greatest.

My real issue with Motor Neuron Disease is that, nearing the end, you are totally reliant on other people. It is such an undignified way to go.

If my issue happened in twenty or twenty-five years' time, when I'm sixty-five or seventy or older, I don't think it would be an issue, as I don't think I'd be having the fight I'm having now. There isn't a good age to go, but in your late sixties isn't too bad, or at least it isn't from where I'm sitting. The issue I'm having just now with MND is that it takes lives. Some are unfulfilled lives, unfulfilled potential, unfulfilled ambitions. I don't categorise myself that way.

A farmer, a businessman, Scotland rugby player, a Lion, a winner, a husband and father to three great sons, a champion for this cause, a doctor, an OBE, a TV celeb. I could have put equestrian champion in there as well if my sister hadn't killed my horse. But you see what I'm saying. That isn't a bad CV to be carrying whenever you move on. Job done.

There are others, however, who might only be setting out in a partnership, or have young kids, or who have just reached a goal with the job they've aspired to. That's when MND is so nasty, so random, so horrible. No warning, no mercy, no chance.

I look at those I know, where fifty must seem beyond reach. I've got a lot to be thankful for.

Friday 28 August

It wasn't because of the 'eat out to help out' scheme where you got fifty per cent of your meal paid for by Chancellor Rishi Sunak. Much as I love Bluecairn, we were getting somewhat sick of the sight of the farm and only the farm, so Kathy and I decided to venture out in public, into this big strange world – well, Melrose actually – and have a lunch date at the Burt's Hotel, a hostelry I may have visited in the past. Yes, the tongue is firmly in cheek here. Great food, good company and still quite quiet. I wasn't expecting hordes of Murrayfield proportions, but I expected there to be a few more individuals about the place, and the town in general. Maybe not what the various proprietors were hoping for, but entirely fine for me and my good lady.

Social distancing was observed, in the main, excessively so for those I knew and who spotted me. Two metres, to remind you, is the size of me, lying down. I think some thought ten feet was a far safer exclusion zone, obviously working on the premise that it was better to be very, very safe than just a tiny bit sorry. But – and I'm choosing my words carefully here – some people, complete strangers in reality, were just a wee bit too familiar with me for my liking, let alone my wellbeing.

It's difficult, being me, not to attract attention, even when the tartan suit is hung up and I'm out in understated clothes. I do stand up and out rather. People have always come and said hello. Currently, though, we are in the midst of a pandemic and have only been released from our homes to, firstly, stop us going completely mad and, secondly, to kick-start the economy.

However, here were people who went out of their way to pat me on the back or my shoulder, tell me how well I was doing with the fundraising, and ask me how I was. I felt like saying I was fine until you felt the need to touch me. What part of pandemic didn't they get? I appreciate that if you have any sort of profile, there is a perception that you are public property. I don't want to end up lost property.

I know, they were being genuine, showing their feelings and wanting me to know how they, as strangers, as supporters, as nice people, felt about me and the Foundation. Lovely sentiments most of the time, but not when we have a pandemic on top of us and a deadly virus dancing around us. I don't mean to sound rude or ungracious, I really don't. But I hadn't spent half a year cooped up within four walls just to feel threatened the first time we venture beyond our driveway.

It was a sobering experience, chilling, if I can say that without coming over as if I'm being all dramatic. Look but don't touch. Nice to see you, nice to speak to you. Now leave me alone. It would never be in my nature to say that. Thinking it? That's a different thing.

It has put me off showing face in public again until such times as we get an all-clear from someone in authority. Och, well, it was good while it lasted.

Saturday 29 August

I'm trying to make arrangements for Rob Burrow and Stephen Darby to come up and see me in the middle of next month, and see what I'm about in terms of what I do in the pool, see my chiropractor Donald Francis and Bruce Scott, who looks after my physiotherapy, and other bits and bobs. I'm interested to see and hear what Stephen has been up to with his involvement in America. He seems to be a busy boy, and has already been in touch to say he's looking forward to it – but . . .

Like all of us who have been shielding – if hide and seek was an Olympic sport we'd be gold medal contenders, individually and for Team GB – you have to be careful, extremely so. Naturally, Stephen wants to know what precautions we can take, because in all of this, we need to be looking after each other. The last thing any of us want is to be exposed to unnecessary risk, which I totally get and respect. It begs the question, however, is this as good as it gets?

Sunday 30 August

I'm lucky to be so well thought after. Others in my position might be running out of people to speak to, definitely not seeing friends, worse still, not hearing from them. Me, I'm getting by thanks to technology. There is always someone or another wanting a quick word, or an interview. It breaks the day up. Other things break my heart. We get a visit from a passing couple, who call in on us to see how we are. Now, remembering everything I've said previously, in one respect this is a nice act of kindness. I am not a mathematician, but I couldn't calculate how many times over this gesture is outweighed by what is misguidedness – is that even a word?

I have extended my stay on this planet thanks to living a monastic existence (okay, maybe not one hundred per cent of the time) if you know what I mean: keeping myself to myself, keeping others at arm's length, keeping the majority at the kind of distance that makes it difficult to see who it is without having binoculars handy. It has worked.

But for the second time in a few days, I'm having my space invaded by individuals I don't really want near me. How can I be speaking like this when they surely don't mean any harm? Is it because I'm frightened?

I don't know where this visitation has emerged from, or where they've been, or who they've been with, or where those they have been in contact with have been, or if they have had Covid, if they have got it, if they have come into contact with it, have they been tested, when was the last time they were tested, have they even washed their hands? Now they want to see me. I am truly at a loss what to think. Am I fighting a losing battle? Am I going to spend the rest of my time worrying and turning social distancing into the kind of game plan or drill I've previously reserved for line-outs? And as we all know, they don't always work out how you'd planned.

My energies shouldn't be about having a dust up with negativity. But then, there are not many ways of showing or enjoying positivity.

SEPTEMBER 2020

Thursday 10 September

There is a routine to my day, in as much as I get up, get dressed and have breakfast, all in the company of my good lady, as without her I wouldn't get up, get dressed and have breakfast. Ach, it's good to laugh – except this is serious stuff. It might sound rather bland, rather samey, but it gives me a purpose on a daily basis, a challenge I need to complete, a mini-battle for the winning.

I need to test myself daily as it would be too easy just to say blow it and stay in bed. Even doing that once every three or four days, that's getting into a habit that could become the norm, and then you end up only getting up every couple of days, then not at all. For me, that's conceding the game when I am very much still in it.

I've had a series of projects I wanted to get into, one of them being building a gym, nothing too fancy, just enough kit – bike, cross trainer and rowing machine – that I can make full use of. To that end I was helped out greatly by Anthony Elliott from Bannatyne's and the good people at Technogym. A good session every two or three days is essential, just to keep the elasticity in my limbs and maintain my strength levels, not always easy if you just don't feel up to it, or it's too cold outside. But it has to be done.

Tuesday 15 September

I cannot think of anyone who hasn't been touched in some form by this pandemic. Kids haven't been to school for huge chunks of the year, their exams have been in turmoil, holidays are cancelled and even playing endless hours of computer games has little or no attraction. People, meanwhile, have seen family and friends pass away, without a proper farewell, and in some cases without even being able to see loved ones in the final months. Weddings, too, have been put on hold, maybe a relief for some, I know, but romance doesn't take you that far only for you to say 'I don't' at the last moment. Work has been brought to a complete standstill in some cases. It's bleak. But is it?

If it's so bad, why am I getting countless jokes, cartoons, videos and funnies through on my phone? Because in all of this, people haven't lost their sense of humour. I mean, who'd have thought women – who hadn't seen a hairdresser in weeks and who normally wouldn't be seen out without their hair done and makeup on – would be able to laugh at their own appearance?

They can laugh about it – but don't you dare!

OCTOBER 2020

Sunday 18 October

There are tens, hundreds, thousands of individuals who have all played their part in contributing to the My Name'5 Doddie Foundation. Every one of them is special, for taking the time to think about us and those we might help. But some take being special to another level, and then keep climbing.

Stuart Thom is a Melrose lad – that makes him special anyway – but over the last few years he has come up with various events and challenges to raise funds for the Foundation and the fight against MND.

As chief executive of Royal Belfast Golf Club, staging golf events as fundraisers was a bit of a busman's holiday for Stuart, but that he did, along with several quizzes, as well as putting up prizes for various raffles and auctions.

Where Stuart has surpassed himself, however, is when he climbs on his bike.

You would be forgiven for thinking that once you've ridden from John O'Groats to Land's End, as he and his team did on the Great Rugby Cycle over a fortnight in March 2019, that you'd done your bit for the cause. I mean, the saddle soreness alone would be enough to quell any thoughts of participating in further tasks, but not for our Stuart – and we are grateful for that.

His major cycling adventure for 2020 was his 'Long Weekend Run', quite literally around Northern Ireland, from Belfast via Portrush to Castlederg, a gentle 161 miles for starters, then 140 miles to Warrenpoint, and a final hundred-mile sprint to the finish via Strangford Lough. All in the space of three days.

Hard enough, but as if that wasn't a test, the intrepid riders weren't sure that, once they had set off, if their overnight accommodation would be open or available as the province was pitched into another lockdown scenario. It didn't deter them. Instead of turning back, they pressed on. That fighting spirit and doggedness has to be admired. It certainly keeps me energised.

I would have joined them on my electric bike, but I was shielding. That's right, roll your eyes as if you don't believe me . . .

Thursday 22 October

We are still in what is a global pandemic with regards to Covid, with figures for deaths and confirmed cases, spikes, waves, how long we've been locked up, or how long until we're released and the likes going up and down on a daily basis. There is probably not a single pharmaceutical business or provider who haven't detailed part or maybe even all of their business to finding a cure or antidote to this dreaded coronavirus.

How many scientists, virologists, specialists and professors have been sucked into this project? And, as yet, they've found nothing. Maybe I'm too demanding or ambitious, then, when it comes to making progress on a cure for MND.

Or again, maybe it is a mission impossible . . .

Friday 23 October

International rugby is back. Scotland beat Georgia 48–7. And on a Friday night. Time for a celebratory cocktail – red wine (half-pint) with an umbrella and decorative straw. What's not to love about life?

Wednesday 28 October

Back in July, before my big birthday, I had the honour of being inducted in the Scottish Rugby 'Hall of Fame'. Normally, such achievements would be heralded and trumpeted at a dinner or banquet. But right now, in these peculiar times, you need a good memory to work out the last time you sat with your dickie bow on in company. In fact, I'm struggling to think.

Covid has rendered the hospitality industry, and the big events they work so hard to put on, completely void. It therefore means that my Hall of Fame trophy – a specially sculpted Scotland cap – is handed over in a one-to-one ceremony.

Now, I totally accept why we couldn't have a dinner.

And I totally get why, because of social distancing and the likes, the handover takes place in a barn, on my farm.

But did the SRU really have to send Chris Paterson to do the honours?

Now, Mossy may himself be a Hall of Famer, and Scotland's leading points scorer, and have more World Cup appearances than anyone else for Scotland (I only know that because he beat the record that once belonged to me) . . .

But a Gala man?

Still, I was able to point out that the hallowed chambers of the Hall of Fame were now blessed by four from Melrose and only two from Gala.

NOVEMBER 2020

Monday 9 November

Open the champagne. I might be premature, but I like a drink. News that there could be a vaccine for Covid is the best news I've had this year. I think you probably can scale that joy up to include the world.

Celebrations all round, and all-round frustration as well. Yes, I'll benefit from getting a jab or several, whatever it takes, to get out and about. I'll happily take my place in any queue and do whatever it takes to get life back to some normality.

But Covid has been on the go for less than a year. Charge the scientific and research world with coming up with a solution, a cure, and they have done it in double-quick time considering a matter of months ago we were being told this could be a five- or ten-year process. Well done, the boffins.

What I'm thinking about is, if you can work so fast, so speedily around Covid, why has nothing happened in terms of drugs for MND? Simplistic thinking, yes, probably flawed thinking and open to derision. But there will not be one MND sufferer who hasn't had that thought cross their mind today.

The galling thing – actually make that the thing that angers me, and it takes a lot to get me angry – is that while we have come a long way in terms of the professors and centres of excellence buying into our plan, trusting us, knowing that if we promise we will deliver, seeing monies come in their direction for trials and research and the likes, there are still those who are dragging their heels on giving answers, or worst of all, being far too slow tapping into the funds that we have ringfenced for them individually and collectively.

I find that extraordinary. Don't complain about funding, then when the funds are put in place, sit on your hands and do nothing. The things I complained about when I was diagnosed are still happening three years on. You start asking, 'Where are we going wrong?' The answer is – we aren't.

We have a charity, a business to run. What we produce is not washers, not elastic bands, not garden furniture (although that would be quite profitable right now), but hope, hope that we will find something that prevents MND being the killer it is, offering the hope that you can survive MND, giving hope that there is a tomorrow, and the day after that, and the day after that, and a week, a month, a year, perhaps several.

I'm not one for calling anyone out. But if you don't want to be part of this jigsaw, go find another box – or, ultimately, we might find one for you.

I may name names in my next book.

Right, give me a hand to get down off this soapbox, safely . . .

DECEMBER 2020

Monday 7 December

Rugby players – Union or League, or Union and League given how many mixed code players there have been in the past twenty-five years – are like a band of brothers. On the field, you get stuck in, afterwards, you get stuck into some beers – or lentil smoothies these days. But there is always the camaraderie, sticking up for each other, supporting your pals.

I've had it in abundance since my diagnosis, since revealing to the world my plight, since the Foundation came into being; from past teammates and room-mates, through to those you have only shared a field with, or shared a dream and a badge.

The actions of Kevin Sinfield typify that bond. Already qualified in the legendary category of rugby league, 'Sir Kev' rose in a nation's affections when he completed seven marathons in seven days to raise awareness in MND and funds for his pal and former Leeds Rhinos teammate Rob Burrow and the MND Association.

His target was £77,777.

He raised £1.2 million, a total that will, inevitably, continue to rise.

Yes, people will say that we needed a good news story to break the tedium of lockdown, and that media agencies, like the BBC, would cover that as part of their news agenda. All very true.

But, you still need an individual – just as I have witnessed first-hand through MN5DF – to get up, get out and do it. If I wore a hat, I'd be tipping it right now to the selfless act of Kevin Sinfield. A legend in every meaning of the word.

Saturday 19 December

When it comes to legends, I'm blessed, honoured, privileged, call it what you will, to have one of rugby's great thinkers in my camp, none other than Rob Wainwright.

If you hadn't noticed, 2020 wasn't the best year when it came to getting out and about, or meeting up with family or friends, or going to games, dinners and events. You know there is something not quite right when even attending funerals is by invitation only. So, all in all, not the greatest period for raising funds for a charity, and not just our Foundation. Every establishment was in the same boat, with the possible exception of the NHS through the marvellous work of Captain Sir Tom Moore, and what Kev Sinfield did for Rob Burrow.

Rob Wainwright's 'Doddie Gump' activities had served the Foundation – and therefore those affected by MND at any level – well since its inception. However, not one to rest on his laurels, or anyone else's for that matter, the bold Wainwright had contrived his most ambitious cash generator yet – Doddie Aid, or #doddieaid as it would become for social media.

Having explained the idea and plan to me, I was none the wiser how it would work – other than it would work, because he was steering this ship. As he said, leave it to me and watch this space. I knew he'd fill it with something.

Sunday 20 December

One thing that sitting watching TV all day, every day, does is give you a real appreciation of the news, domestic and international. Inevitably, be it the news at one o'clock, six or ten, it leads with Covid and coronavirus. Remember how we thought it would be over and done with in the summer?

I might watch a lot of news, but really, where are we? Are we in bubbles, are we in super bubbles, do we even know what level or tier we are in? Does it even matter? However, there is now much speculation going around that all restrictions will be lifted so we can enjoy a reasonably normal Christmas with family. Here's hoping, but it does seem quite regimented, that this window of opportunity will apply to the country. Perhaps it's fine if you belong to a 9–5 world, and if you do, you've probably been working from home for months, that's if you haven't been furloughed entirely.

However, for a great many, this five-day holiday – with a set start and finishing time – won't suit everyone. How can it? What about emergency services, nurses in hospitals and even in our own circle and circumstances. Living – and for me occasionally working – on a farm, our daily business has been going ahead virtually as per normal, with the exception that no one comes here.

Kathy has worked her little cotton socks off, both as my carer but also as this household's main hunter-gatherer. Okay, she might only be hunting and gathering in the food aisles of Asda or Tesco or wherever she visits to find provisions, but you catch my drift. She has to be out and about.

It is the Sunday before Christmas. Kathy has to pick something up from her parents, which her sister Kirsty will be dropping off. My sister, meanwhile, also has to collect various bits and bobs, all done, of course, while being socially distanced. Remember, we are all farmers.

And in all of this, we have an eye on what we'll be doing at

Christmas, who is mixing with whom, and more importantly, who isn't mixing with others. We are so desperate to see one another, properly, abiding by the rules, just so we can have a few days of normality.

Then Kathy's phone goes. I can tell that the news isn't great and it isn't. Kirsty has tested positive for Covid. Not a symptom, not a cough, a sniff, not a fever or a temperature. Nothing, but she is apparently positive. Covid could have been that close to us, to me. It's absolute shock. Christmas is instantaneously cancelled. No visitors, no mixing, no nothing.

Wouldn't you just know it?

That night, Lewis Hamilton wins the BBC Sports Personality of the Year Award, and deservedly so, setting all kinds of records during the course of the season and eventually crowning a great year by taking the world title, his seventh. How many of us – me being one – thought that when Michael Schumacher reached that number of driver's championships it was a tally which might never be matched?

But here was Lewis Hamilton equalling that feat, and well done him. Yet, for everything he did, he missed out on receiving his SPOTY trophy and the acclaim that accompanies it, in front of a huge, live audience. Similarly, Captain Sir Tom Moore, the newest – if you can be 'newest' aged a hundred – recipient of the Helen Rollason award, also missed out on what would have been a massive public showing of love and admiration for everything he'd achieved in raising over £30 million for NHS Charities Together.

Two individuals, doing massively different things during 2020, and both held in great esteem by the British public, but because of Covid denied the chance to have their sporting excellence properly applauded.

A year on since collecting the Helen Rollason trophy in Aberdeen, I have looked at that award, daily – there hasn't been much else to do, being fair – and played that night out a few times in my mind, and just what a special, special event it was for me. Once in a lifetime. I expect it will be the same for Tom. Lewis, though, has every chance of another evening in the spotlight. I hope he appreciates it, just as we appreciate him.

Tuesday 22 December

All that conjecture and speculation about people gathering to celebrate Christmas comes to nothing. In Scotland and England, the festive season is reduced to Christmas Day alone. Kirsty has another Covid test. Negative. I think I'll have a quick sherry ...

Thursday 24 December

It is Christmas Eve, 2020.

Four years ago today, diagnosed with MND, my world collapsed. Metaphorically (and that wasn't a word I used very often before I began writing books), Kathy and I had to pick each other off the floor, firstly because of what we mean to one another, but also because we have three sons who depend upon us.

Four years on, and we are in a different place. But that could be cross-referenced to everyone on the planet. In my case, while my mobility is becoming more troublesome, and my dexterity in my hands especially is virtually nil, I get what I need doing done. I do, however, need help. All MND sufferers need it, but that assistance ranges from someone cutting up your food, to the biggest and best in the scientific world making a breakthrough.

I have been very lucky that I have been able to assist on that front, because of those I've placed around me in terms of trustees, and those inspiring individuals and teams who have performed way beyond anything I ever hoped for to raise the funds for the Foundation so we can explore cures, drugs and the science that might rid us of Motor Neuron Disease, soon and forever more.

All of that said, more than three years into the Foundation's existence, when not a day has passed without someone squirrelling monies into our account from another mad adventure, or rattling a can – virtually in the last year – under the noses of friends and colleagues, I still finding myself geeing up certain members of the scientific community.

If you go to buy a new car, you want to know what it will cost, what it will do, how good it is, what might go wrong, how much it will cost to run, is there a better one to be had, is there a better one I can't afford but I might be able to knock a few quid off? Last but not least, do I need it?

Take all of those criteria and considerations and swap the car concept with that of buying into Motor Neuron Disease and finding a cure for it. All of those questions still apply; however, when our Foundation made moves into that field – the research and science behind MND – there was nothing like the sleek presentations you might get when you walked into your local car showroom. Actually there was nothing, except for levels of secrecy, even suspicion, that I would never have dreamed could have existed among people allegedly with the same aims and goals.

My intentions were to help these people help people like me. However, I was never going to support, back, donate, or spend the monies we had accrued through the endeavours of others without there being a couple of rule changes, the first being these were my rules and if you didn't like them then you weren't in the game. Brutal, yes, but none of the games I've ever participated in allowed folk to make up their own regulations – unless it was the French.

Since those early forays into the world of MND and medicine, I'd say the Foundation's stock has risen, as have the bank balances of various hospitals, universities and laboratories across the UK. It has taken time, but at least we have all the chairs pointing in the same direction, not having debates on whether it is better to work from bed, sit on the floor, face the walls or argue if bar stools are better than couches. The last one depends on how drunk you are.

I have nothing but the greatest respect for the scientists, chemists and researchers who partake in this work. However, maybe the sticky start was made stickier by my approach.

If we had money to spend on drugs and research, you weren't getting any of it unless you could show us exactly what you were doing with it. I was asking questions, making demands and challenging their conventions in a way they'd never been scrutinised before. When I spoke to Martin Turner, Professor of Clinical Neurology & Neuroscience at Oxford University, Nuffield Department, he admitted as much, though he did laugh about it.

The first forum we had was all very tense, with cards being played close to their chests. They didn't know who I was, and I was being a bit of a bull in a china shop, frustrated that they didn't appear to know the answers to the questions I posed, and I vented that feeling. I don't think they'd been spoken to in that manner before, but hey, what had I got to lose?

The first question I asked was, 'Well, what have you been doing for the last ten years?'

The analogy I gave to them was based on rugby, a sport I know something about. I was the player, new to the team, they were the coaches who should know how to win the game, but they weren't really telling me how. Was that because they didn't know, or didn't want to share what they knew? You win nothing like that. Angry is too strong a word. It was all just a bit irritating.

Martin admitted my leading question actually hit a little bell in his head, and he questioned himself as to what had he been doing for years. Another one of the professors said he believed they would find a solution within five years. My counter-question was why not two, or one. Great seeing into the future, but too late for me and many others. Tell us what would speed up the processes, and we'll make that one of our goals. As I've said on numerous occasions, don't give me a problem, give me a solution.

I reckoned they'd never come face to face with a patient, or someone they were trying to cure, who had set or forced the agenda prior to me turning up on the scene. There was an uneasiness, and I felt it as well. I mean, what was I going to do if they all decided I wasn't for them and pissed off?

To be fair, they must have seen some endearing qualities in me because rather than walking out and never coming back, they've hung around and the relationships in the forums we've had thereafter have been fruitful and enjoyable. Even when it's been a bit above my head – and you are in the clouds then – they have taken time to break things down into bite-sized chunks for us to digest.

You have to ruffle a few feathers occasionally to get the business done, and to make certain you are doing it with the right people. Who was it who said one day you are cock of the north, the next a feather duster, gone. Stark, but everything the scientists do is time sensitive to me. These are lives you are dealing with, and one of them mine.

Not just a life, but one that ultimately will be ended as part of an absolutely horrendous sequence of events. I don't forget that, neither should they, therefore a bit of forward propulsion would be nice.

We are comparing apples and oranges perhaps, but my point about ten months to design and develop several Covid vaccines does choke those of us – literally – who have seen one drug for MND in nearly thirty years. Honestly, you shouldn't need a fire lit under you to get moving on this one. It should be a priority. Please.

Merry Christmas. I'm putting my feet up.

2021

MND will make life very difficult for you, at some point. Before that day arrives however, give everything you can to living. I just wish we could bottle that attitude.

JANUARY 2021

Friday 1 January
A happy New Year to one and all. It seems like last week since I was wishing everyone that going into 2020. Remind me, what happened last year?

I've been keeping a watchful eye on the activities of the afore-mentioned Rob Wainwright, and his newest Doddie Gump/Doddie Aid/World In A Day idea. It was now making perfect sense.

Having launched Doddie Aid at the start of December for regis-trations, New Year's Day 2021 was the big start date, and going by what I'm seeing through social media and the likes, there seems to be no shortage of participants or inventiveness when it comes to guaranteeing participation.

Wainwright said this would work. Who am I to doubt him?

The World In A Day plan was to basically circumnavigate the world, encouraging people to put in their miles through cycling, walking, jogging, running, rowing, climbing, sailing, skiing, yomping (although Stewart persisted in calling it 'tabbing'), or any other activity you could come up with, either outdoors or in the cosiness of their own home or torture chamber. That simple.

And just so no one would feel left out or lonely, Rob resurrected the old District Championship teams for a one-off comeback, and individuals became team members for Glasgow, Edinburgh, North & Midlands, South and the Scottish Exiles. Qualification for the teams: well, let's say it left something to the imagination on occasions, as you will see.

Teams need captains, and what a motley crew – sorry, inspirational bunch – we assembled. For South, Jill Douglas and Rory Lawson were in place to lead by example and maintain spirits – in Jill's case, gin, or a case of gin. Just so he wouldn't feel left out, Hoggy was made vice-captain, his main duties being not forgetting the ice and keeping Jill topped up.

Me, with my expert knowledge of all things, especially sitting back and allowing people to put the hard yards in, and then taking the credit, I was manager of the South team. I saw this as the first step towards a job with the Lions.

Kelly Brown, singer and occasional rugby boy, partnered by the ubiquitous star of TV, Emma Dodds, led Glasgow's might, while Edinburgh had my fellow MND warrior, the inspirational Davy Zyw and another lovely face from the telly, Eilidh Barbour, who appears so often you start to believe there must be two of them – even three.

They don't come much more competitive in the world of sport than former Scotland skipper John Barclay and Olympic curler (that's the hurling lumps of granite curling, not using heated tongs curling) Eve Muirhead, so they were natural choices for North & Midlands, which leaves us with the Scottish Exiles.

Captains Jim Hamilton and Paralympian and endurance athlete Mel Nicholls (you'll notice the word 'athlete' only applied to one of them) were the team leaders for those from across the border.

What could possibly go wrong?

Tuesday 5 January

MND has given me a bigger extended family. I hope you understand what I mean when I say I wish we weren't related or had not met. I'm sure you get where I'm coming from. Nothing personal. But we'd all be better without membership of this club.

You notice certain things in adversity: who steps up to the plate, who goes the extra mile, who shrinks into the background. Trust me, sitting back and watching – because there isn't much else to do – you soon get the measure of individuals and institutions.

Sufferers share similar stories, identical situations and certainly the same frustrations, be that in science or just getting your finger on the correct button of the remote control without switching the TV off, or rebooting the digital box, or just dropping the blinking thing.

Who'd have thought life could be so challenging when you can actually do so little?

With Motor Neuron Disease, those affected are in this together, with one aim or goal. To stay alive. That will apply to countless souls suffering other diseases or even having been laid low by Covid. I'd say ninety per cent of the time, they might see a solution. With MND, currently, there is none.

The rollercoaster of emotions can be draining at times. Watching others going through the same – family, friends, carers and the likes – is hard, especially when none of them paid to take that ride.

Maybe it's just because I'm watching TV more that I get to see and hear about mental wellbeing. I'll be honest, there was a time in my life when I didn't even know anything like that existed. Life and attitudes have changed.

I'm in a good place with my life, surprisingly. Others less so. All I would ask is that you take a minute to think about them, pick up the phone, send a text, deliver a message. It's amazing what a wee gesture like that can do to someone's mindset and their day.

I know. I see it from both sides.

Sunday 17 January

The social media campaign around Doddie Aid is in full swing and, among the videos, one from no less than Hollywood superstar Gerard Butler tops the charts with a huge number of views. Well, he is a popular guy and that is his day job I suppose.

However, as anyone who knows anything about the internet, social media and the like will tell you, the one thing people can't resist clicking onto are fun clips involving kids or animals.

If you add the elements into that, then you are bound to have a winner, and after a whiteout in the Borders turned every field into a winter playground, the Weir boys needed no second invitation but to appear in front of the cameras, larking about with trail bikes, surfboards, and being towed behind a quad bike, rendering Mr Butler's cinematic masterpiece null and void.

Well done, lads. I knew I could rely on you to come up with a performance, and to get me thawed out eventually. It was absolutely Baltic, but still worth it.

It was going to take a monumental effort to dislodge that video at the top of the charts. But what did I say about kids, or animals?

Hamish, Angus and Ben's glory was short lived. When the BBC's 'voice of sport' Andrew Cotter posted up a clip of him commentating on the exploits of his Labradors, Olive and Mabel, the lads were relegated to 'B' movie status alongside Gerard.

Never mind, boys, get working on a script and a plot line for next year. Just one hundred million views to beat . . .

Monday 25 January

Happy Burns Night to one and all. A bit strange this year, not having been invited to a Burns Supper, and not having my Addresser-to-the-Haggis-in-Chief Callum Weir delivering the Bard's dedication to the 'great chieftain o' the puddin'-race'. But alas, our national delicacy and the annual celebration of Burns is aff the menu, unless you have a virtual supper. With nothing in the way of festivities, I'm stuck in front of the telly, again, but this time with something worth watching on BBC2.

There are certain quizzes on TV that I'll watch, like *The Chase* and *Tipping Point*. I'm quite good at multiple choice questions – or in other words, I'm a lucky guesser. With that in mind, *University Challenge* is, er, too challenging. If I get one question correct of an evening, I honestly feel quite smug for at least an hour, a day, or for the next week until it comes back on again.

Tonight, I'm tuned in, hanging on every word from Jeremy Paxman and I have immediate success in the observation round. What do you mean, there isn't an observation round?

Well, had there been, I'd have been first, because taking pride of place on our TV screens is the My Name'5 Doddie tartan, as worn by Tom Starr-Marshall, representing the University of Strathclyde, in honour of his fellow colleagues of the Royal College of Speech and Language Therapists, celebrating the work they do with Motor Neuron Disease sufferers. I am, as they say, blown away, touched and moved that an individual would take time out to show his support for our cause, and that, once more, support and exposure is being given to our Foundation.

The buy-in to what we are trying to achieve is utterly bewildering, and this is yet another example of the left-field support and marketing we have achieved in the last couple of years.

And I know the question you are all eager to ask: did I get a question correct tonight? You better believe I didn't . . .

Friday 29 January

This must be a big story given that it is on everything from Sky Sports News to the Shipping Forecast. But it has been announced that Dominic McKay, who has been so helpful to both me and the Foundation in his capacity as the Scottish Rugby Union's CEO, would switch cities and codes, becoming the new CEO of Glasgow Celtic. I can only wish him good luck and every success in his new role. Others, better informed in football matters, would say he might need it.

Saturday 30 January

While Ne'er Day has been the 'b' in bang when it came to the starting gun sounding on the Doddie Gump festivities, some couldn't wait to get started. Glasgow captain Kelly Brown went for a dip in Loch Lomond in his budgie smugglers on 30 December, tiptoeing through the snow to get into the ultimate ice bath. Not to be outdone, his Edinburgh counterpart, Davy Zyw, in his own, inimitable way literally did 'launch' events in the east with his spectacular back somersault, on his snowboard, while wearing just his underpants.

What exotic location did he choose? Chamonix? Verbier? Even Aviemore? No, try Hillend Ski Centre. Oh, the glamour. What a man.

One thing I should have realised – some sportsmen and women just don't do 'friendly' competition. Take Jim Hamilton (just take him, please), for example, who I referred to as being one of the team leaders from across the border. Make that any border.

With qualification criteria that would have left World Rugby, FIFA and the ICC thumbing their rule books, Hammy appeared to have taken a leaf from the recruitment manual of the French Foreign Legion.

The Waltons (the family of my Newcastle and Scotland buddy Peter, not the Liverpool sextuplets or John-Boy, Jim-Bob, Mary Ellen, Grandpa or Grandma from Walton's Mountain) were conscripted, as was Formula 1's very own Lee McKenzie. All above board there.

However, none of us could recall Mike Tindall playing for the Anglos, but up he popped on social media, not only saying how proud he was to be participating, but also claiming to be captain, a mutinous act quelled immediately by Big Jim. Then Matt Dawson and Austin Healey popped up.

David Campese, anyone? A welcome visitor to these parts, anytime, but it appears Hamilton and Nicholls had followed the Eurovision Song Contest regulations by allowing Australians in. And then we had North & Midlands and Glasgow fighting over Ruaridh Jackson. I mean, if it had been someone good or famous, perhaps. Eventually he went for Glasgow because John Barclay didn't show him enough love. Ruaridh, you've changed . . .

The conclusion of the entire programme would come on the day of the Calcutta Cup match in February, but the biggest event had now arrived, the World In A Day challenge, where from the 'comfort' of your own home or garage (or someone else's socially distanced outbuilding) this virtual peloton would circumnavigate Planet Earth. No excuses either if you didn't have a bike. Miles are miles whether you pedal them or walk them or swim them.

The entire movement, however, was blessed to have two utterly amazing guys inspiring those in the saddle, none other than Mark Beaumont and Sir Chris Hoy, working either individually or in tandem. See what I did there? Great supporters of the Foundation in whatever we try to achieve, when spirits might have been flagging, these two constantly stepped up to the plate to kick on. In fact, I don't think they ever stop.

I might add at this point the efforts of Bruce Aitchison – perhaps better known as Happiness Is Egg Shaped – kept up people's interest in the whole thing with a running commentary and some great interviews. This will be scanned and on a T-shirt before you know it.

The support we received was unbelievable, the good wishes from celebs, stars of the small and big screens, the sporting world, and even politics, was both touching and inspiring.

Kenny Logan, okay, maybe not the best example to begin with, but his wife Gabby was right behind everyone. As was Johnny Beattie, Gerard Butler, Will Carling, Todd Clever, Andrew Cotter – along with Mabel and Olive (the dogs who own him) – Hal Cruttenden, Al Dickinson, Simon Donnelly, Craig Doyle, Jenni Falconer, Darren Fletcher, Jason Fox, Bryan Habana, James Haskell, Nathan Hines, Matt Jess, Lorraine Kelly, Greig Laidlaw, Gary Lineker, Lee Mears, Ally McCoist, Ewan McGregor, Drew McIntyre, Lee McKenzie, Kevin McKidd, James Nesbitt, Sally Nugent, Karen Pickering, Francois Pienaar, Keith Senior, Philippe Sella, the band Skerryvore, John Smit, Mark Durden-Smith, Zara Tindall, Dougie Vipond, Hamish Watson.

Plus a cast of thousands who deserve a mention, and credit, and thanks, but who would probably add to the paper bill of the publishers if I listed all of them. You know who you are and what you've done.

One example would be the Brown family from Falkirk, who packed and posted four thousand North & Midlands snoods. What a team effort.

And what of that World In A Day Challenge?

As we all know talking a good game is one thing, delivering quite another and when the gloves came off – or went on given how cold it was – it was everyone putting their rivalries to the side to hit the target and that finishing line.

With 6,300 'Gumpers' taking part, North & Midlands clocked 31,601 miles; the South covered 24,993; Edinburgh managed 23,463; Scottish Exiles reached 17,664 miles with Glasgow accounting for 14,034 of a grand total of 111,755 miles, or six times around the world. They'd smashed it.

The biggest question, however, was would we top the million pound mark. A tweet around lunchtime that Tuesday had revealed all. Some pencil calculations, with a calculator to do the big amount, the readout displaying the sum total of £1,000,094. I'll admit, there was a tear or several that had to be dammed.

But #DoddieAid wasn't over quite yet.

FEBRUARY 2021

Thursday 4 February

Time to splash the cash again by helping the work and efforts of the Motor Neurone Disease Association of England, Wales and Northern Ireland and MND Scotland through their care grants programmes. Thanks to the colossal generosity of many across the country, we are once more able to help the individuals and families affected by MND.

While much of what we raise is targeted towards research, a significant amount is pledged to directly help people who are living with the disease via the Motor Neurone Disease Association and MND Scotland. In total the Foundation donated £400,000 to the MND Association and £250,000 to MND Scotland, directly helping more than a thousand people through these grants.

Home adaptations, ramps and stairlifts, specialist bathroom facilities and riser recliner chairs, as well as respite for carers and families are among the many items covered by the grants.

Those directly in contact with MND face daily battles just to live a moderately normal life. Our vision, focus and pursuit of a cure for this disease have never diminished. However, while we continue to strive for that dream to become a reality, equally we have to try, where possible, to prevent people's last days becoming a nightmare through a lack of provision of key equipment or access to easy fixes that make a difference.

As I've said often enough, I am blessed with a very large support team of family and friends who have made a difference to my life. That facility has to be offered to everyone.

Friday 5 February

On the eve of the Calcutta Cup match we had a gala dinner, the kind of evening that we should all have been attending, somewhere, had it not been for this blasted pandemic.

We had music from Phil Cunningham, Skerryvore and Trail West, a Calcutta Cup preview from former Bath mates (yes, they shared a bath) Jon Hall and Andy Nicol, along with various interviews on the night.

This, however, was a dinner date with a difference and who better to prepare the cuisine, or at least prepare the menu, than Nick Nairn, a champion of the Foundation, and not bad at whisking up some magnificent food, with young Mr Vipond as his sous-chef (French for hinger-on). This, of course, would be a virtual dinner, therefore rather than sitting down in your best black tie, or sparkly black dress, or both, you'd have to get your hands dirty first and do your own preparation and cooking. Easier said than done.

I did offer but was told to sit back and relax. Actually, I was told to keep the hell out of the kitchen and people's way, and as you know, I always do as I am told.

For starters, we had a prawn and smoked salmon cocktail, with Nick detailing the recipe and how to make it. The inclusion of avocado would have confused some in Langholm, as they thought that was only a colour available in bathroom suites.

For the main course, what better than a peppered fillet steak, with whisky and mushroom sauce, potato wedges and salad. I'm relieved that salad was included, a trade off against the whisky used, some of which, in the Weir household at any rate, appeared to have evaporated during the cooking process. Quite a lot of it, to be fair.

And for pudding, I had another steak, but other options were available.

To accompany the food, what better than some lovely wine? Davy Zyw, who knows a thing or two about the grape, teamed up with Ally McCoist, who thinks he knows about wine. Given his involvement, Stewart Weir said he was selling his shares in Blue Nun.

What they came up with was a Rioja, Campo Viejo, and Comte de Senneval, a Champagne Brut, available at Lidl, which proved to be very popular given the levels of hangovers the next morning – just a few hours before Scotland would play England at Twickenham. Maybe having a hangover would be no bad thing.

Saturday 6 February

Given what I did two years ago (it'll be nearer the front of the book), I decided I'd watch this encounter. My 'previous' in this game, both individually and as a player, wasn't the greatest. But one thing we Scots do is live in hope.

Eighty minutes of nervousness and shredded emotions later, and Scotland were celebrating a first win against England at 'HQ' since 1983, when Jim Aitken of Gala, a wonderful friend to me and the Foundation, captained the side, and another Gala man, Tom Smith (not that one, the taller one), scored the winning try. He might even have played with my father, that's how long ago it was. But an amazing result, just a pity there were no Scots there to see it – or did that actually help Toony's team? We'll never know.

What we do know is that that amazing victory brought the curtain down on a fantastic few weeks with Doddie Aid.

Thursday 18 February

Between the weather and the lockdown, I've not been able to test-drive the shiny new trainers I got from Santa. However, they'll get their first outing of the New Year accompanying me on my trip to my chiropractor, Donald Francis, who had just opened a new torture chamber, I mean clinic, in Galashiels, which he has asked me to officially open.

Why does an athlete like me need a chiropractor, I hear you ask. Because I do, is the simple answer. My old adage, if you don't use it, you lose it, still applies, even though I seem to be losing movement and muscle despite my best intentions of working with a specialist. Equally, I don't want to seize up, something that would be all too easy to do.

Life, however, is never that simple and occasionally, in trying to do good, fate conspires to take you in another direction, and in this case, that means downwards.

I'm feeling very good this morning, with my new Christmas trainers on for the first time, but, unlike his old place which is a ten-yard walk from the car, Donald's new premises mean a nearer to forty-yard walk, over the bridge and into the shop, which I did on my own, although Kathy was quite close.

Maybe I didn't cut the ribbon quite as well as I should have – I'd never have made a *Blue Peter* presenter anyway – but with my official duties done, Donald could get to work.

His new premises really looked the part and Donald couldn't wait to show me around the various rooms. All very nice. We walk along a narrow corridor to see the rest of the suite and, on the way back, I trip. The combination of new trainers and a change in surface resulted in my entrance into the chiropractor's chamber being slightly more spectacular than planned. I accidentally stubbed my toe and that was the last I remember.

For normal folk, a stubbed toe probably entails a big step to regain your balance, or a couple of wee stutter steps as part of your self-righting mechanism, and at worst, grazed hands and knees with whatever the landing gear makes contact with first. Unfortunately, it isn't that simple – or as slightly damaging – to me.

Down I go, like a Scots pine being felled, except I can't remotely get any of my branches out to cushion the impact. Wham. I can't remember a thing, knocked cold.

The first connection I make is with the chiropractor's table; the first part of me to connect with it, my head. Not recommended, as I may have said before, and certainly, as I've now experienced a couple of times, painful. Call it an occupational hazard you can do without.

I wake up in the ambulance, with the wife shouting, 'Take him away.'

I feel sore. I feel my teeth with my tongue. One appears to be missing, a tooth that is, not my tongue. Crivvens. I know I've banged my eye, but I can't put my hand up to feel the damage.

This accident results in a day spent in the Borders General Hospital, a head scan and an X-ray, and five stitches – proper big ones which had the boys calling me Frankenstein. I'd once have joked that it was only my head, but it wasn't.

Because of my dilemma, I don't have anywhere near the same bulk of tissue – I was never what you'd describe as muscly – around my shoulders and torso, which means any kind of collision with something solid, and most tables and floors are, means you are going to take a bit of a clatter, an almighty clatter being honest about it.

Imagine picking up a sack of tatties and throwing it down on the floor. That's pretty much what it's like when I tumble over.

While the head hurt more immediately, having my innards bounced around knocked the wind out of my sails. I was supposed to be having a Zoom chat with Stewart, but after sustaining such a battering, breathing, never mind talking and breathing, is a bit mission impossible. He'll just have to talk to himself instead.

If the dent to my head is visible, the dents to my body are less so. As are the dents to my confidence. That can't be seen but it's there, and it hurts. It isn't the falling over, or the structural damage. It's the knowledge that there could be a few more coming this way. To be expected, perhaps, but still unwanted. That is not something I'll dwell on, but equally it is a thought that won't really go away in a hurry.

I'm not one to feel sorry for myself, but I do for poor Donald. There he was, asking me to do the honours by cutting the ribbon, becoming the first patient in his new abode, and an hour later, I'd left a massive pool of blood on his new carpet. Not only that, the paramedics had dented and scratched all his new paintwork getting their big mobile stretcher into that wee passageway. I felt guilty for taking up everyone's time, and more guilty when I hear the damage isn't entirely limited just to me.

Oh, what is happening?

Wednesday 24 February

Less than a year ago, I was meeting Neil Lennon at Celtic Park and he was pledging his support to whatever MN5DF and the Celtic Foundation could do together in the fight against MND. Today, he is the lead story on many of the news bulletins, sacked as the Celtic manager.

This is the hard reality of sport; you are judged on success. But he had been successful. Just a few months ago he led Celtic to victory in the Scottish Cup, thus completing a quadruple Treble in domestic football. That, it appears, counted for nothing when he had been tasked to win an unprecedented tenth successive Scottish league title, and ended up finishing a distant second to Rangers. Even I understand the consequences of that.

All I can say is that I — and a few dozen others — would never have had an international rugby career had we been judged on how we did against our nearest and dearest rivals.

MARCH 2021

Friday 5 March

Taking a tumble has not been infrequent, but not always damaging (although the threat is ever there), or my fault. Indeed, it can be hazardous when receiving a helping hand. For instance, having planked myself down on the couch one evening, a seat which is a bit lower and less firm than other places I plant my backside, Kathy needed to give me a hand up.

The plan was that on the count of one, two, three, up, she'd pull as I stood up. A plan? What could possibly go wrong? Try Kathy giving me a howk on three when I jumped on the 'up'. It did remind me of some of the line-out calls I'd encountered over the years.

We landed in a heap, unscathed, laughing our heads off like a couple of kids (ages don't matter). But she couldn't get me off the floor. Superhero Hamish – 'the human HIAB' – got the call to rescue us. A happy ending, this time.

Monday 8 March

Davy Zyw's name will have popped up a couple of times already in this journal, the guy who kick-started Doddie Aid – if that's the right terminology – with a spectacular somersault on his snowboard. He also had to suffer Ally McCoist for an evening, but he appears unscathed.

Davy, who is an author and a wine expert, has been a massive supporter of MN5DF. During the summer of 2020, he and his twin brother Tommy and their friends rode the North Coast 500, around the north of Scotland, in just four days, raising £150,000 – his initial target was five grand! – an effort which saw him collect the *Cycling Weekly* Fundraiser of the Year award, a remarkable achievement.

Worthwhile mentioning at this point that Davy has Motor Neuron Disease. A bit like me, it was something he noticed with his hand that alerted him to an issue. His thumb stopped working. In my case, I had a loss of power.

In 2018 he was given the news that he feared, and in 2019 made his diagnosis known to those outside his circle of family and friends. He changed his way of life, where he lived, and spoke to me at my cycle ride that summer on the wettest day in history. Unforgettable for him and his stepdad, who needed to be helicoptered to hospital after a crash.

I could tell then he had something about him, an edge, a determination, an inner strength. I sent him my crib sheet on the dos and don'ts of living with MND. I think from memory there were more dos. But was it really my job to give my expert opinion? Whatever, we are both still here.

I've heard him call me an inspiration, and talk about the humility I've shown when speaking and explaining about this disease. I have to say, I mirror that respect for him. For like me, he challenged the medical advice, or what little there was. He wanted to fight back, on his terms, and part of that was through positivity of thought and attitude. As I found out, the doctors don't yet have the answers. So, do it your way.

MND will make life very difficult for you, at some point. Before that day arrives however, give everything you can to living. I just wish we could bottle that attitude.

And why does Davy merit a mention today, of all days?

Today, his wife Yvie presented him with a baby boy, Aleksander. Welcome to our world, Alek. You will be proud of your dad trying to make it a better place. We won't stop chasing that dream.

Friday 12 March

Memories place you at a moment in time forever. There are quite a few things that can be used to capture that instant, although perhaps nothing does it better than music. I'm greatly honoured then that Bruce MacGregor of Blazin' Fiddles fame has put pen to paper and composed 'Doddie's Dream', released today with all proceeds going to the Foundation. Wonderful, and a right wee foot-tapper as well.

This is a collaborative work, which means there's quite a few who have contributed to this recording, among them Anna Massie, Angus Lyon, Jenna Reid, Kristan Harvey, Rua Macmillan, Julie Fowlis, Duncan Chisholm, Gary Innes (no mean shinty player by all accounts), Ingrid Henderson, Breabach, Aly Bain and Phil Cunningham, Ross Ainslie, Ali M. Levack, Alasdair Fraser and Natalie Haas, Donald Shaw, Saltfishforty, Skerryvore, Sharon Shannon, Jerry Douglas, Mohsen Amini, Adam Sutherland, James Lindsay and one Nicola Benedetti, who only picked up an award in the New Year's Honours when I did!

Hopefully all the work of Bruce & Co. will return a tidy sum, and who knows, I might even get on *Top of the Pops*. Is that even a thing anymore?

Sunday 14 March

Mother's Day, Mothering Sunday, call it what you will. Even when your mum isn't here, you don't forget them. A day for a bit of reflection of what you miss and what went before.

A year ago, I visited my mum's grave. It was the first time I had gone since her passing and it just seemed like a nice, and right, thing to do. Mother was laid to rest in the old graveyard at Stow St Mary of Wedale and Heriot Church. As you will have read previously, she had certain stipulations regarding her funeral and resting place, and that was carried out as per her wishes.

Visiting the cemetery this time, two years after losing her, it comes back to me that her funeral wasn't without the odd wee drama. Robbie Brown, the funeral director, and a man I packed down with for several years in the Melrose scrum, knew there would be one or two issues in accessing the grave, because of the location and it being on a hill. No problem, we had plenty of able-bodied men to help him. But, I think now, Mum might have moved around in her coffin a little, given the jiggling and jostling she took finally getting her into place.

Today, I am reminded of that as I make my own way up to her grave. There are several steps, then an uphill pathway that leads to the lair. The steps feel massive, not quite the north face of the Eiger, but trying to lift my legs is nearly impossible. Of course, when my feet are not planted, and they are not heading in the direction intended, I'm as steady on my feet as a new-born foal. I take a bit of catching and a bit of restraining as well. Similarly, the climb is nearly too much for me.

Ben picks some snowdrops and ties a wee elastic band around them to hold them together. Lovely and simple, which, to be fair, is not what you would necessarily be thinking when you had to man-handle me. For what goes up has to come down and that was easier said than done, as firstly gravity takes over, and secondly, I can see where I might end up. That sapping of confidence is becoming telling.

So too is the year-on-year comparison I'm able to make, even if I might not want to. Twelve months earlier, making the same journey, walking the same route was hard but manageable. It was none of the above this time. Not yet impossible, and while it doesn't appear in that category, I'll continue to try it.

What it does do is have you see first-hand the worsening of my predicament. Of course, I'm aware of how difficult it is to do certain things and have been for some time, if only because I can see by the clock or my watch.

But, on a daily basis, I don't really notice any major deterioration in my demeanour. Where it is easier to see, is when there is a gap between activities or escapades, like a trip to the dentist, or the chiropractor, or out our drive and on to the track in front of the house. It only needs to be a couple of weeks, and I can tell that I have limitations that weren't there the last time.

When that is a year, as it was between trips to Mum's grave, I'm all too aware of my decline. What I could do twelve months ago, or what was manageable, is now virtually impossible. If I see it, others must see it. If I don't admit it, maybe others will ignore it as well. But for how long?

Tuesday 23 March

The last year has given me time to spend with the family, time I might not have had with them otherwise. The last four years have been nonstop, full-on, revolving door stuff; another day, another appointment, another place to be, another group of people to see. Solely seeing Kathy, Hamish, Angus and Ben is something I consider a blessing, although I think we are all a bit fractious now. That could apply to every family, probably. In that way, Covid hasn't been a bad thing – dangerous, yes – but not entirely the worst.

However, this virus, this unseen killer, has denied me other opportunities to do things I like, to maybe do things I haven't tried, although I'm limited in what I can do on that front, unsurprisingly.

Life may not have dealt me the best of hands when it comes to MND, but you play it the best you can. Covid is like being thrown jokers. You don't expect the last part of your life to be spent almost entirely at home. Please, I fully realise there will be some who have never had a choice as to how their final months, maybe weeks, are played out. But for those who are lucky enough to still be active, having a giant brake put on normality has been a tough one to take. I left 'why me?' a while back, but right now it's more 'why us?'

Maybe my emotions are heightened by this being the first anniversary of lockdown. Is it really a year? Have we really had a birthday, Christmas and the welcoming in of another New Year? A year – that in some ways felt like a lifetime.

Hopefully, the restrictions we've been living under won't last for much longer. I think I said that last April . . .

Thursday 25 March

This may come as something of a shock to many, but I do like a glass of red wine, especially out of one of those MN5DF pint jugs. Well, it's rude to bother the bar staff too often, don't you agree?

That chance, however, to have my name on my very own red was too good an opportunity to pass up on, especially when the very kind offer came from Sporting Wine Club owner, Simon Halliday, a gentleman I had the great pleasure of facing on the field of play. So, the idea for 'Doddie'5 Red Blend' was born.

Maintaining the rugby connection, the wine comes from the vineyard of Springboks forward Schalk Burger, who has used his wealth of knowledge to blend five different grapes to come up with this unique blend. And maintaining that oval ball connection, the hugely brave and talented mouth-painter Henry Fraser, the ex-Saracens Academy player sadly paralysed by a freak accident, created the label. Another example of the reach the rugby brotherhood has.

Now, if you don't mind, I think I hear a wine tanker pulling up at the farm . . .

APRIL 2021

Thursday 1 April

My wee all-terrain buggy that Santa brought me a couple of years ago – entirely to my specification, coincidentally – has served me well and given me an air of independence around the farm and countryside I wouldn't normally have had. I know, I hear you saying 'what about your tractor?' but it's a bit big to be taking down some of the paths and fields and tracks. My buggy, meanwhile, more than covered all contingencies.

However, it isn't exactly the biggest (although it may be the driver's stature that is the issue), and while I was able to climb in with a bit of a wriggle – being honest, I'd just tip myself into the cab – getting out when you don't have any movement in your arms was proving extremely hard.

I could drive it okay, with just slow and slight movements of the wheel, but once I was in the driver's seat getting out again, when you only have your legs to provide momentum and force, was becoming impossible. That isn't even taking into account the possibility of shoving too hard and landing on your backside in a puddle. And, while it is quite stable and has relatively good traction, I was at risk of serious harm should it tip or roll if I was out and about on my own, which, although I do like the company, is one of the last freedoms I've got.

So, what could give you better access and exiting, while giving off-road capabilities (and remember, it's fields and track we are talking here, not the Paris–Dakar)? Top marks if you've worked it out already – that's it, a golf cart. Dead simple to enter – just stick my rear in the seat and throw the legs in – and equally easy to egress.

The only concern is the steering. Oh, I can steer, but it feels like four turns lock-to-lock, so navigation can be slow on occasions. It has worked up until now, although I have a load of people looking for a solution to the directional issues. If you know anyone with a quick-rack for a golf buggy, I'm in the market.

Friday 2 April

I miss Ceefax. Now there's a statement that dates me. On the other hand, smart TVs deliver all the news with pictures. So maybe I don't miss Ceefax that much.

Anyway, the news hasn't changed much in the last year by the looks of things, other than a bit more positivity about the Covid vaccinations. There might be a light at the end of this tunnel after all . . .

One piece of news has me shaking my head, in disbelief. Kevin Sinfield's '7 in 7' – that of course was seven marathons in as many days – has raised £2.3 million in total. He deserves a medal for his idea, and one every time he completed twenty-six miles, and above all else, one for thinking about his pal, Rob Burrow. What a man to have on your team.

Friday 9 April

Occasionally you have to be honest with yourself. Since my last big tumble (I don't grade them like earthquakes but I know the difference

271

between the innocuous and the enormous), my self-belief –
something I've never lacked – isn't what it was. Walking has become
an effort and dangerous; my balance just isn't there. It seems the
least wee thing knocks my stability, or highlights the lack of it.
And, something I notice more when I hear myself back again, my
speech isn't as strong or as clear. I knew this would eventually
happen. We've given this condition a run for its money, or at least
I think so. But it is catching me up. I fight it, but I see the changes.
Whereas before I was always able to soldier on, I now see that I
tire, show fatigue, and start to falter more often. This condition is
utterly relentless. There is no beating it – but I'm not beaten yet.

Thursday 22 April

As a concept within the sporting world, not many have reached
the heights of the British & Irish Lions. Every four years, four
nations are joined to take on the best there is from the southern
hemisphere. It may be just coincidental, but how often have the
Lions found themselves facing the likes of Australia, New Zealand
or South Africa when they are either World Champions or the best
ranked team in the world.

This year is no different. The Springboks won the last World
Cup, meaning the Lions face the champions of the world this
summer. How very 1997.

That year meant so much to me, my first (I always refer to it
as that, you never know) Lions tour, a real high spot. All these
years on, I may have missed out on selection (again), but only on
the player front. I am delighted, honoured and even humbled that
the My Name'5 Doddie Foundation has been listed by the British
& Irish Lions Charitable Trust as one of their four new charity
partnerships, along with the Matt Hampson Foundation, the Atlas
Foundation and Wooden Spoon.

What this means is that we enter into a one-year partnership, which allows us to use the British & Irish Lions Charitable Trust logo for all promotional activity during that period, as well as using the Lions' digital platforms for promotional purposes, and we also have access to 2021 Lions Tour memorabilia for fundraising. A mega deal for those fortunate enough to be selected.

I can only thank Chairman of Trustees, Gavin Hastings, and fellow trustees Richard Hill, Sam Warburton, and Irish legend Fergus Slattery, for considering MN5DF as worthy recipients.

That Big Gav is my former international teammate and captain, Richard was one of my teammates from the Lions tour in 1997, and former Lions skipper Sam is one of my after-dinner sparring partners, is entirely coincidental. What did they used to say in the old tabloids; 'Our lawyers are watching . . .'

MAY 2021

Wednesday 5 May

You can tell a great deal about someone when you look them straight in the eye. Not many can do that with me, but I could tell this one had what it takes, this one being Doddiethegreat, owned by Kenny Alexander and trained by Nicky Henderson.

Doddie, my equine namesake, had made a winning debut at Ludlow last year, but because of this damn pandemic, it was only now I was meeting up with the four-legged Dodster. What a fine specimen. And so was the horse.

Kenny generously donates all of Doddiethegreat's winnings to the Foundation. Never look a gift horse in the mouth, the saying goes – better in the eye! This one will do for me.

Thursday 6 May

In rugby circles, this is probably as close as you come to experiencing Christmas morning; the 2021 British & Irish Lions squad for the tour to South Africa is announced.

I'm excited as a rugby fan to see who will be facing the World Champions, but also on behalf of the players who will be headed out there to wear that famous red jersey. Not one to get sentimental, the team announcement brings so many memories of being selected myself twenty-four years ago, coincidentally, to visit the reigning World Cup holders.

I remember the buzz around being picked, but also that I'd been oblivious to having been watched during the season. No matter, I was going on that plane, and that's what mattered. Hindsight is always 20–20. Only later did I realise how special it was to have been on that trip, the first in the professional era.

I've never been one to have regrets, but as the team was being listed, there was a small part of me that wished I could recall or feel that buzz again. I think you get so caught up in some things occasionally that you don't have time to enjoy it fully, not that I was thinking that way at the time – the enjoyable part would come on the field, in the training camp, in the hotels, bars and restaurants when you were there with your teammates. And those recollections are still quite vivid, aided I must say, by the regular video clips that appear on social media from *Living with Lions*. Thankfully, not everything was filmed or made the editor's cut!

Scotland's performances in the Six Nations merited eight Scots being named in the 37-man squad – Stuart Hogg, Finn Russell, Chris Harris, Ali Price, Duhan van der Merwe, Rory Sutherland, Zander Fagerson, and Hamish Watson – and Gregor Townsend as attack coach, a bit of a step-up in numbers compared to recent tours.

I am reminded of words of wisdom from older players and coaches, that as a 'wee nation' Scotland benefits hugely from having a decent contingent away with the Lions. In 1983 we had a similar number as this year and Jim Telfer as coach. In 1989 – when Finlay Calder was captain – nine Scots made the tour and Ian McGeechan was coach. And the knock-on effect of that, according to those in the know?

In 1984 and 1990, the years following those Lions trips, Scotland achieved the Grand Slam. I may put fifty pence on history repeating itself, each-way of course.

The regret is that I would have dearly loved to be on the Cape, with Kathy, Hamish, Angus and Ben, and the Lions family who made us feel so welcome in New Zealand four years ago. Like so many things, it isn't to be. Still, a Grand Slam will make up for that . . .

I sent a good luck message via Gregor to the boys, wishing them every success and to do Scotland proud. I don't normally indulge in such things, but after twenty-four years of Jerry Guscott telling the world how he beat the Springboks in 1997, I think it's about time the balance was redressed.

Monday 24 May

In sport, to be the best, you've got to do a couple of things. Having some talent, being lucky, and working hard all progress your chances, as does working with the best. I'm reminded of my time at Newcastle Falcons, where literally from nothing, we went to being the best in the country – some might say Europe – through those four key ingredients.

When the MN5DF was set-up, we knew what we wanted to achieve, but even having those first three commodities by the lorry load wouldn't alone bring about a cure or a way of stymieing MND. We would need expert guidance.

Therefore, in the same way as the Falcons recruited the likes of Andrew, Armstrong and a dozen others, so the Foundation went out to recruit the best talent in the country when it came to understanding MND, its causes and, sadly, the effects that continue to ravage so many.

Over the last few days, courtesy of Richard Scott, Duke of Buccleuch, the incredible location of Bowhill House hosted the Foundation's Scientific Advisory Board, the group we've assembled as the most talented individuals and teams working on MND and related issues.

We had been making steady progress, in terms of planning, research and drug trials – this is where all that generosity provided by our supporters goes – but Covid and the pandemic acted like a massive anchor in terms of the course our good ship was sailing.

This gathering at Bowhill was the first face-to-face meeting with the professors since the pandemic started. You cannot speak to these people without being buoyed and enthused. I know, I may have been quite demanding of them, putting it mildly. But, after this unexpected spell of inactivity, it was encouraging that all had returned, full of ideas, full of thinking and full of chat. There isn't any point in keeping these things to yourself, especially if our Foundation is looking to fund and support your ideas and theories.

Not one to blow my own trumpet, not when I have an entire brass section to do that for me, but when it comes to fighting Motor Neuron Disease, the My Name'5 Doddie Foundation sits at the top table, alongside the professors, doctors and researchers who are the leaders in the UK, sometimes the world, and MN5DF interacts with them as equals.

In parallel, the Foundation has been part of the United To End MND campaign, engaging with the main charities and with patients and clinicians and researchers in trying to secure £50 million from the UK government over the next five years. This has involved numerous meetings with the government, NIHR (National Institute of Health Research), the MRC (Medical Research Council), the Department of Health and others, and we are making progress. Just not quickly enough.

That is no one's fault, given what we've all endured during the past twelve months, the kind of obstacle no other generation has ever had to contend with. And while we will pick up speed again, quite quickly if the chat from Bowhill is a gauge, I can't help thinking of those we had been trying desperately to help who are now no longer here to benefit.

Covid came at a cost to many, and not always directly.

JUNE 2021

Sunday 6 June

Always nice to have a visitor or two, or eight, although I'm surprised Melrose and Scottish Sevens legend Scott Wight, Allan Dodds, Barbara Shiel and Steven Shiel, Mathew Wilkie, Wayne Mitchell, Jamie Murray and Rory Murray have enough energy left to come and see me.

Yesterday, they ran, walked, cycled and kayaked from Portpatrick in the west, to Cove in the east in their Coast to Coast in 24 Hours Challenge, taking in much of the Southern Upland Way as part of the 174-mile route.

Starting at midnight with a ninety-mile bike ride to Moffat, they ran from there to St Mary's Loch, paddled across that, pedalled on to Melrose, walked the ten miles to Lauder, before jumping back on the saddle to reach Cove and the finish line by 11.59 p.m. where a dook in the sea awaited the bravest.

I enjoy hearing and seeing these challenges play out. It's a bit like *Top Gear* but without the supercars! Their aim was to raise a grand an hour, £24,000 in total. No mean achievement given that just eight of them were involved, along with a support crew. But not only did they reach their target but cracked the £40,000 mark. Well done all.

It was the least I could do to offer them a beer, although by the looks of a couple of them, a bed may have been more welcoming.

Monday 7 June

Often, as I've said regularly through this adventure, it's the little things that matter.

The announcement that Heart of Midlothian will have a new shirt sponsor for next season would, in the grand scheme of things, have been something that flew under my radar a few years back. Today, the Tynecastle club take time out to publicise that, for the coming campaign, those famous maroon shirts will carry the name of MND Scotland.

That they are doing such a thing is amazing. However, like so many things, it is because the club have been directly touched by MND with the passing of their Scottish Cup winning captain Marius Žaliūkas, who died from the disease last October, aged just thirty-six.

Raising the profile of MND, of those who have and continue to suffer, all helps in keeping our fight relevant and in the public eye. There aren't many ways in Scotland of doing that better than having a tie-in with football, so well done the Jambos and thank you – although some of my family members may have leanings towards the other side of Edinburgh!

Friday 25 June

Big day today with the Lions Trek For Doddie taking place, which is lots of enthusiastic folk marching the match ball from Melrose to Murrayfield for the Test between the British & Irish Lions and Japan. Just the thirty-two miles, and on average twelve hours on the hoof, but no shortage of participants and some legends in all their glory. And Kenny Logan.

Great to see Jill Douglas going the distance, and in decent time.

She managed to keep up with Jason Fox all of the way, just a few yards behind. I wonder why?

With Thrifty providing the support vehicles and Genius Brewing providing the support lager, a great time was had by all, and while I didn't join in the entire walk (I think I was thirty-one and three-quarter miles short), it was only right that I was at Murrayfield to welcome home that gallant band. If the physical effort could be witnessed first-hand and measured at walking pace, behind the scenes the usual fundraising efforts were going flat-out. At close of play, over £150,000 had been raised for the Foundation, quite a remarkable achievement.

The day was to have concluded with me doing the honours – and what an honour it would have been – of giving each of the players going on tour the official British & Irish Lions jersey. We have countless jerseys accumulated over the years, but that Lions shirt is oh so special. It's a recognition that you have joined an elite group, that you'll get a number to carry with you for evermore, and, that all the car journeys, drop-offs, pick-ups, training sessions when everyone else was enjoying themselves, training sessions when you were the worse for wear, training when it hurt and putting everything on the line for eighty minutes, week in, week out, had been worth it. It might not look a lot, but there isn't a player who wouldn't be thinking some or all of those thoughts when it was handed to them. But, not by me.

These guys didn't come all this way – and I don't just mean from Jersey and their training camp – to suddenly have their tour thrown into jeopardy by an outsider entering their secure bubble. No way.

Saturday 26 June

I'm not sure if it's the age in which we live – with so much televised live sport – but sometimes we lose sight of what a match or an occasion means. The British & Irish Lions kicking off their South Africa tour was one such event. With the game played at Murrayfield, it was the first time the Lions had ever played a game in Scotland, and the first time facing Japan in a Test. And what better way to kick off the trip than with a win. It was, however, at a cost.

I've probably said it elsewhere in these diaries, but Alun Wyn Jones is one of rugby's good guys, and in a world where the tag 'legend' is all too easily attached, he fits that billing both in terms of ability and standing. A few weeks ago, he was named skipper of the 2021 Lions, the outstanding candidate.

Seven minutes into the match against Japan, and his tour – and captaincy – was in serious doubt, a shoulder dislocation undermining his ambitions of leading a successful campaign against the Boks.

It was never going to be just a flesh wound that put this warrior down. He's not the sort to have twinges. As he made his way off the field, I made sure I was helped up onto my feet, to acknowledge an all-time great. I'll admit, I did well up a bit, seeing him being helped off the pitch. He has no shortage of memories and performances with the Lions, but it took me back twenty-four years ago when Doc Robson told me my tour with the Lions in South Africa was at an end. The pain of that news, that reality – and in my case the circumstances behind it – still hurt more than the injury ever did. I'd imagine AWJ would be feeling the same way.

It was, unfortunately, further evidence, if it was ever needed or doubted, of how fickle sport can be. We live for the unpredictability of it, until it throws up something that we don't want – and we certainly didn't want anyone damaged, irreparably, before they'd even boarded a flight and turned left to first class accommodation.

Just to compound the agony, Justin Tipuric damaged his shoulder, taking him out of the equation as well. One man's loss is another's gain, and Conor Murray, the Irish scrum-half, gets to see his name up in lights as the new Lions captain. I wish him well.

I allow myself a rueful smile, not at AWJ's expense, or Justin's either, but at the fact I stood myself down from the jersey ceremonials because of Covid restrictions, and here was rugby being rugby, and sport being sport. How unpredictable.

Oh, and as if to prove that maybe it was wise not to take any chances with the health and wellbeing of the main Lions party, the 'A' game between England and Scotland at Welford Road in Leicester was called off at the last minute because of several positive Covid tests within the Scotland set-up. You can never be too careful.

Sunday 27 June

Under the heading, 'Well, we're up this far so it would be rude not to pay him a visit,' my Sunday breakfast is interrupted by the appearance of a couple of well-recognised interlopers, none other than Will Greenwood and Scott Quinell, two former adversaries, two former teammates, two friends for life.

We've all found ourselves in the same place, at the same time, on a few occasions since, but it was the Lions tour in 1997 that brought us together, for always. After the year we've had, it was just brilliant to see them. Will was officially at Bluecairn to do some interviews and filming, Scott was here to watch a professional at work. Best being honest.

Needless to say, old times were discussed by three old-timers when we became even better players in the space of an hour than we had previously given ourselves credit for. Ach, it's an age thing.

Be grateful for small mercies, it is said, and I'm really appreciative of these boys giving up their time to come and see me and the family. Thinking about it afterwards, it's hard not to be just a bit cheesed off that instead of mixing with guys like this over the last year, we've been confined to barracks. Well, I suppose I should be thankful I'm here to say hello to them.

JULY 2021

Thursday 1 July

I have become aware, through various bits of chat, that one or two people were shocked and upset by my appearance at the end of the Lions Trek at Murrayfield. I don't mean that my hair and attire weren't up to their normal high standards, but more that I looked unsteady on my feet and needed a wee bit of help to complete my 35-mile hike, 34.9 miles of which I completed by car. But, folks, 'we are where we are,' and this is where MND has got me.

It has been interesting, in the past year and a bit, to find out what people's perception of me has become. Yes, I am still here, still soldiering on, and in most people's minds, still relatively intact. This, however, is a bit of an illusion, made entirely possible through the medium of Zoom (other conference call platforms are available).

For the past twelve months, most of my public appearances have been on-screen, wearing makeup, of course, but all at a very safe distance. I have, like others, become a postage stamp, head and shoulders only, as I pop up on TV, podcasts and the likes. In essence, people see the bits that work. The fact is, what folk saw in the video clips from Murrayfield that day is, for me, the new norm.

And the truth is that I cannot now wash, dress or visit the wee boys' room (big boys in my case) without help.

It was always going to be like this, but I might have inadvertently given the disease some assistance along the way. The fall I had at the chiropractor's earlier in the year (number one on my Richter scale) did me more damage than perhaps I was willing to admit to anyone, even myself. The physical damage – what I did to my head, my ribs and limbs – all healed, eventually. What it did mentally is immeasurable. My confidence, where before I was still steady, still walking with more than a casual stride, suddenly became baby steps, even a shuffle, which in itself is more inherently dangerous given the increased 'trip factor'.

When you do have time to think, which is often, either sitting in my chair in front of the telly or outside during the nicer weather, I'm of an opinion – which is always right – that that fall took six months to get over. I could barely talk for a month, as I couldn't breathe and speak at the same time. No bad thing some would say. But everything became an effort.

Those six months I refer to is an incalculable period. Was it six months out of the last year, six months spread out over however long I may last, or has it taken six months off my life? An optimist would like to say 'you're over it'; the pessimist might see it lopped off what's left of my time here. You get time to think things through, sitting in your chair. And I still don't know the answer.

Sunday 4 July

Another year older. Was my fiftieth really twelve months ago? Where have 365 days gone? Like last year, and not through choice, it was another somewhat subdued occasion, mostly family. I didn't get a cake this year, probably because the one I got for my fiftieth – the famous John Deere tractor, made by my nieces Rachel and Esther – wasn't eaten, as I instead turned it into an ornament and refused to cut it. It was a nice keepsake, but they weren't happy I hadn't scoffed it.

Over the past year, the 'ornament' broke (it was actually nibbled at and eaten by Zena (and more on her in a bit) and was eventually thrown out because a) there wasn't much of it left, b) it was a bit stoory, and c) it was past its use-by date by about a year.

Maybe when they come back off holiday I'll get one – and I promise to eat it. Well, unless it looks better on my trophy table . . .

Sunday 11 July

Normally, the last thing you want to see outside your home is a fire engine, but today I'm more than pleased to meet up with members of the UK Fire Service rugby team and members of Scottish Fire & Rescue and they make the most marvellous presentation of a fire fighter's helmet, specially wrapped in the MN5DF tartan. Honestly, it is quite spectacular and has been given a special place on my awards table (as there is no sign of another cake, yet). There is no truth I have been wearing it while watching *Fireman Sam*. The episodes of *London's Burning* on daytime TV are much better. Now, a tartan fire engine . . .

Friday 16 July

Mossyard is a place I like to be. We've visited the Solway coast since the boys were young, somewhere for a do-not-a-lot family holiday. It was also our bolthole when we returned to Scotland having been in New Zealand with the Lions, when I'd made known my condition. And, since then, it has been a place of peace and quiet and, of late, contemplation, like deciding whether or not I want another hangover like the one I had the previous night. But when the sun shines and you are able to laze around, for me, there are not too many places better.

This is the second time this summer we've been here 'on our hols' and how nice it has been just to get away, especially after the year we've endured.

Tuesday 20 July

I'm thinking about my beloved sister, Kirsty, today, for no other reason than she now knows what it's like to feel fifty. Happy Birthday! I would have wished her this in person, but she has taken herself off to Portugal, overcome with the emotion of getting old.

Saturday 24 July

How did we win that? The First Test between the Lions and South Africa ends with the tourists scoring a memorable 22–17 win over the reigning World Champions, memorable in as much as it was a 22–17 win over the reigning World Champions. It wasn't what you would describe as free-flowing, exhibition, Baa-Baas-style rugby. But what the hell, a win is a win and in a three-match series this is the best possible start. Take it for what it is, a victory, and move on.

What was brilliant was seeing so many Scots play a part in this win for a Lions side captained by Alun Wyn Jones. Remember him who'd been written off after being crocked against Japan? What is this guy made of? An incredible recovery.

It goes without saying that it would have been much better being in South Africa, in the flesh, with family and friends, but that was never going to be. I think the disappointment of not being there, despite knowing what a fantastic country it is, and just what an amazing spectacle being with the Lions on tour is, is offset massively by the fact that no one else is out in the Cape owing to Covid restrictions, so the feeling of missing out maybe isn't quite what it would have been. Still, cold Lion lager tastes good whether in South Africa or straight out the fridge at Bluecairn.

Tuesday 27 July

We have a new driver in the Weir household as Ben passes his driving test, a major achievement in any young man's life, giving him the freedom to experience the open road in his 1.2 VW Polo, and go upmarket as well when I need to be chauffeured around in my posh motor. He's happy, and so am I – another red letter day, perhaps one I could never be sure I'd be around to see. But it's brilliant, witnessing your youngest being able to take to the highway, legally . . .

Saturday 31 July

Ian McGeechan said there was nothing as dangerous as a wounded Springbok. How right he was, as the South Africans storm back to level the series with a 27–9 mauling of the Lions in Cape Town. From afar it looked like the South Africans learned from their loss the week before and we didn't find another way to play. I also wonder if the hour-long video released of South African coach Rassie Erasmus, bemoaning the performance of the match officials in the First Test, put some doubts in the mind of the referee ahead of this game. What appeared an incoherent rant might just have been a game-changer. All in all, disappointing, but all to play for in the Third Test. I predict changes now. Wait and see, I'll be right . . .

AUGUST 2021

Saturday 7 August

A right wee crowd arrive to watch the Lions today, among them my old Falcons teammate Dean Ryan, long-time sparring partner Carl Hogg, and my ex-Scotland and Lions colleague Rob Wainwright who, not for the first time, was fashionably late. What had started so well for the British & Irish Lions ultimately ends in disappointment when they are narrowly beaten 19–16 in the third and deciding Test. The Lions put a lot into this series, just to make it happen, but to lose by just three points in the end must have been gutting. Despite the loss, Finn Russell's stock will have risen given his performance after coming off the bench to replace the injured Dan Biggar. Would his inclusion earlier in the series have tipped it in favour of the Lions? Who can say. Everyone is entitled to their opinion, which inevitably is always right.

Four years now until the next Lions tour, Australia, 2025. Would be nice to be there. Would be nice just to see it.

Sunday 8 August

Not too much time to dwell on the Lions loss, although it does dominate the chat as everyone gathers in Melrose for the 2021 edition of Doddie's Ride, expertly engineered and directed by Peter and Trish Winterbottom. Nearly one thousand folk participated, all different ages, shapes and sizes – and that was just the bikes!

I survey the runners and riders from the luxury of my golf cart. No electric bike this time for me. Balance, or a lack of it, and an inability to hang on means my riding days are over, sadly. However, at least the golf cart had one thing bikes don't – a roof.

It is now apparent that if you are looking for a day when rain is assured – like for launching an ark, for instance – then just look at the diary to see what day Doddie's Ride is scheduled.

It came down in buckets. But were spirits dampened? Not in the slightest. Drowned yes, but not dampened.

Saturday 14 August

If you are wondering who the cake-eating Zena is, she is our black Labrador pup we got a few months back. We'd always talked about having another one after we lost our previous black Lab, Doris, a few years ago and finally we'd convinced ourselves. Not as convinced is our wee and ageing Jack Russell, Mavis, who can be seen with a worried expression on her face while she is pulled through the kitchen, into my sitting room, and then back around the kitchen table, at high-speed, while trying to get some sleep in her bed.

Mavis is not alone in being harassed. Zena does a great 'wall of death' impersonation as she comes into the study flat out, laps the room, runs up and over the couch before landing smack on top of me. I can't defend myself against this canine Exocet and her head is as hard as mine. I get licked to death at times, which is better than the occasions when her other end is presented to me.

But given I can't really push her off, for a few months, while she's been going through the teething stage, she has effectively viewed me as a two-metre-long chew stick, with extremely tasty fingers, but best (or worst) of all, a couple of fantastically edible lugs! For someone who wrapped up well throughout my rugby career to avoid cauliflower ears, I am now fearful I might end up like Evander Holyfield did after Mike Tyson took a nibble.

Monday 23 August

All during the summer months, the trustees have met up in that virtual watering hole called the Zoom Bar to have a chat and a blether about what and how we are all doing, and when we can get down to the real business of activities and fundraising again for the Foundation.

Like life in general, we've had a few false starts as we try to come out of lockdown and the restrictions that have dominated our everyday lives. The Foundation work keeps me occupied, giving me something to look forward to. I'm not quite sure the Foundation trustees feel the same way as I spend quite a while scheming, planning and plotting how to move things forward, and how we pick up the ball and run again once we are fully in the clear from Covid, whenever that might be. It is another way of staying positive, looking to the future.

Thursday 26 August

This new book is taking a bit of work. How come it took four months to cover forty-eight years of my life for the first one, but three years to cover thirty-six months for this one? I know things have changed, but not to the extent where I'm struggling with that equation. I'll be honest, there has been a lot of chat between Stewart and myself as he tries to winkle out all the minor details of certain events and how I was feeling around them, a bit of painting by numbers, rather than the broad brushstrokes used to colour *My Name'5 Doddie*.

It has been quite therapeutic, going back over the memories of the last three years – well, some of them. Most folk will have experienced this – nothing to do with MND, but maybe an age thing

– when you can't quite believe something that was in 2018 wasn't a few months ago, while something last year seems a decade ago. I might save some of that thinking for my next book, something along the lines of Stephen Hawking's '*The Theory of Everything*. Well, he got away with it . . .

SEPTEMBER 2021

Wednesday 1 September

You know what social media is like: you don't look at it for several days, then you see something and before you know it, you have eighty browser windows open and are watching an episode of *Top Gear* from 1993.

What catches my attention today is a link to a story concerning Lucy Lintott, who when aged just nineteen became the youngest person in Scotland to be diagnosed with MND. Against all odds – I think she was only the fifth woman to do so – she fell pregnant and gave birth to a baby boy in February last year. Her obstetrician said then they didn't expect to see her back again. Oh, how wrong they were.

For the *Sunday Post* reports that Lucy, now twenty-seven, is expecting again, this time a baby girl. I think it might go without saying, she is believed to be the first MND sufferer to be pregnant twice.

It is not an achievement I am likely to equal or surpass. Firstly, because I don't think I'm kitted out for it, and secondly, the look from my good lady confirmed her thoughts on the subject.

But I am delighted for Lucy and her partner Tommy and the happiness and positivity this news will have brought them.

Tuesday 7 September

Today we are at a sunny and beautifully warm Renaissance Club for the My Name'5 Doddie Foundation Golf Day. A great day was had by all and, again, the Foundation and ultimately MND sufferers will benefit.

It's great being in attendance, seeing old friends and, thanks to Jill's near death-defying all-terrain driving skills, watching them out on the course smashing a wee white ball, although not always in the direction they intended. I'm never one to judge, given my own experiences back in the days of what I'd describe as 'social golf', but there appear to be several who talk a better game than they play.

It was Gary Player (or it might have been someone else...) who said, 'The more I practise the luckier I get.' At this stage I'd like to introduce an exception to that rule, one Kenneth McKerrow Logan, who plays a lot of golf but appears to be exceptionally unlucky.

Someone ought to tell him that what he calls 'fade' and 'draw' is in reality a good old-fashioned hook or slice. Still, he's got some great kit and looks the part, although him constantly shouting 'fore' must put other players off. I should mention that my eldest, Hamish, was part of Team Thrifty, which came second on the day. That he earned a new nickname – that of 'Shark' – suggests he may have to revisit his handicap.

Friday 10 September

The Foundation – including me, Jill and the trustees – receive many messages, letters and emails during the course of the year, and all of them strike a chord because we know what people, patients and carers, family and friends, are going through and the challenges they are being faced with. Some, though, make you think a bit deeper.

In all my time dealing with MND, and speaking to some of the most eminent professors and scientists in the world, there has been a question which has resulted in several answers and theories: namely, what triggers Motor Neuron Disease? Safe to say, you could fill a few books with the ideas and hypotheses around this. I have listened to many of them, but there is something in my mind that says the effects of MND are sparked by some kind of trauma, or shock to the system.

What has got me pondering this matter, yet again, is the correspondence I've received from a young woman – perhaps it was reading about Lucy Lintott that got me guessing even more – that she believed that pregnancy and childbirth brought on MND. Again, I am no expert, far from it. However, I can see where her thinking comes from, that the distress for her of giving birth might have sparked something within her body.

Here, I am referencing my own experience and long-held belief that I was fine until I was injured playing an exhibition game down at Newcastle.

The Falcons Legends were up against our southern hemisphere counterpart in a precursor to the World Cup, back in October 2015. You remember, the World Cup when Scotland were eliminated by a dodgy refereeing decision? Aye, that one; not that I'm still bitter or anything.

One or two of you may be participating in mental acrobatics just now and wonder what a 45-year-old retired rugby player was doing playing a decade after he'd chucked in the towel. I asked myself that after five minutes.

However, I was surviving until I was absolutely smashed at a ruck, and when I say smashed it was of the top end of the Richter scale proportions. Had this been a Test match, Scotland versus England, a Cup Final, I'd have said yes, it came with the territory. But a bounce, in an exhibition game?

I took the blow right on the hip, but the pain went down my leg and up my side, nearly into my ribs. It took a few days for the bruising to start to appear, it was that deep, but when it did I was black and blue, with less of the latter. In all my career, I'd never felt anything like it.

Now, it might all be entirely coincidental, but from around that time, I honestly felt things were not right with me. I say it again, it could be coincidence, fate, chance, call it what you will. But as a one-time (and I recall that time) highly tuned athlete, you get to know your body, how to live with aches and pains. But this was very different.

Perhaps it plays into my narrative of thinking about the shock or trauma. That might explain – or at least open up the debate – as to why some say rugby players and footballers have succumbed to MND, yet the argument or stance falls down when you ask why boxers aren't afflicted; or why a granny from Inverness or a butcher from Fife in his thirties is suddenly diagnosed with MND, having never contested a scrum or ruck in their lives?

To use another big word, this hypothesis of mine could be monumentally inaccurate, but until one of the clever people say otherwise, I'll stick with that belief.

Monday 13 September

If ever anyone embodies the phrase 'it's not the size of the dog in the fight but the size of the fight in the dog' it's my wee pal Rob Burrow. He has been a tower of strength to a great many in the last year and a bit, tackling MND head on.

What with the newspaper coverage of his fight, the fantastic documentary with Sally Nugent, his book, his other TV appearances, and of course, the leverage he's achieved through the rugby league community, especially Leeds Rhinos and the amazing feats of Kevin Sinfield, Rob has played a huge part in raising awareness of Motor Neuron Disease and the plight of sufferers.

Rob and myself, and Stephen Darby and Chris Rimmer have,

each in our own way, lifted the profile of MND and highlighted the daily trials and tribulations facing all those concerned. But so too have the likes of Len Johnrose, who played football for Burnley and Swansea among others. And also Chris Johnson, former assistant chief constable of West Midlands Police, who has had the West Midlands Police dog unit name a litter of pups after MND heroes. There is even a PD Doddie. And there's Emma Moss and her touching YouTube video, telling her story with MND. And, yes, Emma did get to see her daughter go to school. Personal targets like that are such a driver for so many of us. As is raising £50 million.

The United to End MND campaign has been gathering momentum too. The 110,000 signatures on the petition that the Foundation and I began meant we at least had the issue debated in Parliament. The real test is whether we see the £50 million over the next five years that we've requested, for development and research, come to fruition. When those who signed the petition received a government reply stating they have already invested £54 million over the previous five-year term – a figure that has provoked a great deal of scepticism among those in the MND 'industry' – then you get the feeling this is a struggle that won't be won in a day, despite genuine support from various parliamentarians.

A sum of £50 million, against what has been spent to secure a vaccine during the Covid pandemic. Why hasn't it been forthcoming? I've asked the question before. It's worth asking it again.

Government could, if they had the compulsion and the compassion, write that figure off with a stroke of the Chancellor's pen. But as yet, while there have been platitudes and knowing nods of the head, there has been no cash. Unfortunately, time is running out for a great many, and sadly, it already has for others.

The magic bullet hasn't been found, but it is probably out there. Maybe we just haven't looked in the right place – or come across it yet while searching for something else. It could be that simple. The drug trials, similarly, will continue apace. All we need is a bit of luck.

All in all, none of us are quite ready to give up the fight. 'We are where we are,' to quote a famous Borders sage. We just could be in a better place.

Wednesday 15 September

Planning a trip to the swimming pool is now something akin to a military operation. It goes without saying, therefore, that a trip to London has the potential of being a logistical nightmare. However, if we are going to keep this campaign going, we need to be taking the fight to the heart of government. Press releases, TV appearances, Zoom calls and the likes serve a purpose, but being seen to be there carries so much more weight, makes it more difficult to be ignored. It may not surprise anyone when I say that plans are at an advanced stage for me and Rob Burrow to lead a deputation to Downing Street to present our petition to the Prime Minister. That's the theory, anyway . . . but let's rewind ever so slightly.

That term, 'logistical nightmare', isn't referenced without good reason. Do we fly from Edinburgh, or get the train? Neither is terribly practical currently, but who ever gave up at the first obstacle? Consideration is being given to my good pal, Danny Sawrij, flying us there by helicopter, although I'm not sure if his chopper has reclining seats! Or we could just drive, possibly with the prospect of making more pit stops in four hundred miles than Lewis Hamilton makes in an entire F1 season. We will find a way. A bit like beating MND itself, I'm determined to.

Tuesday 21 September

The Downing Street visit is on and we finally hit upon the best mode of travel: the good old motor car, regardless of how many stops we may have to make on the way south. We can even get the car deep into central London so it becomes a no-brainer, really. Me, Kathy and our pilot Gary head off first thing, and all is going well until we arrive around Leeds. Then *ping. Kathy gets a message on her phone to say that she has been in close proximity to someone who has tested positive for Covid, namely our sister-in-law, Anne.*

To say this was a bit of a bummer is an understatement. We have a quick confab, trying to decide what the next course of action should be, or indeed, what we are allowed to do. Do we carry on, drop Kathy off, or take Kathy home and start again? It is a debate which in truth doesn't last very long. Within a few minutes, I get a message as well. Again, our thinking isn't exactly crystal clear, but much as I would love to be in Downing Street, rules are rules and we have to turn around and come back home. I wasn't going to put anyone at risk, and someone might have noticed me in the photographs outside Number 10.

Oh well, another day.

Thursday 23 September

Christmas comes early to Bluecairn, or at least it does for me with the arrival of the 'Harley Davidson' cool trike electric mobility scooter. Here is a classic example of how MND and any disability changes your perspective on things. Whereas before I'd have been desperate to find out how fast it could go, whether or not I could pull wheelies in it, and just how far you could tip it on two wheels, I am today satisfied having the wheels and the wherewithal to simply pootle around the farm without turning it into a special stage from the Dakar Rally.

Of course, if you have been a good boy – and I have – you get more than one pressie, and I must have been extremely well behaved because who pops in? None other than the brains behind the Doddie Gump and my old captain, Rob Wainwright, bringing gifts from afar in the shape of calves to Bluecairn.

OCTOBER 2021

Monday 4 October

The Trustees of the Foundation meet up for a couple of days at The Renaissance, where we get a state of the nation report and throw some ideas out there about what we might do over the next twelve months. It does resemble the meeting we had a year ago as normality didn't arrive back quite as quickly (if at all in some areas) as we might have expected. But at least we know what the plan of attack is going forward.

Thursday 7 October

Dan Schofield, from the *Daily Telegraph*, is coming to do an interview about the new book, Doddie's Diary, which has been well received thus far and hopefully, many more will receive it in time for Christmas.

Monday 18 October

Another book interview, this time with Rona Dougall from STV. Can it really be four years since we met up at The Greenyards to chat about my diagnosis and the launch of the Trust and Foundation?

In some respects it seems a few months ago, in other ways it feels like ten years, which may tell you how much I've packed into the last few years, and I enjoyed every moment of it.

NOVEMBER 2021

Thursday 4 November

Another day, another flirtation with technology, this time a Zoom chat for the ISF Cambodia Virtual Dinner (of which our good friend out in Hong Kong, Martin Murray, is a major player). For this event, I'm joined by Rangers managers past and present, Alex McLeish and Steven Gerrard. They are both very entertaining. A few days later, however, it becomes two 'past' Rangers bosses when Steven Gerrard leaves Rangers for Aston Villa. To think, all that time we were on air, he never mentioned it, or gave me a wee tip as to who the next Villa boss would be . . .

Sunday 14 November

While there had been concerted efforts and considerable pressure put on the Government to support the fight against MND, no one really expected that late on the Saturday night the *Sunday Express* – a fantastic champion for our cause – would inform us that Boris Johnson had pledged to give £50m over the next five years as part of a bigger strategy in overcoming MND and other neurodegenerative diseases.

A wee whisky is in order.

Friday 19 November

Best glad rags on for the MN5DF Anniversary Dinner at Prestonfield House, where we can say thank you to a great many people who have gone above and beyond in helping the Foundation. To be honest, we could have awarded 250 'Doddies' to those who have played a significant part in fundraising and events, but those who did receive the accolades and plaudits have been exceptional and deserved. And a good night was had by all, particularly some of the younger generation, who showed their generosity by outbidding the room (and I might even say themselves) to purchase a table and tickets for the Cheltenham Festival. What happens when drink is taken; a warning to all.

Thursday 25 November

I'm old enough to remember bad weather when it was just called winter. Now, each and every gust of wind or downpour seems to have its very own title, and this week it was Storm Arwen's turn to hit – and hit Bluecairn it certainly did.

It left us, literally, in the dark for five days, until those nice people from Scottish Power hitched us up to a generator. Hallelujah. I've got my Sky and telly back. I can say it was an inconvenience; however, there are worse things in life to contend with.

DECEMBER 2021

Friday 10 December

I team up with Stewart to do a live interview with Stephen Jardine for BBC Radio Scotland. The intrepid Jen has everything set up at my end, but for some reason, Skype keels over a minute before we go on air. Sixty seconds of panic ensued but we go live to the nation on time. Technology is great when it works. When it doesn't, your blood pressure doesn't half rise.

Christmas 2021

In past years, I've recalled that fateful day in 2016 when I was given the news I had MND. That day, 23 December, has had its time in my life. I'm still standing (with a bit of help) as Elton John once sang, so I no longer dwell on what might have been or on the past. I look forward to the festivities, some kind of normality after Covid, and that Hamish has a significant birthday (his 21st) next week, and in February Ben hits 18, which to be honest, like other significant dates and events, I wondered if I'd see. But I have. Things are a bit slower, ponderous even, but the optimism levels haven't fallen. There is still a lot of living to be done.

2022

While there are a great many things happening around the country, and indeed the world, it's always nice to know that the support of your own community is there, and as ever, a huge thank you for that.

JANUARY 2022

Saturday 22 January

January in the world of My Name'5 Doddie Foundation can only mean one thing, and that is Doddie Aid. There are countless events, with thousands participating in them, but few are as popular as our Big Curry Night. While Covid has curtailed many activities, the one great thing to come from it is how we have suddenly opened up the world through Zoom. It has meant that individuals who might struggle to give an evening or a day of their time can dial in for fifteen minutes or half an hour to entertain and get people to spend some money.

Nick Nairn and Dougie Vipond were our intrepid chefs yet again as they prepared and showed us how to serve up a starter of chilli garlic king prawns with kachumber, with simple chicken tikka and butter sauce for the main course.

To wash that down, Davy Zyw selected various beers, while Ally McCoist offered up his expertise during a whisky tasting experience.

Brilliant! But what happened to my mango chutney?

Monday 24 January

We have a My Name'5 Doddie board meeting in Edinburgh today and a delayed Christmas lunch. Nice to see the old faces and some new ones who will be helping us press ahead with the work of the Foundation. Plenty to keep us busy, trying to play catch-up after what has been a two-year hiatus because of the virus.

Friday 28 January

Not too far to travel for our latest appointment at the Scottish Borders Council offices to unveil the MN5DF flag in the company of Kathy, Gary, Councillor Sandy Aitchison and Convener David Parker and his guide dog Clive. He was on his best behaviour – Gary, that is, not Clive.

While there are a great many things happening around the country, and indeed the world, it's always nice to know that the support of your own community is there, and as ever, a huge thank you for that.

FEBRUARY 2022

Tuesday 1 February
Kathy has Covid. Usual drill, although this week it means that I won't be at Murrayfield for the Six Nations opener against England. Blast.

Thursday 3 February
Kathy, being the sharing sort, has passed Covid on to me. Double blast. That said, I don't feel as threatened as I once did, for two reasons. The first is I've had all of my injections and do put a lot of faith in that. Secondly, my dad had it as well. Taking into account his age, that he has some underlying health issues and may be a pound or two over his fighting weight, and yet survived it, I'm positive I can do the same.

Saturday 26 February
Scotland's second home game of the Six Nations is against France, but inasmuch as I came through my latest Covid drama, it has left me a tad low and recovery has taken a bit longer than I'd have liked. Again, nothing to worry about, although missing another match at Murrayfield isn't great. Then again, this might not be a bad one to skip . . .

MARCH 2022

Wednesday 2 March

The one thing that has remained a constant over the past two years is that people have tended to give me a wide berth at the mention of Covid, which has left me grateful and frustrated in equal parts. I want to be mixing with folk, but better to be safe than sorry I suppose.

Wednesday 16 March

Gary and I hit the road, headed for Jesmond to say a fond farewell to Steve Black, aka 'Blackie', a man who was the heartbeat of Newcastle Falcons and who endeared himself to hundreds within sport.

It was not a great few days that week in February, when news of Blackie's passing was followed by the untimely death of Va'aiga 'Inga' Tuigamala, another of my Falcons team mates. It is difficult to put into words what the arrival of Inga was like at Newcastle, both in what he gave the team but also in terms of his standing in rugby, both League and Union. Imagine Hibs signing Messi. It is no exaggeration, in my mind, to state that that's what he brought to the Falcons. His purchase for £1 million put down a marker that professional Union had arrived. He was like a chieftain, a leader and an inspiration. I heard a story about some campers who were looking to pitch up for the night and approached Inga to see if they could use his land. 'No, you can't,' said Inga, 'but you can come in.' He had a room made up for them, shared dinner with them and wouldn't take anything for his hospitality. An amazing man, sadly missed.

Blackie, on the other hand, brought you just as much off the field. A man – a motivational guru in today's money – who would always have an encouraging word, a sympathetic ear, but above all else, the ability to impart knowledge, perspective, genius and belief in any player. He had an uncanny knack of saying the right thing often when you found yourself in the wrong place or time. I think that's why so many loved him, because he treated everyone exactly the same, whether or not you belonged to his club.

You saw that at the service in St George's Church. Craig Quinnell came up from Wales to be there, Danny Cipriani was there and I saw Rob Andrew, Jonny Wilkinson, Dean Ryan and Tony Underwood. Blackie was also greatly involved with Newcastle United, and it was great to see my old boss Sir John Hall, who was in superb fettle, and the likes of Peter Beardsley, Joey Barton, Steve McClaren, Steve Watson, Terry McDermott, John Carver and Alan Thompson. We even had Glenn McCrory from boxing and Jimmy Nail.

Hard to believe Inga and Blackie have gone – and I'm still going. Life, eh? I shared a huge part of my career with these guys, a time I'll never forget. I was lucky to know them.

Friday 18 March

I receive a visit from Stewart as we need to update 'the Diary' because it is coming out in paperback. Good news. He brings his 18-month-old retriever Flo with him, and she and Xena (although

I prefer Zena) spend the afternoon chewing each other to bits and running themselves to a standstill. Oh, to have that energy.

There is a bit to catch up on, but again, because of the dreaded Covid, we are behind schedule, and worst of all, Cheltenham is on and I'd prefer to be watching that – and even losing money – than talking about the past several months. Still, it has to be done. I mean, people need to have something to read on the beach now we can get away again.

Co-author Stewart Weir is a former sports reporter at the *Evening Times*, chief sportswriter at the Scottish *Mirror*, and Head of Sport at the Herald & Times Group. He has worked extensively in PR, for governing bodies and individuals such as Sir Chris Hoy, Stephen Hendry and Ronnie O'Sullivan, and is also a regular on talkSPORT. Stewart and Doddie have been friends beyond rugby and media for well over twenty years. And it's the strength of this friendship – steadfast, upbeat and shot through with irreverent humour – that makes DODDIE'S DIARY such a candid, warm-hearted read.